The Catholic Church in Modern Africa

A Pastoral Theology

The Catholic Church in Modern Africa

A Pastoral Theology

JOSEPH MULLIN

HERDER BOOK CENTER
NEW YORK

Geoffrey Chapman Limited
18 High Street, Wimbledon, London, S.W.19

Geoffrey Chapman (Ireland) Limited
5–7 Main Street, Blackrock, Co. Dublin, Eire

First published 1965
© 1965, Joseph Mullin

Nihil obstat: R. D. Dermitius Fogarty, D.D., L.C.L., Censor deputatus
Imprimatur: H. Gibney, Vicarius Generalis
Datum Southwarci die 3a Maii 1965

Made and printed in Great Britain by BLACKIE AND SON LTD., Bishopbriggs, Glasgow

To my brother priests, the African-born clergy

Contents

Preface

LATE in 1961 I was invited by Bishop Blomjous of Mwanza, Tanzania, to write a pastoral guide for his diocese. Out of that guide this book was born. I had access to a library receiving some four hundred reviews a year; likely articles had been noted and classified in their appropriate files, so that on almost every subject discussed in this book I was able to read a fairly wide range of the periodical literature of the last thirty or forty years, and contemporary literature in particular. It was not difficult to discover in what matters there was a consensus of opinion and for the most part this is what I have presented, only very occasionally, I think, taking sides.

Not all pastoral theology is to be gained from reviews or books, and I owe a great deal to many African and missionary Fathers in Nigeria, Sierra Leone and Tanzania who helped me, each in his own skill: the urban parish priest, the head of a pastoral institute or catechetical centre, seminary or social institute, canonists, moralists and dogmatic theologians.

My practice was to discuss the subject with them before writing and then to submit the manuscript to them afterwards. To them all I now express my warm thanks. Particularly I thank Bishop Blomjous for his invitation to Mwanza and the ample facilities he offered me. I thank also Father John O'Donohue, W.F., of Mbarara diocese, Uganda, who kindly undertook the labour of the revision of the text.

One caution: wide areas of this book will be of equal value to the European reader as to the African. But differences run deep and may not always be noticed. This work is a pastoral theology *for Africa*. In a pioneer study of this kind, I may beg the reader to make allowances for me wherever I seem to have failed.

4 May, 1965.

Introduction

WITH a deep sense of the pastoral inspiration of present-day theology, Mgr. Mullin has devoted long and patient research to his pioneer work on and for *The Catholic Church in Modern Africa*. The result is gratifying as a synthesis of past efforts, and a powerful stimulus to future study.

Africa has entered the dynamic modern world with its ever-expanding scientific horizon and its ever-changing cultural patterns. While some may regret the tranquil days of a definitely lost past, Pastoral Theology looks ahead. Without any claim to prophetic foresight, it humbly tries to follow and enliven, with the grace of Christ, the watercourses flowing into the mainstream of the future. Knowing quite well that it cannot draw a final picture of modern Africa with hard and fast rules for the priestly ministry, Pastoral Theology studies the concrete African situation, the living inheritance of the past and the new political, economic and cultural trends. The Pastor must see the complex change and learn to understand its creative elements.

The author certainly helps us to meet the challenge of the moment. He describes the forces everywhere at work in our cultural revolution and the factors underlying widely different situations. One of his main concerns is to integrate the rich African inheritance of cultural and religious values into our future way of life. African civilization cannot be saved like a museum piece. Our age-long religious longing will be lost in the modern technical world and the religious soul of Africa will succumb to materialism, if it does not find new life and true fulfilment in Christ. An African Pastoral Theology must choose the best elements of our past and incorporate them with the new, so that they may become part and parcel of our future. Mgr. Mullin has opened a path with new vistas. He declares it foolish to think that he could say anything like the last word on the subject (p. 182). His task has not been to give adequate answers to our questions, but simply to make some remarks which may help those better equipped, in the course of time, to refashion African life according to the mind of Christ (p. 147).

A word to missionaries: Mgr. Mullin's work inaugurates a vast plan. Further study is required to fill in the particulars and to map out new solutions. You bring to Africa the living tradition of the Universal Church. You feel unable to transmit Christ's message without understanding the people. Often you are puzzled: What do the Africans think? How do they react? Despite your efforts at sympathetic understanding, you grope in the dark. The emerging Africa does no longer answer to the traditional image. The character of mission work changes with the changing African scene. New inquiries along the lines of Mgr. Mullin's suggestions are needed. With your experience of the technical world and of the modern Pastoral Theology, you can offer invaluable help to complete the mission work and to find solutions to so many problems old and new. With the courage and dedication of your predecessors, do the pastoral work of today and help us to incarnate the full Christian life in the modern African society.

A word to African priests: Mgr. Mullin would achieve his main purpose if in 6–12 years time, a new edition of his Pastoral Theology could be published by African priests. The time has come for us to play an active part, not brushing aside the suggestions of the missionaries but correcting and complementing them. We are inclined to criticize the European writing on Africa, because we deeply feel the inadequacy of his descriptions and the insufficiency of his solutions—yet we refuse to take the risks of scientific progress and to commit ourselves to the necessary tasks. Many of us have studied abroad. Only a few continue study and research at home, and fewer still publish their findings. This is a very serious lack. Bishops and priests, together, must try to find a remedy for this sorry plight. Pastoral studies are not a loss of time. They should have top priority in our planning, because they are absolutely essential to the African Church with the growing complexities of its problems. Patient field work, frank discussion of problems and possible solutions, and bold experiments are as necessary in Africa as anywhere else, if we really wish to make the Church relevant to the new Africa. All those who engage in such work may be sure that they, like Mgr. Mullin, contribute to the realization of the aims of the Council, which 'desires to impart an ever-increasing vigour to the Christian life of the faithful; to adapt more suitably to the needs of our own times those institutions which are subject to change; to foster whatever can promote union among all who believe in Christ; to strengthen whatever can help to call the whole of mankind into the household of the Church' (Constitution on the Sacred Liturgy, article 1).

CARDINAL RUGAMBWA

PART ONE

The General Background

1 The New Africa

THE Church's mission is eternal, but she has to fulfil it in time. The worldly circumstances of her children are not directly her concern, but she cannot remain indifferent to them; it is in this particular context of time and place that Christians have to work out their salvation. A book like this, therefore, which attempts to lay down guide-lines for the conduct of the Christian apostolate in modern Africa, must say something of the present situation in Africa—social, economic, political. We shall try here at the outset to uncover some of the current political trends in Africa, to discuss the major forces which are seeking to influence the development of the continent, and conclude by considering the impact made on African society by the new industrial revolution.

SOME POLITICAL TRENDS

The Church has no politics, but she has to live with various political systems. It is therefore important that her leaders understand the political forces at work among the people whom they are called upon to serve. Before speaking of the relations between Church and state in modern Africa, we may conveniently consider the political life of the continent under the four headings of nationalism, totalitarianism, socialism, and neutralism.

Nationalism

The word nationalism has acquired unpleasant overtones in recent years; it suggests an exaggerated exaltation of one's own country, idolatry of the state and racism. Nationalism in some degree is a temptation for most men. Confronted with his own inadequacy, the individual is tempted to console himself by dwelling on the glories of his country.

As far as missionaries are concerned, Pius XI said the last word on nationalism when he declared that it was the greatest single social obstacle to the work of the Church in the new countries. Every missionary in Africa today appreciates the dangers involved in associating the Church with European prejudice of any kind; nothing could be more disastrous than for the Church to become identified with European culture.

It is not however European nationalism, but African nationalism which is the greatest concern of the Church in Africa today. Here it is the priest's duty to educate his people. Like all heresies, nationalism starts from a truth and perverts it. Love of one's country is good and necessary, and this should be insisted upon by Christian teachers; it becomes evil only when it generates contempt for, or hostility towards, people of other countries. Patriotism has always been recognized as a Christian virtue, and the Church has nothing but sympathy for this healthy nationalism. It is right that the citizens of a country should seek to protect their independence and their traditional culture, and they should be encouraged to co-operate with each other and interest themselves in the political and social life of the community. The priest will urge respect for one's country and for its leaders, who have a right to the same respect that children are expected to show towards their parents; Christians should be taught that, while they must love all men, they have special duties towards their fellow citizens, and that they must be prepared even to die for their country, if necessary. Obedience towards legitimate authority should also be insisted upon. Enlightened instruction of this kind from the pulpit and in schools will go far towards preventing the growth of that distorted patriotism which we call nationalism.

Love of nation should be truly nation-wide, and not narrowly parochial or tribal. If federations are formed, as they may be in parts of Africa, the people should be taught that they owe their loyalty to this larger homeland, provided it has been set up by common consent, and with a view to the common good of all the people involved. Patriotic attachment to one's own country, in the narrow sense, rather than to the larger cultural or religious group, is a comparatively recent phenomenon in the world, and there is no reason why one's own nation should be regarded as the only possible focus of patriotic sentiment.

Totalitarianism

A totalitarian state is one which permits no rival loyalties or parties. Under such a system, the government is identified with the state, which in turn is regarded as co-extensive with society, so that the government invades every department of the citizen's life.

Sound political philosophy recognizes on the contrary that the government is not the state but only its executive and legal arm. The state is the politically organized community, the body politic, and it is evident that it covers a much wider area of life than that controlled by the government. The citizens themselves, public opinion and its organs, opposition groups: these too are authentic parts of the body politic and exist independently of the government. Moreover, the state is made up of individual citizens, each of whom exists independently of, and prior to, the community of which he is a member; the state exists for the benefit of the citizens as private individuals, and subordination of the interests of the citizens to those of the state can only lead to disorders of all kinds, and to the suppression of basic freedoms. Even considered as a body, the citizens are more than members of a political community: they have social rights which are independent of their political life and over these the government cannot claim exclusive control. The religious life of the citizens, for example, is outside the scope of the government's authority, and while the political power has a duty to promote the social and cultural welfare of the people, it may not claim exclusive competence in these matters. If the individual and the family are to retain their natural dignity and independence, it is essential that organizations other than the state play a part in providing social services.

Complete totalitarianism involves an affront to man's dignity as an independent person and must be condemned. But we must be sure before we condemn. In a developing country, uninformed opposition can cripple government plans that are already beset with difficulties enough, and the government is justified in suspending customary freedoms when these are being abused to the detriment of the common good. The priest must defend the rights of individual citizens, and of ethnic or religious minorities of every description: but equally he must urge all citizens to fulfil their duties to the state (for example, just taxes must be paid). The common good is the yardstick, and where minority views or customs are really harmful to that common good, they must be abandoned. Further, under-developed countries cannot afford waste or inefficiency; their slender resources are all needed for constructive purposes, and there may well be circumstances in which a political opposition party, whose approach is purely negative and obstructive, may justifiably be restricted. In the same way, intimidation by private citizens or by political groups is rightly held to be intolerable and may be repressed by suitable measures. The private rights of citizens have to be defended, but the government too has to be defended from un-reasonable criticism or obstruction on the part of the citizens.

African statesmen frequently compare the present emergency situa-tion in Africa to a state of war, when all the resources of the country must be mobilized for the common good. Though the analogy should not be pressed too far, circumstances in Africa today plainly require more interference from the government than would be acceptable in the normal way. Thus while the state may never lay claim to absolute control of the nation's social services, it has the clear right and duty to organize them where they do not yet exist, and to draw up appropriate regulations for their efficient functioning. The Catholic body should be encouraged to anticipate the government's action in such matters by offering to co-operate in the creation of unified social services for all the citizens of the country.

A final word on the 'strong man' feature of totalitarianism. The idea of one man as the strong leader of the state is part of the African tradi-tion, and it is a tradition which should be respected. Evidently there must be no adulation of political demagogues, who do not merit respect; but it would be a mistake to think that the Western forms of democracy are the only forms suitable for Africa.

Socialism

There is much talk today of African socialism, although the words seem to mean different things in different mouths. President Nyerere has proposed the word *Ujamaa* as aptly expressing the type of society he is seeking to create in Africa; the term may be rendered 'family spirit'.

It certainly seems susceptible of a Christian interpretation. It would be a mistake to conclude automatically that African socialism necessarily involves the materialistic conception of society which we associate with European communism. We should study African socialism before we pronounce on it; it may in the end prove to have the right answer to many problems.

The social distresses of Africa are manifold, and they can only be met by adapting the social teaching of the Church of the Poor to African conditions. It is clearly important that the Church's social doctrine be known by all Christians; practical means of ensuring this are suggested elsewhere in this book. The Christian's first task is to ensure that his individual relations with others are inspired by the principles of justice and charity, which are at the basis of the whole social teaching of the Church. When the same principles are applied to relations between families and groups, then we have a Christian society. Credit unions are a good example of the application of the Church's teaching at a local level.

Mater et Magistra should be our guide here. This remarkable document, the fruit of wisdom and wide charity, is a practical manifesto concerned with facts rather than with theory. Pope John wished us to be realists and to accept the facts of the situation. Instead of seeking to change what is in fact unchangeable, the Christian should do what he can to apply Catholic principles to the situation as he finds it. Pope John condemned especially an attitude of withdrawal on the part of Christians. We may not contract out of our duties as members of human society in order to take refuge in a self-centred spirituality. Our task is o lower barriers, not to heighten them, to play a full part in society and so bring a Christian influence to bear on it. The Christian who remains aloof from the society of his fellows is doing his duty neither as a man nor as a Christian.

Non-alignment

Neutralism has become the standard foreign policy of independent Africa. The first prime minister of each newly independent country is expected to proclaim in his maiden speech that his party stands for a foreign policy uncommitted to either of the great world blocs. This attitude may suggest that principles are or no importance, that there is nothing to choose between the philosophies of the West and of the communist East. This cannot be accepted. The principles of communism are false, unchristian. European Christians cannot help feeling alarmed when they see African countries entering into trade and cultural agreements with countries under a communist regime. If however the policy of neutrality is adopted for the purpose of security, and does not imply approval of communist ideas, then it is perfectly justified; African countries have every right to refuse to be sucked into the quarrels between East and West. This protective neutrality, of which Pius XII spoke, is legitimate, provided that it is not inspired by moral indifferentism.

Church and State

The new countries of Africa have, for the most part, promised freedom of religion for all. This is excellent, but one may regret that there is no legally binding agreement governing the relations between Church and state. Such an agreement should be concluded as soon as possible. It is understandable that the new governments like to have their hands free when assuming their responsibilities, but the future is likely to be beset with all kinds of difficulties if the mutual responsibilities of the spiritual and the temporal power are not clearly set out in a written instrument accepted and understood by both sides.

Church and state are each perfect societies, with God-given authority over their different spheres. This notion of two separate and independent societies in the state is as alien to African tradition as it was to the ancient civilizations of Greece and Rome and to the early primitive cultures. Christian revelation alone brought the truth, expressed in clear terms by our Lord himself when he urged his followers to render to Caesar the things that are Caesar's and to God the things that are God's. Respect for the two authorities and for their different areas of competence is something that the priest has to teach his people. Infringement of the rights of either side has to be avoided. It is important at the present moment for the Church to emphasize the rights of the state and to go as far as she can in meeting them. If the government wishes to set up a unified education system, or to organize other social services at a national level, the Church should co-operate. Catholic schools should welcome all the children of the area they serve, and conversion efforts in these schools should be avoided, while the Church should offer her help in bringing the state schools up to standard where this is necessary. She should also, where necessary, take active measures to meet Moslem needs.

Wherever the ruling power tends towards totalitarianism, there is a danger that the Church will come into conflict with the civil power; but Church leaders should beware of exaggerating the rights of the Church, and should be alive to the fact that in an under-developed country there will inevitably be more government interference than in a developed country. In a positive way, it is for the Church to do all she can to ensure that her children play a full and even leading part in the temporal affairs of the state, for this is an essential part of the Church's mandate, and if undertaken whole-heartedly can bring immense benefit to the state.

A possible source of friction with the state is the Church's position as a landowner. In many cases, missionaries were granted their property in freehold by the colonial governments. Freehold is a concept alien to African tradition, and if the independent governments wish to abolish it, the Church should accept that ruling, and be content with the same title as that enjoyed by African landowners. Obviously, Church property should be invested in the indigenous Church as far as possible. Land and buildings should be owned by the diocese and not by missionary bodies, and the boards of trustees of diocesan and missionary institutes must include at least some African members. The Church should not retain more landed property than is necessary for her needs; any surplus should be either sub-let, if the title-deeds allow, or (with the permission of the Holy See) sold or simply made over to the people.

It need hardly be added that the Church cannot be associated with any political party; she must insist on political freedom for all, but must be detached from all political groupings. Non-Catholics especially are suspicious of priests who meddle in politics. It is no exaggeration to say that such priests can be a curse to the Church.

Four Forces Struggling for Africa

There are at present four forces struggling for the soul of Africa: Islam, communism, secularism and Christianity. We shall say a word about the first three of these.

Islam it everywhere in Africa and its successes are obvious to all. It is to be met by kindness and co-operation. Christians should adopt a friendly attitude to Moslems, and seek to join with them in working for the material welfare of the country. Only thus can Christian influence be brought to bear on Moslem society. Of the direct apostolate to Moslems we speak elsewhere.[1]

Communism has not so far achieved much success in Africa. Russian tactics were initially clumsy, largely because Russia lacked any experience of the African background. They will certainly become more refined with time, and are already showing increased knowledge and know-how. The Chinese communists are more subtle and devious in their approach; although China is still poor, they are offering bait to African leaders in the form of the material aid which is so desperately needed, and may well prove the greatest menace in the long run.

Africans are naturally religious, and atheism is repugnant both to their traditions and to their instincts. Nonetheless, communism is a threat to be taken seriously, and one which Christians must be prepared to face. The best preparation is a solid course of instruction in the social teaching of the Church, about which so many Christians still know nothing. As far as the individual is concerned, his immunity to communist propaganda will be according to the depth of his conviction of God's personal providence for every man.

Islam and communism are obvious and well-understood obstacles. Secularism has received less attention, but in many ways it is a greater danger; it is the greatest enemy of the Church in the West, where it has lost whole nations to the Church, and it has certainly infected the African educated class.

By secularism we understand a philosophy, often unformulated, which admits that religion has a place in human life but seeks to restrict this to the individual conscience; religion is a private affair, and has

---

[1] Chapter 21, p. 228.

nothing to do with a man's public life. Such a divorce between religion and life is unnatural, and, as Christopher Dawson and other Catholic writers have pointed out, once religion loses its hold on social life it soon loses its hold on life altogether.

The African is at first baffled to see how religion in Western Europe and America is apparently restricted to private life, for he views life as one whole. Yet he is gradually adopting the secularist approach, perhaps mainly through the influence of those Europeans in Africa who are clearly good men, and convinced and practising Christians, but whose faith seems to make no difference at all to their public life. Naturally it is the educated African who is most contaminated by this pest of secularism, and his Christian teachers can often be held partly to blame, for they have failed to heed Pius XII's warning about the dangers of separating doctrine from life when imparting religious instruction.

The educated African today, the man who is influencing events in his country, has probably begun his education at a Christian school at home; then he goes abroad perhaps to some secular institution in Europe or America; if he has not lost the faith by the time he returns, he is only too likely to have become a self-enclosed Churchman, a Christian in private only. He is not opposed to religion, and perhaps even earns respect as a practising Christian. But he carefully excludes religion from his public life, and his public utterances are deeply marked by the secularist mentality.

The dangers presented by this insidious philosophy should be recognized; they are all the greater in that secularism hides its fundamentally anti-religious character behind professions of respect for religious belief. It is for Christian education to emphasize the Church's social aspect, the part she has to play in all sectors of life, bringing with her everywhere Christ's message of justice and charity. Christian laymen must be brought to realize that they are Christians quite as much in public as in private.

The division of life into separate and independent compartments may partly be due to a false conception of the meaning of the separation of Church and state; care should therefore be taken to explain that this separation concerns the different areas of competence of the two authorities and does not mean the recognition of separate standards of behaviour for private and public life.

THE IMPACT OF INDUSTRIALIZATION AND THE
NEW PATTERNS OF SOCIETY

If foreign investment in Africa continues at the present rate, industrialization may be expected to increase rapidly. Experience has shown that the growth of an industrial society can easily be accompanied by abandonment of faith and a decline in moral standards. Men and women of all beliefs and none are thrown together on the factory floor and in crowded working-class housing areas, and the usual result is the levelling of all down to the lowest common denominator. There are special difficulties in Africa, for the African has been accustomed to live in a community where he has a recognized and well-defined place and which provides him with security; he is totally unprepared for life as a wage-earner, where he must fend for himself. To separate himself from the family and clan group and become part of a mixed community of strangers is perplexing for a man accustomed to live in a homogeneous society, where all think and act in a predictable, familiar way. Only Catholics who understand their faith, and live it in its full dimensions can hope to survive when thrown upon their own resources in the welter of an industrial society.

This situation will be one of the great pastoral challenges to the priest and layman in Africa in the years ahead, and they will have to be prepared to cope with all the moral and religious problems which face the industrial worker. We shall speak of these later when discussing the urban apostolate. Here we may note that the Church is also concerned with the social side of industrialization; wages, housing, working conditions, the recruiting of labour. The Church must keep a vigilant eye on all these matters and do what she can to see that the principles of justice and charity prevail. She cannot remain indifferent when she sees urban slums developing and shanty towns going up, and she must lend all her support to government plans for providing decent accommodation for African workers and their families. The industrial firms themselves should also accept responsibility for the welfare of their workers, at home as well as in the factory. In some places, successful schemes are in operation which enable the lower-paid workers to build and own their homes. These too are to be encouraged. Recreational facilities are also necessary in urban areas: cinemas, cafés and clubs of various kinds all help towards creating a better atmosphere. There should also be provision for adult and youth education. Firms that employ large numbers of workers may be asked to set up model villages, perhaps with a village for each tribe where possible.

Materialism is already rife in Africa, and it may be expected to grow as industrialization increases. As Pope John pointed out in *Mater et Magistra*, preoccupation with material things, however necessary and excellent in itself, brings the danger of obscuring man's spiritual vision. Material well-being has become the one interest of many of those from older countries who are trying to help the young countries of Africa and this mentality can only too easily be passed on to the African people themselves. Further, the African naturally tends to identify himself with his surroundings, and in his understandable desire for improvements in the material conditions of his life he may well be tempted to abandon his private beliefs and adopt the mentality of those who are trying to help him. In a wider context, it is clear that the scientific spirit and technology are setting a mark on all cultures and giving rise to a world-wide civilization, changing mental attitudes and social structures.

A change in African society which the Church has to take into account concerns the shift of power from the chiefs to government officials. The rank and influence of these new officials has to be acknowledged, and much caution is necessary when the Church is asked to intervene in a dispute between civil servants and customary chiefs. She must not become involved in civic affairs of the wrong kind, and delicate and perplexing situations can arise, as, for instance, when priests are asked to help in supervising elections. Social work too, apparently of the most innocuous kind, can turn out to have unforeseen political implications.

Central government and the growth of urban and industrial societies are disturbing the old tribal and clan structures of African society, and tribal life is clearly doomed, however slow the dissolution. In its long-term planning, the Church must take this into account. Individualism is replacing the old good life of the community; this may be regrettable but it is inevitable, and the Church's effort must be directed towards preserving what can still be saved of the generous and humane values which the African inherits from his old way of life.

Anti-clericalism is a frequent product of education, and is showing itself among the Christian body as well as among non-Catholics. Zealous lay apostles may be heard to complain that they are being kept in leading-strings. We shall have to remember that even the totally uneducated are much in advance of the African whom the first missionaries met in the last century, and they must receive the respect which is their due. The lay apostle knows his responsibilities, and it is galling for him to be treated as a child by the clergy. Power corrupts, spiritual power no less than temporal, and it is easy for the priest to exaggerate the importance of his position. A willingness to delegate to the Family and People of God the authority to which they have a right in the Church would reduce tension between clergy and parishioners.

The Church and her leaders may also be the object of attack on the part of non-Catholics. One hears talk of Catholic power-politics, of undue Church influence in education and elsewhere, of a state within a state, and the like. Often such talk is unreasonable, and has simply to be endured; but priests would do well to make sure that their attitude is not contributing to anti-clerical public opinion outside the Church.

To conclude this review of the new African society, it may be useful to point out that education is gradually splitting the community into three broad social groups, each with its own characteristics. There is still in many countries a quite large class of 'traditional' Africans, who have received no formal education, or none that has left any permanent impression, and who continue to live largely by the standards of the old Africa. Then there are those who have followed a complete or partial course of elementary education. Finally there are the educated Africans from secondary schools and institutes of higher education. It is worth our while to recognize the difference between these three classes, and to adjust our approach to the mentality and requirements of each.

A major problem which everyone concerned with the Christian mission in Africa faces is that of communication. The Christian still uses an idiom which our contemporaries do not understand. The new insights into the eternal truths which the Church is seeking can be transmitted to the men and women of today only in terms intelligible to them. Africa, now in transition from traditional patterns to the twentieth-century way of life, has bewilderment enough: the Good News must come to it with an African accent and using everyday vocabulary, rather than scholastic terminology.

2 Knowing the Circumstances of Our Time

THE APOSTOLATE AND THE LAITY

This is the era of the Christian layman. Thus, early in this book, it is worth laying down once for all the fundamental principle that *all* lay Catholics are expressly called to collaborate with priests and bishops in building up and perfecting the Mystical Body of Christ. The whole theology of the apostolate of the layman (which will be dealt with in more detail below) is based on this principle, and recent theological reflection on the nature of the Church has further underlined this principle. So pastoral theology, which has as its object the theory and practice of the apostolate, must include a theology of the apostolate of the layman, and not confine itself to a discussion of the theology of the Church and the apostolate of priest, bishop and pope.

A LAY APOSTOLATE ADAPTED TO THE AFRICAN SCENE

The problem is to find a formula for the lay apostolate which really is adapted to the African situation. One must look not only at one's own parish, diocese and nation, but at the other developing African states, whose problems all have much in common. The proposals which follow, worked out against this larger background, are widely accepted in the African Church, and follow recent papal and conciliar guidance.

First, the whole body of Christians must participate in the apostolate. Certainly it is imperative to train an elite, but this alone is not enough. To this end, the structures and methods of the lay apostolate must be widened.

Next, since the lay apostolate can only be based on the parish, we must turn the parish into a living, apostolic and fraternal community; we must give the parish an apostolic dimension which is still lacking after eighty years of missionary work. It is not enough to preserve what we have, to maintain the status quo; our times demand a programme of conquest.

The fact that the African has a strong community sense has not been sufficiently taken account of. The African lives and thinks collectively, in his religious affairs and practice as in other matters; as a Christian and an apostle, he needs to be part of a group. If we can make a vital and unified group of the parish a new dimension will be added to the Christian practice of the individual. This is something that cannot be achieved overnight, but only by radical rethinking on the part of the clergy and sustained training of the people. This training must take place through the new approach to the liturgy, through the Sunday Sermon, which should develop the communal and apostolic sense of the Sunday Mass, and through the new catechetical methods in schools and in the adult catechumenate: all of these need to be inspired with the urgency of apostolic conquest. In the harsh trials of the Congolese Church, most Christians were passive, and in the towns, adults defected *en masse*. This would seem to point to a superficiality in religious instruction, and certainly indicates the necessity of a sense of purpose in the teaching of religion and of vital apostolic communities whose life is founded on this sense of purpose. The people can only receive this sense of purpose from teachers who can relate doctrine to life.

Finally, the priest must not be content merely to speak of the apostolate and train his parishioners for it; he must associate them with his own ministry and explain his problems to them; and, above all, he must let them take the initiative.

A Continent in a Hurry

Things are changing so rapidly in the newly-independent countries of Africa, that one might be tempted to sit back and wait to see what will happen. For the Church, such a negative attitude could be fatal. Only by keeping one step ahead of events by imaginative thinking is there hope of riding the winds of change and emerging stronger, not weaker, than before. There is a danger that precipitate political events could change the situation so radically and suddenly that there could be no catching up. But an even greater danger, and a more likely one, is that the gradual evolution of new patterns will not be taken note of in time, and the Church will try too late to adapt itself. One must at once distinguish between what is changeable and what is unchangeable in the Church. The Church is not tied to any particular set of historical circumstances.

A new outlook is demanded not only in the parish clergy, but in all responsible for the training of future priests, Brothers, nuns, lay teachers and lay apostles, be they African or non-Africian. Clearly much planning lies ahead, much patience will be needed, a grappling with the unfamiliar and the untraditional which is bound to lead to strain and mistakes at first. But the first essential is to realize that a new era has begun for the Church in Africa, and methods and strategy must be transformed accordingly.

CATHOLIC INSTITUTIONS, THEIR ORIGINS AND PRESENT PURPOSE

Pastoral theology is a practical science, and it adapts its methods to the contemporary situation. The aim is always the same, the building up of the Mystical Body under the direction of the hierarchy; but the means change.

When we look back over the Church's pastoral activity down the ages, we can distinguish three separate periods. In the early days, the Church's activity was conditioned by persecution; Christians lived apart from the world, seeking and finding the mystery of salvation in an intense liturgical action. This was the first stage. In the Middle Ages, human society became Christianized and was co-extensive with the Church: to be a citizen of the state was to be also a citizen of the Church. The third stage—the post-Reformation—was ushered in by events. Since then the ideal of pastoral action seems to have been to institutionalize the world into a Christian form. Today, in the spirit of *Mater et Magistra*, the ideal would seem to be to put the world into a state of mission, to make the Church present in the world. The Church must resume her mission by direct action on society; self-withdrawal must be abandoned, and those who sought its shelter sent forth to mingle with society at every level to make known the Christian message.

When we speak of Christian institutions, some of which we may now abandon, we are clearly not referring to those which are of divine origin. The sacraments, the teaching authority, the hierarchy: these come from Christ himself and are unchangeable. Nor are we referring to institutions provided for and organized by the Code of Canon Law. But in the Church there are other, purely human and temporal institutions, of whose suitability to these changed times we must make sure. The Christian state, Christian political parties and trade unions, Christian hospitals, schools and newspapers: all these are institutions that have a human origin.[1] They have done great work for the Church in the past, but what are we to say of them today?

It will help in this discussion if we draw a sharp distinction between two kinds of Christian institution: power institutions and educative institutions. By power institutions we mean those which are wholly secular in their object, and have been founded in order to provide Christians with alternatives to the anti-religious and dangerous institutions set up by worldly bodies: for example, Catholic trade unions, Catholic political parties, professional and social organizations of every kind, business enterprises (plantations, for example), and works of charity, such as hospitals. Educative institutions run by the Church include schools, youth movements and newspapers.

Power Institutions

Power institutions are partly a heritage from the Middle Ages, when the Church managed pretty well everything in society: they certainly reflect a medieval mentality, which considered that the normal thing was for Church and state to be united. Educative institutions are especially a relic of the counter-Reformation. Each has been considered a mainstay of the Church in its day. It is widely felt that the emphasis should now shift from the institutional to the personal approach, especially as more and more institutions are being taken over by the state.

We may note here that the early Church had no institutions.

[1] The terminology is at first confusing. We are distinguishing between: 1. purely divine institutions (frequently called 'ecclesial'); 2. institutions not of divine origin, provided for and regulated by the Code of Canon Law (frequently known as 'ecclesiastic'); 3. all other institutions in the Church (frequently called 'Christian'). These 'Christian' institutions are either (a) power (pressure, prestige) institutions, or (b) educative institutions.

Her only pastoral activity seems to have been the Sunday Mass–liturgy, with the catechumenate and instruction for children. Even schools, even non-Christian ones, did not begin until the fourth century. Yet this was the period in which Christianity triumphed over paganism, and succeeded, as we have not yet succeeded, in transforming a non-Christian society into a Christian society. How was this achieved? Leaving aside the action of God, always present but unseen, the Church's success would seem to be attributed to the power of a dynamic liturgy and of parishes alive with charity. Parents whose formation had been through the liturgy were able to associate Christianity with life and to hand on to their children a truly living faith. There was no organized lay apostolate, no youth movements, no clubs; yet young people were able to win a pagan world to the faith. There is little point in attributing the source of all this to the early charismatic gifts: these did not endure up to the Edict of Milan.

In modern Africa, the Church's Christian institutions, both power and educative, can be sources of difficulty. They may have fitted the needs of the apostolate ten or twenty years ago, but we cannot assume that they still do so today. We can frustrate God's purposes if we cling to patterns determined by merely historical circumstances which no longer obtain. There must be no fighting for lost causes. In Africa the time to pass from an institution Church to a true Church of mission has come.

Several objections may be made to power institutions today. In the first place, they may very easily seem to be in competition with those under secular control, and so drive Church and state into opposition. The dualism between the Church and the world was foretold by Christ, and it will continue until the end of time. The Church's task is to enter into a fruitful missionary dialogue with the world; by establishing power institutions of her own, she artificially suppresses this dualism, which should be accepted as a fact of life. The Church must not seem to be setting herself up as the rival of the state, least of all in a developing country. In Cardinal Doepfner's words: 'Renewal is necessary . . . as a corrective to false developments. Her presentation of Christ's love can be defective if the Church, for instance, uses power rather than humility, force rather than service.'[1]

[1] Address to Katholische Akademie, Munich, Feb. 1964.

Secondly, the Church's power institutions can do damage to Christians. They have about them, these organizations, something of the sterner forms of the Old Testament. Keeping God's law becomes less a matter of personal conviction than of obedience to an external authority. Under the new dispensation, men are called upon to draw their life and their inspiration from the sacraments and from the Word of God, and to make a willing surrender to the sweet yoke of Christ; if the Church hedges them about with regulations in power institutions, Christians may too easily be satisfied with external conformity. Further, an excessive desire to protect the faithful from the world drives deeper the division between men; inevitably there will grow up a tendency to divide mankind into two groups: the good (inside the Church), and the bad (outside). There could be no more effective way of killing the apostolate of the temporal order than for Catholics to consider themselves as quite separate from, and better than, those outside the Church. There are not two kinds of men, but only immortal souls. Those souls who are in possession of the Good News have the duty of handing it on to the rest. A holier-than-thou attitude is no help to the Church in her attempt to mingle with all men and prepare their eventual entry into the Church by the indirect apostolate, that consecration of the natural world which brings with it the doctrinal and moral truths of natural religion.

These Christian power institutions, albeit conditioned by Christian thought, are very near to humanism. They postulate a Church which is rooted in a Christian order both religious and disciplinary, whereas the Church, in the last analysis is a mystery, the Paschal mystery, and in any case is in a state of mission. By building up an institutional Church we do not thereby build up the Mystical Body of Christ which is the Church. There is also the danger of basing our pastoral strategy on an immediate political context, cashing in, as we say, on the policy or tactics of this or that particular government or party, nationally or locally, as opportunity comes. There are not wanting clergy and laity who think this is the key to all Church–state co-operation. But such influence is a boomerang, as recent African experiences have shown; it would be disastrous to the Church in Africa at this time.

What we have called power institutions, then, seem to be undesirable and should be abandoned when convenient. They are much less acceptable than the educative institutions. Evidently we cannot withdraw at once from all power institutions, for many of them are rendering a service to society and cannot easily be replaced. The common good, once again, is the measure, and the Church should only give up her existing power institutions when she can do so without inflicting damage on society. In certain cases, she may even set up new institutions, to satisfy an urgent need. But this should be by way of exception, however frequent the exception may be in some places. The general principle must be that it is no part of the Church's task to provide for her children institutions whose objectives are merely worldly ones.

Educative Institutions

Schools, youth movements and the press are in themselves excellent means of the apostolate. But they always remain means; when they are turned into ends, something has gone wrong. Catholic schools help the Church's apostolic mission only to the extent that they fit into the contemporary scheme of things. What really matters is that the Church be present throughout national education. There is a real danger in Africa that if Catholics resist too strongly government pressure for some change in the running of schools, the governments will be provoked into taking measures which will damage the really essential interests of the Church. As things are at present, missionary bodies have what amounts to a monopoly of education in Africa. Will the independent governments be prepared to accept such a state of affairs permanently? Or will they not be understandably anxious to educate the youth of the country themselves, and impart to them the spirit which they are seeking to develop in the country?

We are not advocating the abandonment of Catholic schools. We only wish to say that the subject should be considered dispassionately in the developing countries, and with an eye on the Church's essential interests. 'The Church,' said the Bishops of Tanganyika in 1961, 'has the right to possess her own schools, and to educate Catholic children as the delegate of the parents.' But it should be observed firstly, that even if the worst comes to the worst, and all Catholic schools are nationalized, all is not lost; secondly, should this happen, the Church must continue to co-operate with the state and seek to make use of any means which will secure the Catholic education of the child (for example, providing Catholic teachers for state schools); thirdly, the state has the right to supervise the whole of the secular side of Catholic schools, and Catholic co-operation in this matter must be willing and complete; and, fourthly, Catholic schools have two functions: they provide Catholic education for Catholic children, but they also provide a service to society.[1]

A spirit of 'hang on to our institutions at all costs' soon leads to competition with non-Catholic institutions, and a desire to keep our own institutions by raising standards (gaining the best results in examinations, for example). This creates the exact opposite of the state of mission and co-operation with every class of society and that penetration of the temporal order which is the whole aim of the apostolate of the new era to which we are now come. Again, it creates a Catholic ghetto, in direct contrast to the appeal of Pope John XXIII, in *Mater et Magistra*, for full social co-operation. In his speech at the opening of the Second Vatican Council, Pope John went out of his way to call his children 'citizens of heaven *and earth*'.

Finally, these works absorb money, time and personnel. One need only recall, for example, that a third of the Church's total effort in Tanzania is in education. In particular, the priest is being taken away from his proper work, which is the ministry of the word, the liturgy, and the transformation of his people into ardent Christians and dedicated apostles. As far as he can he must leave the institutions—when they are necessary—to the laity. Throughout the Christian world we see this unfortunate channelling of the priest away from his true role. Typical of many such cases is that of a boys' school one recalls, that absorbed thirty priests as teachers, in a diocese with a Catholic minority which was short of priests. State universities are often allowed less than a tenth of that number to act as chaplains for several thousand Catholic undergraduates; yet these young men are the leaders of the future. There can, of course, be no question of returning great numbers of priests to the parishes at once, any more than there can be question of closing institutions which constitute a public service, such as the

---

[1] See the balanced appraisal of this question in L. W. ROBINSON, M.M., 'Church Schools and Religious Liberty' in *African Ecclesiastical Review*, Jan. 1965, especially pp. 91–3.

hospitals. The common good comes first and it is our duty to serve society. Abrupt changes would be disruptive. But we must begin now to adapt the Church to the new trends and the new structures.

Today the Church is absent from entire areas of arts and letters, industry, culture, politics and the broader streams of intellectual life. Yet her mission is to influence the full range of civilized activities. The Gospel of Christ implies more than a purely spiritual message. Might not one reason why the gap is widening between secular and Christian life be that the Christian has met the world by organization rather than by personal encounter? In the present reappraisal of pastoral strategy there is need above all for personal responsibility. It is the work of the Church's leaders everywhere to convince Catholics of this individual involvement.

At no time has it been easy effectively to balance the needs of the institutional and the personal approach. But it is at least clear that first things have not always come first.

We hope that in this delicate question what we have written will not be misunderstood. Little has been written by pastoral authors about the possible passing of the institutions, although this is occasionally discussed. We have relied principally upon the statement (stronger than ours) of the Congo-Leo hierarchy, and on contributions by Father Liégé, O.P., of the Catechetical Institute of Paris.[1] What we have written has been at the level of seminal thought rather than practical application. The European or American reader will remember that we have the developing countries, Africa particularly, in mind. Our remarks do not refer at all, for example, to Catholic schools in European and American countries with Catholic minorities. And it must always be remembered that it is solely for national conferences of bishops, or the Ordinary as the case may be, to decide when and if any particular Christian institutions have ceased to serve.

[1] Cf. *Actes de la vie. Assemblée plénière de l'Episcopat du Congo*, Leopoldville, 1961, pp. 107–34; and the course of pastoral theology given by Father Liégé, O.P., at the Catechetical Institute of Paris, and also his article in *Parole et Mission*, no. 15. The Congo-Leo hierarchy acknowledge their debt to Father Liégé.

3 Africanization

The Church has been planted in Africa, but its roots in its new soil are not strong. The reasons for this are not far to seek. Christianity, to the African, is revolutionary. It completely alters his attitude, not only to his religion, in its social and personal aspects, but also to the structure of his society and to his relations with his community. It draws him away from the society which hitherto was his support, and he feels rootless. His conversion was a leap into darkness and for some time he is unable to grasp the underlying unity between his new faith and his old social and cultural patterns. So, in time of stress, he slips back to seek security in the old patterns of life. The cleavage in his spirit goes deep, far deeper than that of the Western Protestant or agnostic who enters the Church.

This is undoubtedly the chief cause of the restlessness of the faith in Africa. There are others. The Gospel was brought by non-African missionaries, who have sometimes been criticized too glibly: however much they desired to adapt to African culture, they brought with them the only culture they knew, their own. As a result, the African Church still has a European face. Again, Christianity has rarely been presented as a dynamic, living reality, a force which engages the individual's whole personality. Instead, the people were given a code of things not to be done; doctrine was taught theoretically, and lacked the personal impact and simplicity of the Bible, to which the African has a much closer cultural affinity than the missionary Fathers of that time, or of our own.

Unwittingly, the position was made worse by the ex-colonial powers. In the former English-speaking territories, an attempt was made to preserve the original system of rule as far as possible, but the impact of the new culture went deep. To this, now, is added the disruption of urban life and industrial work, with their blurring of moral standards and the loosening of the ties of tribe and clan. Again, the missionaries were Europeans, as was the colonial power, and they had to work with it. For the African, religion was tightly linked to the animistic and communal society; it seemed to him natural that the Christian religion should be equally closely linked with the alien society of the colonial powers.

Adaptation: the Essential Catholicity of the Church

In any discussion of Christian adaptation, the fundamental fact to be grasped is that the Church founded by Christ is a universal Church in which men of all races and cultures find their natural home. Its coincidence with Greco-Roman culture, however providential, is a historical accident. It must be clearly understood where essential Christianity ends and Western culture begins. Christianity absorbed and developed the old pagan cultures of Rome and Asia; the task of both missionary and diocesan priest in Africa today is to ensure that Christianity absorbs the culture of Africa in the same way, and becomes incarnate in this way. All that is valuable in African culture, whether in its thought, its moral standards, its social life or its art, must be used as the material out of which to build the African Church. The use of the vernacular in the liturgy, the adaptation of Church ceremonies to African thought and way of life, the use of African music and art for Church purposes, the study of the social life and moral customs of Africa in the light of Christianity: all this is hard and slow work, but it is essential if the Church in Africa is not to remain what she very largely is today, rootless, a stranger from Europe. The melancholy story of the Chinese Rites provides all missionaries in Africa with an unforgettable lesson: the loss of China to the Church was due in part to the lack of a profound approach to Oriental culture by Western missionaries. The Church must adapt or perish.

In spite of some tragic exceptions, on the whole the leaders of the Church have long recognized the necessity of missionary adaptation. In 1659, the following directive was sent from Rome to the missionaries in China: 'In no way persuade these people to change their rites, customs and manners of life, unless these practices are flagrantly opposed, not to the customs of your own homeland, but only to the faith.'[1] Recent popes have repeated the same idea in even stronger terms: 'The Catholic Church,' said Pius XII in *Evangelii Praecones*, 'does not despise, nor reject, pagan teachings, but she rather completes and perfects them . . .; in a certain manner, she has consecrated the customs and ancient traditions of peoples; she has taken their pagan feasts and transformed them into memorials of the martyrs and of sacred mysteries.' Similarly Pope John XXIII in *Princeps Pastorum*: 'The Church is ready to welcome and indeed to encourage all things that honour the human mind and heart, even if they have their origin in places that lie outside the Mediterranean basin which was the providential cradle of Christianity.'

If, so far, little has been done to incorporate Christianity into the indigenous culture of Africa, this is not due to any want of encouragement from the Apostolic See. Today, unhappily, islands of faith have been developed in the midst of African culture; they may often be flourishing islands, but they are still islands, separated from the mainland of traditional Africa and with hardly any influence upon it. The reluctance of the African Christian himself to see theological thought, liturgy, sacred art and music, adapted to his traditional heritage, is a serious difficulty in all parishes; often he resists the priest who urges adaptation.

Again, we do not blame the early missionaries; they did magnificent work and the contemporary Church in Africa owes everything to them. But our task today, with the new light which is ours, is to make good what was wanting in the past, and turn the Church into a genuinely African thing. If we avoid the painful intellectual effort involved, we are acting against the wishes of the universal Church, so clearly expressed in the Council, and by the popes.

Towards a Practical Solution

'To give life to men, the Son of God took their life. To proclaim the Word, he adopted their language. To give them the Spirit, he incorporated himself in humanity.' (Plenary Assembly of the Bishops of the Congo, 1961.) This is the principle which must guide the development

---

[1] *Collectanea*, I, p. 42.

of the African Church. As God became a Jew to preach to the Jews, so the ministers of God's Church in Africa must identify themselves with the people in every possible way.

First of all at the material level, this will mean that in some cases priests and missionaries will be called upon to accept a lower standard of living than that to which they have been accustomed. In rural areas particularly, it is not fitting that the clergy's material conditions of life should be notably superior to those of the people around them. Furthermore, everything belonging to the mission or parish should be at the disposal of the people as far as possible.

We would pay a bitter price if we waited for shocks such as those of the Congo and the Sudan to precipitate this adaptation. The Africanization of staff, the adoption of African methods of working, speaking, living—not too much abstraction, not too much haste in conducting interviews—these and a myriad of similar things loom big in African eyes. Church administration methods are still Western. More responsibility must be given to African laity: this is not proceeding as briskly as it should in the parishes. Responsibility is developed by giving responsibility; that thought should brace the hesitant who are not obeying the instructions of the Holy See. We should Africanize our educational system as quickly as possible. This implies that the actual management of the schools be entrusted to the laity, instead of an attempt to maintain the system of priest managers in those places where it still exists. It also implies the possibility that European staff, even when better qualified, should occupy posts subordinate to Africans.

Ultimately, only the African can Africanize the Church to its full extent. The missionary's role is to make himself dispensable. Let us be frank and say that both he and the African priest have sometimes lacked whole-hearted participation in the Africanization programme. The privileged classes, which are evolving so quickly, present a delicate problem. It is quite common to find among them the feeling that whatever is not Western is lacking in civilization, and little desire to go back to the past. Yet in many of them, the old values are still strong, and there is no reason why they should not borrow from the two main cultural streams which have influenced Africa: the English and the French (how much Rome borrowed from Greece). The Catholic Church, in its African context, could unify these two streams, incorporate them into her universality, and by integration with African values and forms, provide the genuinely African cultural unity which is now wanting.[1]

THE DEEPER CULTURAL VALUES

How, in practice, does one apply these ideas? There is a hiatus, most of us feel, between theory and practice. It is indispensable to have a knowledge of customs: sociologists agree that the life history of the individual is before all else an accommodation to the patterns handed down in the community. But one must see the relevance of these customs in the context of the practical science of pastoral theology; their impact here is not always immediately obvious. (In passing, we must remark that one does of course adapt to contemporary customs, not to former ones—archaism in this is as bad as archaism for its own sake in the liturgy.) What we are seeking are the deeper cultural values, all those values that make up the fabric of the African's life. It must be said that more study and field research is needed here: a proof of the need for the methods of religious sociology in all branches of pastoral work. I myself feel, as I believe many others do likewise, that failing scientific work of this kind, it is best to group together what seem to be the few hinge values, examine their substance, and consider their pastoral implications. The central values would seem to be four: three society values, family, community, natural religion; and the fourth, the African way of thought, which we might call subjectivism.

The Family

Ethnologists agree that the African universe is a unity, the centre of which is the family (whereas the centre, in Western civilization, is the individual). By family we mean both the immediate family and the greater family, the clan. Deceased ancestors are part of the family; they received from God springs of vitality, a vital force which was to be perpetuated by the family. The first point of interest for our study here is that the individual is immersed in the clan and in society. The key to African society lies largely in the effacement of the individual before

[1] Cf. Joint Pastoral Letter of the Nigerian Hierarchy, 1 October 1960.

the collective. He will not, for example, take decisions without consulting the clan. Hence, the lessening of the sense of personal responsibility which is detrimental to his Christian practice.

What are the behaviour patterns of the immediate family and, above all, what are the childhood behaviour patterns? The education received by the child in the family and the clan is all directed towards driving home his responsibilities towards his kinsmen. There was no formal education in the tribal system,[1] but the example of his elders, and the sanctions which enforced the child's acceptance of the group values, have left an abiding impression on the African mentality. The African child finds security in being accepted and noticed by his parents and by the older members of the clan. When he leaves the traditional environment and goes to a European-type school, he may have the feeling that he is being left to himself, that nobody cares about him any more. The individualism of the school, the competition, the loss of family support: all these weaken the African schoolboy's sense of security. The strikes in secondary schools may often be no more than a cry for attention.

In Western culture the child's sense of security is built on the sustained affection of parents and the inculcation of general principles and beliefs. Natural religion and the collective group take the place of these patterns for an African child. Applied, say, to the school and cate-chumenate, one must distinguish in Western education in morality between what is properly natural and Christian law, and what is quite a different thing, the application of this natural and Christian law to Western conditions. The unchangeable principles are what we must apply to the patterns of the African family.

Current shifts in values must also be taken into account, as must modern influences from outside the family group, such as school education, which is replacing the family ethos, the growth of individualism, urban development and industrialization: all of these are tending to lessen the security of the individual and weaken the hold of family, clan and tribe.

[1] Cf. 'Eléments constructifs d'une civilisation d'inspiration négro-africaine', in *Présence Africaine*, Feb.–May 1959, XXIV–XXV, especially pp. 263–5.

The African's Religious Attitude to Life

Religion is not kept in a separate department in the life of the African: it penetrates the whole of life, individual, family and social; no aspect of life can be kept separate from it. This applies, for example, to the material universe, to agriculture (where it acts to prevent new and productive methods being introduced): all that exists is under the influence of the divine. All events are explained by these religious beliefs: the African has no true sense of causality. This deep and pervading religious spirit has been a great help for the conversion of the African to Christianity, and clearly this natural religious belief and sense of morality must be made the basis of the supernatural and revealed truth we are to communicate to the African. From religion he expects an answer to all the problems of life. This we can give, not by a formal methodology of theory, but by initiation into a new life, a supernatural way of daily living, a supernatural way of looking at the universe about him, animate and inanimate, a grasp of the wonder of the life of grace which replaces and surpasses the vital force principle of his former days, which he believed to come from the ancestor spirits to the family and the clan. And we should show him in detail that the Church answers every problem: 'How have we not, having Christ, received also all things?' The Faith will preserve and enlarge his African instinct to see the universe *sub specie Dei* and it will counteract his involvement in the Western analytic spirit which divides religion, together with all other aspects of life, into separate compartments.

The priest, Brother, Sister, or lay apostle from abroad are told that they must know the mental outlook, temperament, religious beliefs and customs of the tribe or tribes they are to serve. They are aware that they must fight to preserve whatever is good in a tribe's religious beliefs and customs; that, having found the good, they must make it the foundation of their Christian teaching. Thus no one can communicate Christ's message in depth unless he has discerned the good as well as the false elements in the pagan notion of the virtues, particularly truth, justice, chastity, charity, obedience and humility. And always he has need of the sure anchorage of the principle of substitution: if a belief or custom must go, it is to be replaced by a corresponding Christian belief or custom: the saints and the holy souls, for example, instead of the spirits; the blessing of seeds and crops, instead of rain-making ceremonies, and the like.

Community Consciousness

The strength of the African community spirit, built on family and clan, is well known. To this we must add the lesser bond of the village community. The principle of kinship and the principle of the identity of the members of the clan binds tight even a large community: each member of the clan is a kinsman; fathers' brothers will be called 'father' also, fathers' and mothers' sisters 'mother'; male cousins 'brother', female cousins 'sister'. The African submits his thoughts to the group for judgement. That which is good for the community is morally good. Life is lived not as an individual, but under the pressure of the group.

Here, as in all four manifestations of the traditional textures of society of which we are speaking, account has to be taken of the new, alien factor, the insertion into that society of Western values: in this case, the individualist approach of the Greco-Roman pattern, with its structure of individual obligations and its weakness in stressing social obligations (a weakness which it is only now beginning to repair), its treatment of religion as something between the individual and God, with insufficient emphasis on his belonging to the community of a living Church.

Perhaps no aspect of traditional society has been so well understood by the clergy as this community consciousness, and it is easy to point to its pastoral relevance. Unfortunately, many of the Christians are ashamed of it, and think of it as a primitive characteristic. In catechizing, we should use this fact of community consciousness to stress the Communion of Saints and the Mystical Body: these truths it does illuminate, even if it is not a help to an understanding of the eminent dignity of the free person. Baptism should be shown as the entry into a community, incorporation into the holy unity of the body of Christ; wherever possible, the ceremony of baptism should be a communal one. The parish must be shown as the local community, a cell of the Mystical Body. Christians are in communion with the Church Suffering and the Church Triumphant. The catechumenate is a preparation for entry into the Christian fellowship, where the eucharistic banquet makes all Christians one.

We have already mentioned the value of the community sense in the lay apostolate. More use could be made of purely African organizations; we could reach the people through these and fashion our own organizations on them. What comes nearest to the organizations they know appeals to them most. Locally, they could be organized, more than is at present the case, around the catechist or a lay apostle.

If educational bodies and all the social bodies concerned, including the Church, would foster the community spirit of Africa, this spirit could be raised from passive to active 'socialization' without incurring the searing personalism and individualism of Western experience.

The African Mentality

After these three social factors, family, religion and community, we come to the special mentality of the African. The African's reasoning methods are not discursive; he knows nothing of the syllogism, he thinks inductively rather than deductively; nor is his thinking analytic: it is intuitive and synthetic. In this sense he is subjective—the word is not used here to suggest in any way that he lacks objectivity. He looks for meaning rather than sign, for the deeper reality rather than the appearance of the object. He feels what he sees; hence his vivid sensibilities and emotions. He is in sympathy with all about him, including the cosmos, the ordered universe; his sensitivity to external forces coming from other beings is acute, whether they are material, animal, human or spiritual. He identifies himself with nature—the fields about him, his plantation. This is a mentality different from the European, and to be respected as such. Its physio-psychological note is plain. One consequence of it is a circular manner of thinking, a collecting of impressions, a feeling of the way before coming to the kernel of a problem (this must be borne in mind when conducting a palaver or *shauri*). A more important consequence is the primacy in his thought of the concrete over the abstract, and the human over the institutional.

When we consider this manner of thought coming into contact with the Western mentality, we at once come to practical implications. In our schools and elsewhere, the African is following Greco-Roman forms of thought in a purely exterior way. European teachers, trained in deductive thought, pass on ideas in a way impossible for the African to assimilate. They do not square with his reasoning, and from this springs formalism in the application of the law and principles, and bureaucracy in the running of institutions. Care must be taken in the teaching of religion that formalism is not introduced into the moral law and the commandments of the Church (so that, for example, marching into and out of the confessional matters more than sorrow for sin, the act of receiving communion matters more than personal dispositions). The link between the African and Christianity must be by way of African humanism and African reasoning.

The African's natural sense of communion with the cosmos and all nature is a preparation for the life of grace in which this natural unity is raised and completed by spiritual oneness with Christ. All that is good in the primacy he gives to human relations must be kept; at the same time he must be taught the need of institutions, and the relative, not wooden, fixity of the law. Religious instructions must be concrete, without abstractions, with often repeated examples and practical applications to his life, and there must be frequent turning to the Bible, to which he, like the Oriental, is so akin. The Church's rich, instructive liturgy might have been designed just for the African—see how, having received Christ, he received all things.

There are two final points, and neither of them is trivial. Etiquette, usually formal, is part of the fabric of everyday life in Africa: it matters, and must be observed. The African is a cheerful person: those who can smile with him come close to his heart.

4   Some Consequences of Africa's Plural Society

IN FORMER times, when communications were slow and primitive, society in all parts of the world was for the most part stable and uniform. Each nation, each village even, was to a large extent self-contained and homogeneous, all its members were of the same race and shared the same culture and religious beliefs; the vast majority of mankind lived and died where their fathers had lived and died for generations. Such was the general situation in Africa down to very recent times.

Modern transport facilities have already changed this situation, and it may be expected that as the years go by the changes in African society will become progressively more profound. Men come and go now throughout the world, and there are few countries today which do not have a plural society, a society, that is, containing diverse and often conflicting elements.

In this chapter we consider how the Church is affected by this pluralism in society. We discuss five kinds of pluralism: ethnic, cultural, political, social and religious.[1]

Ethnic Plurality

Under this heading we include all differences arising from diversity of race, nationality or tribe, and we seek to find the principles which will enable different peoples to live peacefully in a single society.

All men have been created by God and all have the same fundamental dignity of creatures with an immortal destiny. At the highest level, the human race is one; differences at other levels can only be of relatively minor importance. The bishops of Tanzania declared in their letter:

[1] See joint letter of Tanzania hierarchy, *Unity and Freedom*, Christmas 1962.

'The same human and civic rights must be guaranteed to each and every member of every nationality, race or tribe living in any country. All are equal as human beings and must be held equal before the law, regardless of their ethnic origin. Discrimination against any nation, race or tribe would be clearly contrary to the natural law.'[1] It is by insisting on these obvious truths of the natural law itself that the Church seeks to bring peace on earth.

The duty of the priest is to instruct his people in the essential solidarity of the human race, and to teach them to make charity the guiding principle in all their relations with other people. This means that we must cultivate an attitude of respect and tolerance towards those who are of another race, nationality or tribe than ourselves. Tribal rivalry goes deep in Africa, but persistent efforts must be made to eliminate it, at least in so far as it leads men to offend against charity. Great tact is needed in schools, where there will nearly always be several tribes, and often different races, represented among the pupils. The Church too must keep an eye on commercial life, and use all her influence to prevent racial or tribal discrimination in trade.

Cultural Plurality

Cultural diversity is a natural result of ethnic differences. Every people has its own special intellectual, legal and artistic heritage, and this is to be respected. The state has the duty of seeing that people with a culture differing from that of the citizens as a whole are protected, and enabled to follow their traditions. There are occasions when the common good may make this impossible; but care must be taken not to make an imaginary common good an excuse for doing nothing to help minority groups.

As the natural leader of Christian culture, and the zealous patron of all that advances the spiritual welfare of mankind, the Church has a special role to play in helping to preserve the different cultures of the world. She should therefore take every possible means to protect minority cultures from neglect or oppression.

Differences in culture are, however, not confined to people of different races or tribes; within the same ethnic group, there will

[1] *Loc. cit.*

always be people who are culturally more advanced than others. All men have a natural right to develop their talents and to improve themselves so far as the circumstances of society allow, and in a developing country a special responsibility for the uneducated is laid on those who have received the advantages of a sound education. The state clearly has a duty to do all in its power to provide education for the citizens; in the meantime, it must grant the same civic rights to the uneducated and to the educated, and give to all the opportunity of living a life which is in accordance with human dignity. Catholic people should be instructed in the duties both of the state and of educated citizens towards those who are culturally less advanced.

Political Plurality

The question of allowing different political groups to develop in a country has already been mentioned in our discussion of current trends in Africa.[1] Here we repeat that political freedom is a natural right and must be respected, though there may be exceptional circumstances when the common good will demand some measure of limitation on the exercise of this right. Secondly, we note that political life, as much as any other sector of life, must be governed by the Christian principles of justice and charity; lying of any kind, and especially the spreading of malicious calumnies about one's professional opponents, is as sinful for a politician as it is for any other man. Thirdly, the Catholic politician must have the interests of the whole people at heart; it is as wrong for him to favour his own co-religionists as it would be to show special favour towards his fellow tribesmen. Here again, the common good is the measure, and the Catholic elector should vote for the candidate who will most advance the common good, be he a Catholic or not.

Social Plurality

We have already stated[2] that is is desirable for other organizations apart from the State to play a part in providing a country's social services; we have noted too that the Church must be prepared to co-operate in, and even to initiate, a nation-wide social service.

[1] Pages 3–8.   [2] Page 8.

The priest's role in social affairs is to take the initiative in launching schemes for the common good, and then leave them in the hands of laymen, while always being ready to offer advice when asked. In modern Africa, it is important that every priest have at least some knowledge of social development. Certainly the spiritual apostolate comes first and it is not normal for a priest to spend more time in social action than in his own specifically priestly work; but he should be in a position to explain to the layman the moral and doctrinal issues involved in social work of various kinds.

It must never be forgotten that where the Church is herself running a social service, she must not allow sectarian considerations to restrict her sympathies. Catholic hospitals must accept patients of all religious beliefs, and any patient in a Catholic hospital must be able to obtain the religious minister of his choice.

Religious Plurality

In most African countries, Islam and various non-Catholic Christian denominations are found existing side by side with the Catholic Church and the old animist religions. Citizens of different religious beliefs must live together in charity, and priests should be at pains to preach respect for those who have not received the faith. Every religion contains an element of truth, and all truth comes from God; the realization of this fact should be a bond uniting those of different faiths. We must emphasize in all ways, not what divides us from unbelievers, but what is common to us all. The immediate norm of morality is a man's conscience, and the rights of conscience, even of an erroneous conscience, must be respected. It would be foolish for Catholics to take personal pride in having received the free gift of faith, and they have no right to look down in any way on those on whom it has not been conferred. It is true that we must not teach that all religions are equally good; but while condemning indifferentism, we may not fall into bigotry.

Giving Glory to God in the Affairs of This World

The Church's answer to the pluralism of modern society is plain enough: her children must seek to secure the presence of Christ in all sectors of society by whole-hearted co-operation with other citizens and by doing their full duty in the temporal order.

It is a mistake to think that Catholics should prefer to work under a Catholic employer or that non-Catholics should be refused Church employment. The aim is to lower barriers, not to make them higher, and Catholics reduce the divisions between themselves and non-Catholics by incorporating themselves in society at large. The Church's mission is the eternal salvation of mankind, but her secondary, civilizing mission is inseparable from this task. She seeks to transform the world at the temporal level also and the Catholic citizen should be encouraged to see himself as a representative of the civilizing Church when he plays his part in the public life of the nation. By bringing to his fellow men the notion of God and the basic principles of the natural law, he is preparing the way for the Christianization of his country, laying the moral foundations on which grace can build at the moment designed by God. He must not regard his work in the world as a camouflaged apostolate; by simply doing good in the affairs of this world, the Catholic layman is playing his part in the pattern of redemption, for he is helping to build up the Church and renew the face of the earth.[1]

Charity, like all good, is *diffusivum sui*; it is infectious, and the Catholic in society is spreading the good infection. There must be no question of intrigue or hidden motives, as if God could bless such means in any circumstances or for any purpose; by doing good simply and humbly, the Christian layman is bringing Christ to the world in the most effective manner possible. It is charity—real, genuine, disinterested love for all men—that has been at the root of the successes of the Church down the ages as the mistress of civilization; and only a humble charity on the part of Christians will turn Africa into a Christian continent.

---

[1] In the past a dualistic anthropological conception misled Christians into considering grace and redemption as a matter for God and the soul of man to deal with, so much so that the whole range of earthly life and of human responsibility for the terrestrial future of mankind seemed to be relegated to the fringe of Christianity; one ran the risk of disregarding the truly Christian value of building the world and of promoting the advancement of peoples, thereby relinquishing the chore to those who called themselves non-Christians. How easy it is to discern in that behaviour one of the many factors through which the institutional Church alienated men from herself.' E. SCHILLEBEECKX, in *Concilium*, Jan. 1965, p. 42.

PART TWO

The Structure of
the Local Church

5   Pastoral Theology in a
Changed World

WE HAVE already observed that pastoral theology is a practical science, and that its methods are continually changing to suit the conditions of the age. The last word can never be said. It is in fact largely true to say that pastoral theology has to be not only revised but rewritten for each generation, for new situations are continually arising, bringing problems that have never had to be faced before. In our own day the tempo of change is so fast that many of the books on pastoral theology written since the last war are already out of date.

Let us begin discussion of the new look required from pastoral theologians by insisting that pastoral theology is a science and not an art. Too often it has been regarded as individual, rather than universal, in its scope: an appendix to the moral tract on confession, maybe, or a collection of commonsense methods compiled by experienced priests in the sunset of their days. It is doubtless because of this view that some theological faculties have so far been chary of including pastoral theology in their courses. Yet the object of theology in general is divine revelation, and pastoral theology treats of this revelation with regard to the apostolate; how, then, could it be simply technology, a mere know-how? We have said already that it presumes a theology of the Church, hierarchy, priesthood, laity. Its essential sources are the Bible, the magisterium of the Church and ecclesiastical history; other sources are simply auxiliary—modern psychological methods, medico-pastoral aids and the like. Its major divisions are based on the three powers of the Church: to make holy (liturgy and the sacraments); to teach (preaching and catechesis); to govern (direction of missionary activity, the apostolate of the laity, works of charity and the like).

A contemporary and authentic pastoral theology will, therefore, be hierarchical—included in this term is the living community of the

41

baptized; this will mean that it must be carried out under obedience to the divine command and to the Church. More, it will be based on the doctrine of the Mystical Body; it will not be concerned with individual groups as in the past but with the whole Church which is the Body of Christ in all its members. And it will also be eschatological; it will look still more to the universal resurrection, to the final kingdom of God, 'the life of the world to come'.[1]

A good example of the present approach is a contribution of Father Bernard Häring, *Macht und Ohnmacht der Religion* (Power and Limits of Religion).[2] Here are his chapter headings: Theological Fundamentals of Religious Sociology, Relationship between God's Kingdom and the World, Church and State, Main Problems of Religious Sociology, Theology of the Milieux, Religion and Society in General, Elite and Mass in their Religio-Sociological Aspect, Religion and State (covers politics), Religion and Economics, Religion and Culture, Religion and Present Trends, Religious Sociology in Pastoral Work, Purpose and Reason of Sociography. There follows a résumé and two final chapters, The Value of our Findings and The Plan of Action.

The ideal work on pastoral theology might be a first volume like the above, followed by a second in the usual empirical style but underpinned by the principles already laid down.

The Rediscovery of the Church

There is, however, a more profound cause for seeking a new look in pastoral theology than changing society and changing problems—and this is the Church's new awareness of herself.

Theological reflection on the mystery of the Church, particularly since the First World War, marks the breakthrough to a new Christian age. As this reflection deepened and widened it was seen that its insights came more and more to touch a broad span of Christian teaching and life. To the narrow counter-Reformation concept of the Church as a

[1] See L. DE CONINCK, 'Current Trends in Pastoral Theology' in *Theology Digest*, vol. III, 1955, pp. 15–18, condensed from *La Nouvelle Revue Théologique*, Feb. 1954. The author mentions that the term pastoral theology dates from 1851 with BISHOP BINSFIELD'S *Enchiridion Theologiae Pastoralis*. Strangely, its history began in 1792 with Maria Theresa of Austria, who ordered that the clergy be taught a minimum of dogma and a maximum of practical theology.

[2] OTTO MÜLLER, Salzburg, 1956; English translation to be published by Desclée, New York, late 1965.

hierarchical and juridical structure, it brought awareness of the Church as a supernatural reality and mystery, first as the Mystical Body of Christ, then, more recently, as a community, the family and People of God. Today this idea of the People of God is taken as the fundamental concept of the Church.[1]

This rediscovery of the full reality of the Church has meant the end of the old pastoral theology. Theology indeed it scarcely was; rather was it a practical guide with an occasional observation on dogmatic or ascetical theology. Good material, from which all benefited, but it was not enough. The supernatural reality which is the Church has pastoral activities; these of necessity are supernatural activities and therefore must be the subject of theological reflection. 'Every fresh consideration of pastoral questions, every new initiative in the field, must issue, ultimately, from a deepened understanding of that which is at once the medium and the goal of all pastoral work, namely the Church.'[2]

The empirical, the contingent, remain: bulk large indeed. But they are set in the context of a genuine theology, underpinning deductions and ratifying applications that touch the mission and work of the Church.

We have attempted in this work to follow this approach, particularly by describing the theology of the Church's mission, the theology of the lay apostolate and the theology of the parish. Perhaps it is hardly necessary to add here that missionary activity, which belongs to the whole body of the Church, derives directly from the nature of the Church and is its expression; that is why the missionary bishops requested the transfer of the dogmatic content of the schema on the missions to the schema on the Church, where it now is.

The Necessity of Planning

Given this sound ecclesiology, we may now, with Heinz Schuster[3]

[1] This is the ecclesiology of the Dogmatic Constitution on the Church, the pivotal document of the Second Vatican Council (English trans. C.T.S., London, 1965). The whole of this document deserves not only study but prayerful meditation. See, on this point, especially Chapter II.

[2] KARL RAHNER, S.J., *Mission and Grace*, Vol. 1, p. 174, London and New York.

[3] Cf. HEINZ SCHUSTER, 'Pastoral Theology: Nature and Function', in *Concilium*, March, 1965.

offer this general definition of pastoral theology: it is *that branch of theology which deals with the Church's self-fulfilment in the ever new contemporary situation.* So its primary aim is to plan the fulfilment of the Church for the present and the future. The word pastoral must not be taken, as in the past, to refer only to the pastoral activity of the pastor; this is unecclesiological. Christ's redemption is carried on by all members of the Church, not just by priests. Following our definition, we may well call pastoral theology, as do the Germans, practical theology: it is an existential ecclesiology, providing a scientific and theological meeting-ground.

Many priests have a fear of organization. The essential thing, they say, is that the apostle be a man of God and filled with zeal for his cause; form-filling is simply a waste of time.

We cannot accept this as a true analysis of the apostolate. Certainly personal holiness and apostolic zeal provide the motive-power of the apostolate; if they are absent, nothing is possible. But dedicated individuals can do little by themselves; if the motive-power is to be effective it must be harnessed and that means organization. If there ever was a time when the Church could best be served by the dispersed efforts of gifted individuals, that time has certainly passed away now. Only by combining the generous efforts of all through careful planning can the best use be made of the vast human resources which are at the disposal of the Church and which have so often been squandered in the past. We need have no fear of over-planning if we all maintain our spiritual lives. Here indeed is one important sphere of individual responsibility.

It is of course important to know, before we start planning, what it is that we are planning for. What exactly is the aim of the apostle of the young churches? We have already mentioned it several times: it is to build up the Mystical Body and to renew human society by establishing the Church. To this end, all Christians are grouped in parishes, deaneries and dioceses, and the dioceses themselves work together to ensure common action at the national level. We can imagine what an impact even a small Christian community would have on the life of a nation if all its members were inspired with a sense of missionary urgency and working harmoniously together in well-knit communities. Such a community would indeed renew the face of the earth and the immediate aim of our planning must be the formation of a large number of living and apostolic-minded communities, working together under the direction of the hierarchy to bring Christ to the world.

We speak of the witness which the Church is to give to the world, and it is important here to lay down an order of priorities. In countries where the Church is well-established, it may well be that the whole of a priest's time is devoted to looking after his parishioners; in countries of mission, however, the Church is still in the process of foundation, and her attention must be directed in the first place to those who are still outside the fold. The bishops of East and Central Africa, in their 1961 meeting, stated plainly that the aim of apostolic work in Africa is 'to establish the Church, and therefore its first care is to the non-baptized, then to the baptized non-Catholics'.[1] This is the special task of the missionary Church, to preach the Gospel to non-Catholics, and here we find the specific element which distinguishes the missionary vocation from the priestly vocation in general. Of course the faithful must be cared for, and as the years go by this will take up more and more of the priests' time; but the final aim must be to organize all Christians in working for the spreading of the Gospel.

The Use of Religious Sociology

In planning the apostolate, we have at our disposal today an invaluable instrument in the findings of religious sociology, the science concerned with the laws and development of religious society. By the use of scientific methods of research, the religious sociologist is able to provide exact statistics concerning, for example, the number of Catholics in a given area and the proportion who receive the sacraments; he discovers where conversions take place and why; he is able to find out which people are most likely to lapse from the faith and to suggest the educational and pastoral methods best suited to prevent this; he is aware too of the general changes taking place in society, and is able to indicate the pastoral approach for different classes of people.[2]

Religious sociology is more than an aid to the apostolate: as a branch of sociology it is a science in its own right. It studies the social forms of

[1] *Record of Interterritorial Episcopal Meeting*, July 1961, p. 31.
[2] There is an excellent bibliography of religious sociology in *Concilium*, March, 1965, pp. 72–7.

religious life (hierarchical organization, for example); the relations between the different structures of one particular religion (say, the parish and the apostolate of the laity); the relation of a religion to secular groups and structures (social classes, say, and civil institutions).

The religious sociologist, then, provides the Church with the data essential to her mission. Too often priests set about their work in a haphazard way which no modern business organization could tolerate; effective action must be based on established and well-understood facts, instead of on guesswork or 'hunches', as is only too often the case. We have no right to jeopardize the Church's work by taking risks which are no longer necessary.

It is unfortunate that the immense value to the Church of the methods and findings of religious sociology have not yet been everywhere realized. Clearly the findings of religious sociology need careful and indeed expert handling; there is some truth in the cynical remark that statistics can be used to prove anything; but intelligently used there can be no doubt of their value. How often does it happen, in Africa and elsewhere, that a great effort is made to put up a church which in a short time proves to be much too small or, which is perhaps worse, far too big? A demographic survey of the parish before the plans for a new church are drawn up greatly reduces the risk of such tragic miscalculation. This is one obvious example of the use which we should make of sociology. There are many others. Clear findings on such subjects as plural society, Christian institutions and current social trends would provide the parish clergy with much-needed information. Our own suggestions in earlier chapters would no doubt have gained much in breadth and depth if they had been based on a skilled and patient sociological survey, which might well have uncovered embryonic trends which we have all missed. Alas, we have not the means in Africa for professional surveys but we can sometimes learn from the findings of other parts of the Church.[1]

All priests are not expected to conduct detailed sociological studies on their own account; but care should be taken in answering questionnaires which may be sent to them from time to time on such subjects

[1] We are delighted to learn, as these proofs come from the press, that F.E.R.E.S., the International Conference of Religious Sociology at Louvain, will shortly begin such a survey at Nyegezi, Tanzania.

as tribal customs or religious practice in their area. This is their contribution to a survey which, when completed, will provide the leaders of the Church with the knowledge they need to adapt their policy to the real requirements of the apostolate. It need hardly be added that it is necessary to carry out instructions received from the bishop; we have higher motives for obedience, but it may sometimes be a help to realize that these instructions are usually based on a wide and carefully conducted survey, and are not simply the result of a bright idea which came to the bishop one morning.

The Importance of Team Work

The Church is not a club for freelances, but a living community where all work together for the realization of the aims of the apostolate. This means co-operation with one's fellows and loyal submission to authority. There are perhaps some Christian denominations which provide us with an example of what can happen in a religious society when each member feels free to act as he thinks best. It may indeed seem occasionally that an individual would be able to achieve more for Christ by branching out on his own; but nearly always this will be an illusion, even as far as material results are concerned. What is certain is that there can be no supernatural fruit from any work performed outside obedience; our Lord is the life-giving vine, and if we cut ourselves off from his authentic branches, we cannot hope ourselves to receive the life of Christ, much less to be able to pass it on to others. The intelligent co-operation of all, under the guidance of the hierarchy, will alone enable the aims of the missionary church to be realized.

We speak later on of the details of parish and deanery organization; here we simply give the broad outline of how the apostolate is to be planned. At the parish level, all the priests must work together; they discuss all problems in common and act as one man. The priests in turn unite with the other apostolic workers in the parish—Brothers, Sisters, lay apostles—to form again a single team. (The presence of Sisters at the parish council is expressly mentioned, Cardinal Suenens reminds us, in a letter of Cardinal Cicognani, written in the name of Pope John XXIII.) All come together for regular meetings; no matter how specialized the work of some may appear—in schools, for example, or hospitals—they are all contributing to the single, fundamental work of building up the Church and renewing human society, and they all have something to offer when the apostolate is under discussion. Next comes the parish council of laymen, whose special function is to co-ordinate the various types of Catholic action in the parish, including of course the general lay apostolate which is the business of every parishioner. In towns especially, these meetings of laymen will often cover more than one parish; a town is one social unit, and there must be full co-operation between the different parishes. Public authorities are sometimes shocked when they find this lacking. In the deanery meetings of the clergy, and of the laity (for deaneries should be envisaged as lay as well as clerical organizations), plans of action are drawn up to be submitted to the bishop.

Above the deanery comes the diocese, with its head, the bishop, to whom all owe obedience. In most dioceses it has been found necessary to set up specialized teams at the diocesan level, for the parish organization is too small for certain types of apostolic work. Five kinds of diocesan teams will usually be required, one each for the urban apostolate; the rural apostolate; the apostolate in schools; the liturgy; and youth problems.

By careful planning and team work on this scale, we enable the Church to meet the challenge of the twentieth century. There is no other way.

Lest, not only here but throughout these pages, we should seem to our brother priests to aim too high, to fail to appreciate their burden or the difficulties of carrying out what we ask, let us say here, once and for all, that we are grievously aware that their difficulties are crushing. How frustrating it is, for example, not only to try to find but to try to train lay apostles. It is God who gives the increase and we have a right to set our sights as high as his power; do not blame us if sometimes we seem to reach for the stars.

6   The Growing Church

The Establishment of the Hierarchy and Some of its Implications

IN THE early stages of the evangelization of a country, missionaries come from abroad and seek to plant the Church. They receive their mandate from the pope, who bears the ultimate responsibility for the Church throughout the world, and they work under a vicar apostolic, who is usually (though not necessarily) in episcopal orders, and who receives his jurisdiction directly from the pope.

At the end of the missionary phase, a local hierarchy is established. This means that the Church has now been planted, and, to borrow the terminology of politics, is ready for self-government. Dioceses are set up, and the bishops placed at their head govern by 'ordinary' jurisdiction, that is, by powers attached to their position, and not simply by virtue of delegation from the pope.

We discuss in this chapter the general significance of the establishment of the hierarchy and three associated points: the permanence of parish priests, the deanery organization, and parish finance.

THE ESTABLISHMENT OF THE HIERARCHY

The last fifteen years have seen local hierarchies set up in almost the whole of Africa. In 1950, the hierarchy was established in what was then British West Africa; during the next decade, the same step was taken successively in South Africa (1951), East Africa (1953), Southern Rhodesia (1955), former French Africa and Madagascar (1955), Gambia (1957), Northern Rhodesia and Malawi (1959), and the former Belgian territories in the Congo, Ruanda and Burundi (1959). The Holy See has thus recognized the existence of an African Church. Strictly speaking, the missionary period in Africa has come to an end, and the Church in that continent is now governed according to the general rules of Canon Law, and no longer according to the law of territories of mission (or, at least, not entirely).

Nearly all the decrees setting up the hierarchy in Africa mention two specific points: the consultors of vicariate days are to be replaced, when and where possible, by a chapter of canons; and each diocese should have at least a junior seminary to prepare the local clergy of the future. It is well to note these legal points, but of more interest to us are the wider implications of the establishment.

In general terms the end of the missionary phase of the Church in Africa means that the young churches of Africa should aim at living from all points of view as diocesan churches just as the diocesan churches of the whole world do; this in spite of the fact that the Church may not yet be fully implanted in these new dioceses owing to the need of inner growth and development. Above all, more responsibility must be given to local church leaders; this supposes an even greater effort than in the past to train a complete African clergy, a numerous body of African religious of both sexes, and a zealous African laity. The missionary is still needed in Africa, and he will probably be needed for a long time, but the nature of his work is changing; the pioneer work has largely been done, and the fundamental task now at the parish level is the religious formation of the African laity; a fervent laity will certainly produce the vocations which are so badly needed, and will ensure that the Church strikes those deep roots in the local soil which we have already spoken of as the first objective of the Church in Africa today.

Although in the technical sense the missionary phase of the African Church is over, in a broader sense the Church in Africa, as indeed in the whole world, must remain a Church in the state of mission. The Code of Canon Law implies this when it urges all ordinaries and parish priests to consider non-Catholics living in their territories as 'commended to them in the Lord' (Can. 1350, §1). The Church is always in a state of mission, and all priests in Africa, whether missionary priests or diocesan priests, have pastoral duties to non-Catholics. It would be as wrong for the foreign missionary to consider that the mission to non-Catholics was confided exclusively to him as for the local clergy to think that foreign priests had no longer any right to minister to the faithful. All priests working in Africa have exactly the same task, first, to preach to those outside the Church and second to care for those who are inside.

With the end of the missionary period, the expression 'Catholic Mission' becomes obsolete. Parishes should be referred to simply by their patron and the name of the place, according to the universal practice of the Church, thus: St. Joseph's, Chilosa. Notice boards should not therefore be inscribed 'African Clergy, Roman Catholic Mission', or 'Such and Such White Fathers' Mission'; these expressions suggest a church within a church. The term 'Roman Catholic' has undesirable overtones in countries where there are also Protestant Christians, and is best avoided; the term Catholic is specific enough.

The parish priest is to be known as such, and not as Father Superior. A parish priest who is also a member of a missionary society or of a religious congregation is Father Superior only with regard to those curates working under him who belong to his society or congregation; any African or volunteer priests working under him are simply his curates, and he is their parish priest and nothing else. It is also desirable that the faithful get into the habit of speaking simply of the parish priest; whoever he is, he is not their Father Superior.

THE PERMANENCE OF PARISH PRIESTS

The Code of Canon Law (Cans. 2147 and 2157) recognizes two kinds of parish priests, movable and immovable, but it clearly assumes that all parish priests are more or less permanently appointed. It is true that there is a healthy tendency in the universal Church today not to multiply parishes from which the parish priest is canonically immovable, but it is in the interests of general order and stability that parish priests be not changed too often. In early missionary days, when the work to be done is so vast and the priests so few, it is natural for there to be a good deal of movement; new situations are continually arising, new opportunities are continually presenting themselves, and pioneer missionaries necessarily form a kind of flying squad, ready to go anywhere at almost a moment's notice. With the establishment of the hierarchy and the arrival of a more settled state of affairs, it is desirable that parish priests stay longer in the same place than the superiors of mission stations were often able to do. Mission stations are hastily erected, temporary structures, and their staffs are likewise provisional; parishes on the other hand are more like permanent buildings, and they need a more permanent staff. Bishops of course must be free to change their priests according to the requirements of the common good, but they will be inclined to consider the appointment of even 'movable' parish priests as more or less permanent. This is according to the recommendation of Can. 454, §1, and is reflected in the common practice of formally inducting parish priests into their office.

Official appointment and formal induction are normally required for the validity of a parish priest's jurisdiction; if this has been overlooked the Church may be considered to supply the jurisdiction according to the principle of common error, and after three years the title becomes convalidated by prescription.

The erection of the hierarchy entailed parish status for what formerly were only missions. Many of the clergy think this means that these parishes are only quasi-parishes. This is not true.[1] What is true is that parish priests in countries under Propaganda are movable. And, in any case, the term quasi-parish is, as the canonists agree, obsolete for all practical purposes. Further confusion comes from the proviso of the *Sylloge* (no. 85) that whatever is stated in law of quasi-parishes still applies to mission parishes.

DEANERIES

The Code of Canon Law (Can. 217) makes provision for the parishes of a diocese to be grouped together in a number of deaneries, and in many parts of Africa it may now be considered opportune to put this provision into effect, for it is a normal part of the structure of a canonically erected diocese. The great advantage of the system is that it unifies pastoral planning, bringing neighbouring priests together at regular intervals, so that they can discuss common problems and, not less important, simply enjoy each other's company. The priest who is on intimate terms with his brethren is supported in his vocation, both spiritually and psychologically, and the deanery organization encourages this desirable fellowship among priests.

[1] See BISHOP DE REEPER, 'Juridical Aspects in Newly Established Mission Dioceses', in *Novella Ecclesiae Germina*, Dekker and Van de Vegt, Nijmegen-Utrecht, 1963, pp. 39–40, especially his reference to *Sylloge*, no. 85; also, ibid., 'Parishes and Parish Priests in Mission Dioceses', in *African Ecclesiastical Review*, Jan. 1965; note what he has to say on installation.

The different priests of the deanery are united principally through the deanery meeting, when all come together to take part in a theological discussion and to talk over pastoral planning. Such meetings take place at intervals fixed by the bishop; in many places it is the practice to hold them four times a year, during the Ember weeks. The dean fixes the place and time of the meeting, draws up the agenda and distributes a copy to each of the priests of the deanery in good time before the meeting; it is also the dean's task to send a report of the meeting to the bishop, embodying any proposals which need the bishop's sanction.

The dean is chosen by the bishop, usually from the parish priests of the more important parishes, and may be changed by him at will. By virtue of his appointment he takes precedence over all the other priests of the deanery. He looks after his brethren with fatherly care, taking an interest in each of them personally. In particular, the dean must see that any sick parish priest receives all the temporal and spiritual assistance he needs, and he makes the funeral arrangements when a parish priest dies. If a parish is vacant, or if the parish priest is prevented by illness from fulfilling his duties, the dean is responsible for seeing that Church property is safeguarded. The dean too is obliged to see that the priests of his deanery live in a fitting manner and carry out the bishop's instructions and all other priestly duties. He makes an annual report to the bishop, noting the good that has been done, and making any criticism that is called for, though of course here he must be prudent and objective.

The dean presides at the deanery meeting. This will usually include a talk on some subject of practical importance by a qualified priest or layman. Obvious topics will be pastoral liturgy, catechetics and social problems. The meeting should be followed by a fraternal meal where all relax together.

In some places there is a custom whereby the dean presides at the induction of a new parish priest; often the occasion is the object of a special paraliturgical ceremony. The dean introduces the priest to the people and urges them to show him love and obedience; the parish priest then addresses his new flock for the first time. Such a ceremony helps the spirit of the parish, whose welfare depends to a great extent on the relations that exist between the parish priest and his people.

There is every reason why the priests of the deanery should come together socially, in one of the presbyteries of the deanery, even outside the occasions of the regular deanery meetings.

PARISH FINANCE

The establishment of the African hierarchy means that the Church in Africa is moving towards a situation where it will be completely self-supporting, not only as regards personnel but also as regards material resources. There should therefore now be an increased effort to make each parish financially self-supporting. The economic conditions of many countries will make it impossible to realize this aim fully at present; but serious and sustained effort is essential. One day missionaries will withdraw from Africa; they must not leave the African clergy with an impossible financial burden. The Church cannot be said to be truly planted in Africa until it is able to support itself completely.

For the sake of convenience we group together here everything we have to say about parish finance. After speaking of the education of the laity in this matter, we add a note on church dues, and a second on the methods to be employed in collecting money.

Education of the Laity: Financial Priorities

The idea that the members of a parish are responsible for the support of the clergy and of all parochial works is a matter of education. It must be seen above all as a spiritual duty. A parish where there is genuine fervour is a giving parish; people who have really understood the meaning of religion, people to whom their faith is their life, want to give material support to the Church; material generosity is a spontaneous expression of the religious spirit. On the other hand, good habits in the matter of giving to the Church will increase spiritual fervour; even on the purely natural level, people value more what they have paid for themselves. Thus fervour and generosity go hand in hand, and by teaching the people to be generous, we are also helping them to be fervent.

In many parts of Africa, priests have waited far too long before insisting on this essential duty, and it is by no means uncommon to meet Christians who consider that finding money is the priest's job, not theirs. All priests in Africa, but especially priests from abroad, are aware that the people regard the clergy as possessed of boundless riches. There is nothing surprising in this. Priests who come to Africa from Europe or America are often unable to reduce their standard of living to the level of that of the local population, and this causes mis-understanding. Missionaries have the right to be provided with the necessities of life and with a degree of frugal comfort, even though this style of life may seem luxurious to those with a different background. All we can do is to do our best to live very simply and poorly, while not sacrificing our health, and trying not to be a source of scandal to our people. Another way of showing our people the real nature of the situation is to refrain from putting up large, imposing buildings, out of any private sources of income to which we may have access; it is much better to wait until the people begin to contribute themselves, even if this means a fairly long delay, and then to erect a modest structure in keeping with the general surroundings of the country. An endemic disease of missionaries is *morbus aedificandi*, building disease.

Priests all over the world know how disagreeable is this duty of instructing the people in their responsibility for the upkeep of the Church; but it remains a duty. Our Lord praised the widow who contributed her mite, and in the same spirit even the very poor should be encouraged to give something, as an act of religion.

The priest cannot resort to unworthy arguments in urging generosity on their people. The fact to be insisted on is that this is a permanent and natural duty of the faithful, whatever other sources of income the Church may or may not have. Thus priests should not say that support from overseas has been reduced, or that the bishop has been obliged to cut down the allowances for the upkeep of priests or catechists, or that schools have had to be closed; these things are irrelevant. Much less should appeals be made to unworthy motives; any comparisons with Moslems or Protestants, any reproaches to the effect that the people are still living on foreign money, are harsh and discourteous and can damage the spiritual tone of the parish.

Instruction on financial responsibility should be given from the pulpit, in parish meetings and in private talks; the confessional is not the place for such subjects. The people must be brought to realize that we preach the necessity of generosity to the Church as part of their spiritual formation and for their own benefit, not for ours. Our preaching must bring no bitterness, but if the lukewarm are driven away from the Church because they are unwilling to give, this must be tolerated; we cannot alter the law to suit all tastes. If we work with patient and gentle persistence, we shall eventually succeed in bringing our people to a sense of their duty. As long as we ourselves are visibly spiritual men, living lives of personal poverty, there is no danger that we shall alienate the people by asking them for money. What matters is to have the approach of a priest and not of a commercial traveller. We are not out to enrich ourselves, but to enrich our people, and that principally in their spiritual lives.

The same spiritual approach must determine how we fix our priorities in spending Church funds. Prestige projects and unnecessary luxuries like church bells must be resolutely abandoned; it is no use preaching to the people that giving to the Church means giving to God if they see us spending their money on such things. We must remember that it is the Church that we are building in Africa, not churches, and regulate our spending accordingly. We need to keep things in their true perspective and realize that training good catechists, for example, means far more than putting up the finest church in the diocese. The available money must be allocated in the first place to the upkeep of the parish staff, both priests and catechists, and to the travelling expenses they incur in the course of their pastoral work. The second priority is a contribution to the training of seminarists and catechists, and the third to the central funds of the diocese for common purposes. Priests as well as people need to remember that they have a duty to support wider, non-parochial works, which benefit the diocese as a whole. Independence means that the diocese, as well as each parish individually, is self-supporting. Only when a just contribution has been made to each of these three priorities should we see what is still left for the maintenance of existing buildings and for the erection of new ones. 'Il faut avoir du pain', said Dupanloup, 'avant de chercher des ragoûts.'

As part of the education of our people, it is important to keep them informed of the financial position of the parish. Accounts should be published regularly, so that the people know what money was received, and from what sources, and how it was spent. For this purpose, a simple, business-like system of book-keeping is essential. Well-kept accounts also make it possible to send in accurate returns to the diocesan treasurer, who is thus able to know how far the diocese is becoming self-supporting, if it is not already so. The order of priorities should be explained to the people. Unfortunately, they see things happen whether they give or not. It is often better to defer a project such as a better church until they begin to ask what has gone wrong.

Church Dues

A principal source of church revenue is the tithe, or church dues. In some places, the money collected in this way belongs to the diocese, but in Africa at present the bishop will often prefer to leave it in the hands of the local clergy for parish purposes.

The bishop fixes the amount of the tithe, and the faithful should contribute the sum he determines. It is usually based on the wage for a certain number of working days; in Africa's situation at present, it might be the wage for four or five working days per year, and about half that sum for women and working youths.

It is the parish priest's duty to see that Church dues are properly collected, though it will often be preferable to leave the actual collection to the catechists or churchwardens. Receipts should be issued when the dues are paid, and the money should be placed in the bank on a deposit account, where it will gather interest. To keep the money in the presbytery not only exposes it to the danger of theft, but it also means depriving the Church of precious revenue from interest. The interest of course accures to the parish and not to the diocese, but it is advisable to bank the money in the name both of the priest and of the diocesan treasurer, so that in the event, for example, of the sudden death of a parish priest, the money may still be withdrawn.

Methods of Collecting Money

Priests should be careful not to use any kind of force in collecting money. Deducting church dues at source from the wages of church workers is an objectionable procedure; people cannot be educated against their will and behaviour of this kind will only lead them to refuse to give voluntarily. The same is to be said of the practice of attaching fees to every possible religious act—fees for baptism, fees for marriage banns, collections in season and out of season. When nothing spiritual is free, religion becomes odious.

In spite of all efforts, the Church in Africa will probably remain dependent on financial help from overseas for a long time. It is therefore a natural duty of missionaries to seek help from generous benefactors abroad; again, however disagreeable this may be, it is a necessary part of the missionary's work. A word of caution however is perhaps necessary here. It is clearly very undesirable for the people to make comparisons between rich priests and poor priests, and missionaries who have more money at their disposal than others should be careful to associate their brethren in their projects, so that whatever is done is regarded as a common achievement of all the priests. Fraternal charity demands that we avoid any suggestion of glorying in our wealth; it is probably not really ours anyway, for we will seldom have earned it personally. Class distinctions are unpleasant; between priests they are intolerable. There would be something wrong with the spiritual life of a priest who considered himself superior to his brethren because he was richer. Team spirit and a refusal to use one's own money for private, pet schemes will help here.

It need hardly be added that a priest who relies wholly on money from abroad, because he is unwilling to train his people to give, is failing in his duty. Paternalism has shown its fruits sufficiently by this time to reveal that its source is sometimes pride, and the pride of man cannot do the work of God.

Conclusion

We mention two last points to conclude this question of finance. All clerics, of whatever race, secular and diocesan, are forbidden by Canon Law to take part in trade or commerce (*negotiatio* and *mercatura*) for the sake of gain, whether personally or through an agent. The priest must be above any suspicion of money-making for his own benefit; he is storing up treasure elsewhere.

Secondly, it may be pointed out that all Church employees have a strict right to be paid a just family wage. It would be strange indeed if the Church, while upholding the rights of employees in her social teaching, failed in her own duty in this field. Our own house must be thoroughly in order before we can expect to be listened to by others. Part-time employees must be paid enough for their own personal needs. It will hardly be possible in most parts of Africa to consider paying pensions to former Church employees, but those who retire after a long period of service should receive gratuities.

7 The Parish, Its Theology and Structure

Its Theology

It is a healthy sign that the theologians are now focusing attention on the parish. As the basic unit of pastoral strategy and, still more, of liturgical worship, this was necessary. It results from the new thinking on the nature of the Church. The Church, that is, not only in its juridical, hierarchical sense but the Church as the People of God. So now we have what many are calling a theology of the parish. It might be objected that the parish cannot be in itself the object of theology since it is not a supernatural object revealed by God. But it can, indeed must, be the object of theological reflection: this is clear from consideration of the nature of the Church.

The danger here is unreal thinking. Priests and layman have been bewildered by theological writing on the parish which did not square with the facts of their experience of it. Here too the outlook is brighter. Increasingly theologians are taking notice of the findings of religious sociology and the daily experience of clergy and laity. Necessary as a theology of the parish is, a more immediate need is religious sociology. Religious sociology would strip the parish of its present rigidity and adapt it to a changed world.

Naturally, in a subject which has only recently begun to come to the front of the stage, there is a certain difference of thought concerning the theology of the parish.[1] We shall sketch out briefly a few ideas on it which, we believe, would find general acceptance.

First, the parish is a territorial unit. Good; provided that this legal aspect of it does not receive excessive stress. It is also a living unit.

[1] There are some five schools of thought, not mutually exclusive. The position is clearly and fairly exposed in C. DAVIS, 'The Parish and Theology', in *The Parish and the Modern World*, London, 1965.

How otherwise, since the Church herself is a living unit, the Mystical Body of Christ? The Mystical Body lives, and Pius XII, ending all controversy, has told us that the Mystical Body and Christ's Church are one and the same thing. So the parish is not merely an administrative or territorial unit, a local subdivision with a supernatural end. Nor, as it is so commonly considered, is it primarily a place. The definition of the Code (Can. 216, §1) is for legal purpose; lawyers define social organizations, not natures.

No, the parish is a cell of a living unit. This is its most conspicuous structural feature, both intrinsically and also in its relation to the diocese and the Church. 'A parish,' said Pius XII, 'is not only a church, a priest, a territory, all expressed in more or less eloquent figures; a parish is a cell of a body which here is the Mystical Body of Christ.'[1]

The parish is a form of community as well as a living unit. Note, however, that it is normally composed of several Christian communities, not one: the priests, the family, religious, the small band of the working and praying devout. It is a community of faith because all believe in Christ and his Church, a community of worship, principally because of the sacrifice and the banquet, a community of charity because of the great commandment given by the head of the Mystical Body that his members love one another. These three characteristics of the parish correspond, following the Thomistic doctrine on faith and sacrament, to the three offices of Christ: Prophet, Priest, Shepherd. The writer to whom we are indebted for this analysis makes the suggestion that this analysis of the three characters of the parish deserves to become classic.[2]

Dominant in the story of the Church's origins is the missionary character of the parish. First in the cities, under a bishop parish priest, then later in the villages under a simple priest, the parish served the need of missionary expansion, and was an organization of conquest. *Plantare ecclesiam*, to plant the Church: growth, not merely conservation—this from the beginning was the organic law of the Church and the parish. A vast literature has grown up since the last war on this missionary character of the parish; it is worth dipping into.

[1] *Osservatore Romano*, 21 August 1957. Address to a parish group.
[2] *Die Pfarre, Gestalt und Sendung*, a report of the study week of the Pastoral Institute of Vienna, Freiburg, 1953; reviewed by P. M. Gy in *La Maison-Dieu*, no. 36, 1953.

We conclude by saying that the parish has these characteristics: it is a supernatural reality even though it is not a supernatural object of revelation; it is not an instrument of democracy—rather it is part of the supernatural Church founded by Christ; it is, according to its limits, part of the Church as an institution, though it is not of divine origin. It is supernatural in that the Church is in it supernaturally active. It issues from an astounding supernatural revelation: the Word was made flesh, and the Church and its living members are the Mystical Body of that Word.

One Consequence of this Theology

One clear consequence of reflection on the nature of the parish is the necessity of integrating the apostolate of the laity in the life of the parish. We mention this here not only because it flows so immediately from what we have said but also because this is in itself an important fact. If the parish is a living unit of the Mystical Body, it certainly has an indispensable role in the whole apostolate.

Without this integration it will be impossible to realize two central principles of all lay apostolate. These are first, that it must be in collaboration with the hierarchy; second, that it must draw its life from the Mystical Body. It is in the parish that they will draw life from the life of the Mystical Body—around the parish altar at the community sacrifice and banquet and, at the hands of their parish priest, the sacraments from which flow grace and charity. This is confirmed on the practical level by the impossibility of co-ordinating without it the different activities of the lay apostolate. Not otherwise can useless competition between one group and another be avoided. It is confirmed too by the impossibility of keeping in existence without it the different forms of the laity's apostolate, which would otherwise be anchored to individual leaders and all the inconstants of thrust and change. As in business, so here: the organization is built on the smallest unit, thus ensuring (one hopes) the flow of vertical communications within the Church; from top to bottom and from bottom to top too.

Its Structure

Africa, ninety per cent rural, is a sparsely populated continent, and priests are in short supply. This means that both in geographical extent and in population an African parish will nearly always be far bigger than a parish in Europe or America. Rural parishes of 40,000 Christians, staffed by two priests, are by no means unknown.

The typical parish in Africa has three elements. There is first of all the parish centre itself, with the parish church and the house of the priests. Secondly, there are the principal outstations, or sub-parishes as they may be called; they would be parishes if more priests were available, but as things are it is impossible to provide them with a resident priest. The congregation of the sub-parish constitutes a real community, bound together above all by the solemn weekly assembly in the central act of Christian worship, the Sunday Mass, as far as is possible. (In practice they are true parishes; the canonical aspect is another matter. But having one parish priest helps unity and co-ordination, and also is a witness of unity to those outside.) Provided that weekly Mass is assured, and that there is an adequate tabernacle, with a trained catechist in residence, the Blessed Sacrament will usually be reserved in the sub-parishes; the catechist however should in this case have a separate building in which to give his instructions. Baptisms are conferred and marriages solemnized in the sub-parishes, and the whole preparation for baptism should be given there, provided there is a competent catechist. Thirdly, there are the minor outstations. These are small centres where regular instruction is given to the people by a catechist or by lay apostles, such as Legionaries of Mary; the same leaders conduct a Sunday service for those Christians who are unable to attend Mass in the parish church or in the sub-parish. Mass will be said here as often as circumstances permit. These small outstations are very important, and the aim should be to multiply them as much as possible; it is through them that the Church reaches out to every family and to every individual within the parish boundaries, and they provide excellent centres for the apostolate of the laity. They are to the Church what communist cells are to the party: it was by means of such cells that the faith was kept alive for a century in Korea, and for three centuries in

Japan, when there were no priests in the country. To reach each family and individual a true cell movement is required; it is needed in the whole parish, but especially in these outstations. The cell movement here implies centres of prayer; lay apostles, not necessarily belonging to a special society, should go into houses and pray with the family.

All these three units—parish centre, sub-parishes and cells—are of course under the direction of the parish priest, who represents the bishop to the whole Christian community of the area. They all combine to form one canonical parish. We proceed now to speak of two councils which must be formed if the parish is really to achieve unity: the priests' council and the parish council. We conclude with some suggestions for a third council, the parish education council.

The Priests' Council

The parish priest and curates, whether they are diocesan priests or missionaries or a mixture of the two, should meet weekly to give reports on their work and to draw up plans for the coming week. This council is the best means of ensuring that team-work among the priests of whose importance we have already spoken; it enables every priest to know what his colleagues are doing, and prevents parish priests and curates from conducting a private apostolate of their own, to the detriment of the common work. The African Church is fortunate in that in many places it enjoys this tradition of a weekly meeting of the priests of the parish; in other parts of the world, we understand, it is hardly known. Here certainly is something which these parts of the Church in Africa already have to offer to the Church in older countries.

The parish priest directs the council, and his decision is final. This does not however mean that the purpose of the council is simply to enable him to communicate to the curates his decisions and his instructions. There must be truly common discussion before the final decision is taken. Obedience means much more than the passive execution of the orders of the superior; it also obliges the curate to make known his views and to contribute positively to the elaboration of the final decision, for which he too has responsibility. Once the decision has been taken, the subject must act loyally in accordance with it, even if he does not agree with it; but he cannot abdicate all prior responsibility and simply wait to be told what to do. The ultimate authority of the parish priest, however, must be recognized by all; no curate has the right to consider any part of the parish work as his own private affair in which the parish priest may not interfere.

One of the curates will usually be appointed as procurator of the parish, and it is he who will correspond with the diocesan treasurer on financial affairs; but even here the parish priest remains ultimately responsible, and it is a good plan for him to arrange for the procurator to present his accounts once a month to the priests' council for approval and discussion.

We must seek above all to prevent any jealous refusal to tolerate interest or interference in each other's work; there must be distribution of work among the different priests, and the special responsibility of each must be respected, but there must be no saying, 'This is my business. Keep out!' In a team, each member has his own work to perform, but only as a contribution to the work of the team as a whole. This must be the spirit of the parish clergy—a fraternal sharing of the common burden, seeking neither to live our own lives in isolation nor to abdicate all interest in, and all responsibility for, the work of our colleagues. We shall have occasion to come back to this point when speaking more directly of the parish clergy; for the moment we are concerned to point out that the parish cannot hope to function effectively as a pastoral unit unless the priests are fully united; and of this union the weekly council is the most powerful agent.

The growth of parishes in Africa and the great development of the Church in general means that priests must organize their time properly. It is no longer possible to live in a free-and-easy fashion; timetables must be drawn up, and followed strictly, for the giving of instructions to different categories of people, for meetings with the catechists and the leaders of the lay apostolate. It is also advisable to have fixed office hours when the people can come and see us about their problems; but we must not be too rigid here: it is good that our people feel that they will receive a welcome whenever they come to see us, within reason. We are not civil servants, but servants of Christ, who was so often besieged by the multitude out of season. Nevertheless, it is good to aim at a certain degree of regularity, consistent with our position as fathers of our people.

The Parish Lay Council

The parish lay council is an advisory body of laymen who help the parish priest in both the spiritual and material development of the parish (cf. Cans. 1182-6; 1521-3). It is a most precious means of uniting priest and people in the common apostolic work of the parish; it should be regarded as indispensable. So useful has it been found that many priests of churches abroad have asked for information about our way of running it, and have imitated our methods.

It has usually been found best to fix the number of members of the council at between ten and fifteen, depending on the size of the parish. All the members must naturally be practising Catholics, and they should also be endowed with plenty of energy and commonsense. Methods of choosing the members of the council vary. If a suitable system of election can be devised, this is probably best, though the parish priest must retain the power of veto. If election is not feasible, then the members may be appointed directly by the parish priest, normally for a period of two or three years. The bishop may reserve the right to nominate members of the council, and he may also dismiss them for a serious reason (Can. 1183, §2). Meetings should be held at least once a month, under the chairmanship of the parish priest.

It is desirable that all the outstations of the parish be represented on the parish council. The parish priest should take the council into his confidence, especially in all that concerns the material and financial business of the parish, for in such matters it is possible that laymen will be more competent than he. The members for their part represent the parishioners, and they should make known the desires or criticisms of the people at large. The council can provide the priests with invaluable information for their work, and it should be encouraged to bring to the attention of the clergy anything which they should know concerning the spiritual welfare of the people.

We have spoken already of parish finance, and here especially the council is of great value. The members should have the right to inspect the parish accounts (even if these are not displayed to all the faithful, as we have recommended); they should also prepare the annual budget and suggest means for raising the necessary income. They fix the amount of church dues, arrange for their collection, and decide on any special collection that is to be made. They may also be entrusted with the payment of salaries to catechists and other church workers; the priests, of course, must see that money is available for this purpose, and that it is paid promptly.

A well-run parish council will free the catechist from many material tasks which at present fall to him, and will enable him to devote himself to his proper spiritual work. The parish priest must learn public procedure as it is called, the method to be followed at meetings. For their effectiveness these depend to a great extent on how the chairman conducts the business. There is plenty of literature in English available on this subject. The chief rule is that everyone must keep to the point, and the chairman must insist on this if the meeting is not to degenerate into a social occasion. The different points of the agenda must be taken in order, and any irrelevant topic, however important in itself, must be resolutely excluded for the moment. The chairman must relegate questions out of place to 'other business' quite ruthlessly. 'May I reserve your point until later? At present we are discussing the code marking of eggs.'

We add a few words on the parish education council, which many dioceses have found it useful to set up in order to encourage the Christian community to take more interest in the Catholic schools of the parish. The future status of Catholic schools in Africa will probably vary from country to country. Wherever there are truly Catholic schools, the faithful must be taught to regard them as their own and not as something belonging only to the clergy. Catholic primary schools form an integral part of the whole parish organization, and the people should not consider them as Government schools which happen to have Catholic teachers.

To further this aim of involving the people in their schools, there should be a committee for each school; on this will sit some local notabilities, *including non-Christians*, representatives of parents and of teachers, and perhaps a catechist and a lay apostolate leader.

In addition, there is the parish education council. Each of the primary school committees is represented on this council, and there are also representatives of the teachers, of the parish council, of lay apostolate leaders and of the catechists. The parish priest is chairman of the education council, which should meet at least once every three months.

A principal aim of every parish is to make sure that parents fulfil their duty of obtaining a Catholic education for their children. Both school committees and the parish education council are a help in realizing this aim; attendance at Catholic schools will certainly improve once the parents realize that they have a real stake in them.

We have tried in this chapter to give some idea of the true nature and function of the parish, and we have suggested some ways of ensuring its effectiveness as an apostolic instrument. We go on now to speak of the men on whom above all the prosperity of parish life depends, the parish clergy.

8 The Parish Staff

I⊤ ɪꜱ through the priestly power that the Church sanctifies the souls of men. The priest is thus the central figure in our Lord's plan for the redemption of mankind. His sacramental power is independent of his personal qualities, but evidently much of his influence, and therefore of the Church's influence, will depend on his natural and supernatural metal. The great need of the Church is for a holy parish clergy, for only on such can a dynamic Christian community be founded. This requires high holiness, nothing less than Christian perfection: *volo fieri sanctus, et magnus sanctus, et brevi tempore.*

The early Church, following on the work of the apostles, was built up by local clergy who were themselves newly Christian. The Holy See today lays the same great responsibility on the African-born clergy. The salvation of their fellow countrymen is placed in their hands: it is for them to ask God humbly that they prove not unworthy of the call. In every land the task of building up a newly founded Church has been heavy and at times brave hearts have been tempted to throw down the burden. If the issue depended on themselves, well they might. But it does not: it depends on placing no trust in themselves and total trust in God. To lead their people to God, to be the living link between Africa and Christ, and always in an African way: this is how they will fulfil their charge. No need to ask how they will be capable of it. 'There is only one thing necessary, that we ask for everything and give everything' (Péguy). The African priest who does that will lead to God the land which he so loves and for which he has worked so hard.

We discuss in this chapter some of the qualities required of the priest in Africa today, whether missionary or diocesan, and then go on to speak of the problem of vocations. We conclude with some remarks on African nuns and Brothers, and on lay apostles.

THE PRIESTLY LIFE

This work is not a handbook of spirituality for priests. We are however specially concerned with Africa, and we venture to think it useful to say something about those priestly qualities which seem to be of special relevance in that continent today. We shall speak of poverty and charity and add a note on the spiritual life of the priest.

Poverty

The apostles were poor men, and when our Lord sent them out on their mission he insisted that they remain so. 'Do not possess gold, nor silver, nor money in your purses, nor scrip for your journey, nor two coats, nor shoes, nor a staff.'[1] Priests are not expected to apply these instructions literally to their own lives; but the spirit behind them, the spirit of dispensing with all that is not either necessary or useful, must animate the messengers of Jesus Christ in every age. St. Paul admonished Timothy in a similar fashion: 'But having food and wherewith to be covered, with these we are content . . . for the desire of money is the root of all evils.'[2]

History has shown only too plainly what happens to the Church when her priests become a moneyed class, and many African priests have said that their chief peril in years to come may well be the temptation to acquire money and property. We have already mentioned that missionaries in Africa must be prepared to accept a standard of living lower than that which they would have enjoyed had they stayed at home. We must have what is necessary for our personal life, and we need too whatever is useful for our ministry; but we have abandoned the right to all else. When priests are known for their contempt of money, the spiritual tone of the parish is safe and the generosity of the faithful assured.

Gladys Aylward, the famous Protestant missionary in China, was thus described to her mother in a quaint letter from a Chinese friend: 'She won't mind the bitternesses, difficulties and poverties. Most foreign missionaries come to China not purely for preaching the Gospel, and

---

[1] Matthew x. 9–10.   [2] I Tim. vi. 8, 10.

most of them are very comfortable, and therefore very few people in China believe Jesus Christ. Because the people see it is not same what saying in Bible when they have it compared.'[1] Gladys Aylward was different; the Catholic missionary has to be different too.

Priests must live frugal lives: this is one side of the Church's poverty. The other side concerns the Church's public image. The Church, insofar as she has a sacramental form, is not only an effectual instrument of the grace of Christ but a sign lifted up among the nations, a city set upon a hill. Therefore she must in her dealing with men be filled with the Gospel spirit of charity, humility and poverty, so that those who are searching for Christ may descry even in the visible face of the Church the spirit of Jesus. She is the servant Church, fashioned by a servant Lord. Her presentation of Christ's love is defective when she uses power instead of humility, force instead of service; and her presentation of Christ is also defective when she appears rich where Christ was poor. The missions *Propositiones*, as discussed at the Second Vatican Council, asked that we be 'followers of the poor'. Too often the image the Church presents to the world is of a proud and worldly institution, surrounded by a pomp and ceremonial rather remote from the evangelical and apostolic ideal. Many Council Fathers have spoken of the necessity for public poverty, and many are uneasy about the titles and costumery with which they, and holders of honorary titles such as 'Monsignor', are perforce surrounded.

Poverty and simplicity were characteristics of our Lord, and they must be seen as characteristics of his Church. Pope Paul VI, addressing in Rome the general chapters of several religious congregations, urged the necessity for corporate as well as individual poverty. 'But, apart from the poverty in which the individual members must live, it is not proper to neglect the poverty to which the religious order as a whole should aspire. Religious institutes should refrain, in their buildings, and in all their doings, from luxuries and ornaments which are too fine; they should reject all things which are ostentation or luxury, and think upon the social condition of the men who live around them.'[2] It is clear how this principle is to be applied to the Church in Africa. There must be no grandiose buildings, but only buildings which show to mankind in a living sermon the poverty of Jesus Christ. The fact that the African

[1] ALAN BURGESS, *The Small Woman*, Pan Books, p. 123.   [2] *The Tablet*, 6 June 1964.

likes to see civic and religious leaders surrounded with circumstance cannot annul the teaching and example of the servant Christ.

Charity

Communitas calamitas, said the monks of old, and throughout the world priests know that one difficult feature of their chosen life is learning how to live and work together. There is nothing surprising in this; at every level of society 'other people', just as they are the source of most of our human joys, are also the source of many of our human difficulties. This is the law of life since the fall, and priests must be prepared for tensions in their common life and not grow discouraged when difficulties begin to show.

The human principle which must guide us in our relations with the other priests with whom we work is that we are not competitors but collaborators. Unity and co-operation are essential for our own personal happiness and for the success of our work, and experience has shown that when initial difficulties have been overcome and tensions resolved, even the most oddly-assorted communities can live together in great happiness and in fruitful collaboration. Racism and nationalism, as we have said in our first chapter, are to be abhorred. Their source is pride, and they divide men. The priest represents the saviour of the whole human race, he is the disciple of a master who was meek and humble of heart; his own humble search must therefore always be for what can bring men together, and he must strive to banish, from his own heart in the first place, whatever tends to division.

Both missionaries and indigenous priests need a high degree of cultural, racial and national humility if they are to live and work in harmony. We all know the temptation to exalt ourselves, whether individually or collectively; it is a temptation we must resist if we are not to bring ruin on the Church. There must be no criticism of our fellow priests or of other parishes; we are all one, and in damaging the reputation of other priests we are damaging our own. We preach charity often enough; let us be sure that we practise it at home.

Language can cause some difficulty in the multi-lingual society of modern Africa. Elementary good manners demand that the language of the presbytery be one that is understood by all the priests. There may well be a diocesan ruling on the subject, and this of course must be carefully obeyed. Usually, at present, the language will be English or French, but when at all possible it should be the local African language.

The biggest single factor in the happiness or unhappiness of a curate's life anywhere in the world is the parish priest. It is true that African presbyteries usually have a more democratic atmosphere than is commonly the case in countries where the Church has a longer tradition; but there is always a danger that the parish priest will take undue advantage of his position. Parish priests who reserve to themselves all the more spectacular duties, and leave humdrum and laborious tasks to the curates; who are zealous in supervising the curates' work, but show little willingness to share their burdens; who listen too easily to the parishioners' complaints about the curates: such parish priests are failing in their first duty. Charity begins at home, and it is hard to think well of a priest who reserves his affability for outsiders and is difficult in community. A presbytery is a home, not an institution, and one of the parish priest's first responsibilities is to make it a happy home; he will be amply rewarded for his efforts to make his younger brethren happy and comfortable. Certainly the parish priest should guide his curates (*paterne instruat ac dirigat . . . ei invigilet* says the Code), but he would usually be well advised to regard himself more as a brother and a friend than as a superior. There are parish priests who break their curates; God will surely ask them for an account of this. The old rule for superiors is best: *omnia vide, plura dissimula, pauca corrige*.

We must love our fellow priests, and we must also love our people. Then we can do almost anything with them. There is no defence against love. Patience, gentleness, goodness: it is these we must cultivate if we are to become even in a small degree worthy representatives of him we serve. Otherwise we shall drive people from God, and shall deserve the fate of the sons of Heli who 'withdrew men from the sacrifice of the Lord'.[1]

These are commonplace truths, but we could not omit all mention of them here.

---

[1] I Kings ii. 17.

The Spiritual Life of the Priest

The Code of Canon Law[1] sets out the general laws which safeguard the personal spiritual life of the priest. He must go to confession frequently (universal custom interprets this as once a week); he must devote some time each day to mental prayer, and to an examination of conscience; he should say the rosary each day and pay a visit to the Blessed Sacrament. These regulations are not just for religious or for members of missionary societies: they are inserted in the Code for the special benefit of diocesan priests, who are not bound by a religious rule. Many dioceses in Africa have a special directory for diocesan priests, giving a daily timetable which includes the spiritual exercises asked by Canon Law. These timetables resemble that followed by the members of the Apostolic Union, an association of diocesan priests which has a large number of members throughout the world. This Union also asks the reading of a portion of the Bible every day, and encourages priests to extend their professional knowledge by half an hour's study each day of ecclesiastical subjects when possible.[2]

All priests of course have a serious obligation to study; it would be fatal for their ministry as well as for their own interior life if they were to lose the habit of reading and the taste for intellectual work. A missionary needs a deeper understanding both of Christian truth and of the milieu in which he works than a parish priest in a country where the Church has been established for centuries. The latter can sometimes presume that things will go on more or less as usual; but the missionary has no past on which to draw, for he is founding the Church. Some of the worst mistakes in the history of the lands of mission have been made by men who were full of zeal, but whose understanding of theology and of local customs was imperfect. It is expected that the fourth session of the Vatican Council will require bishops to draw up general pastoral guides for their clergy; this is suggested in the draft decree 'The Pastoral Duties of Bishops'.

A well-established custom for diocesan priests throughout the world is the practice of an hour's adoration before the Blessed Sacrament,

---

[1] Cans. 124–6.

[2] The Pan-African Study Week at Katigondo, Aug.–Sept. 1964, suggested a pastoral study year for priests four or five years after ordination. See report of this Study Week, ed. R. LEDOGAR, *Katigondo, Presenting the Christian Message to Africa*, London, 1965.

either every day or every week, and this should be encouraged among the diocesan priests of Africa. The holy eucharist is the centre of the Christian priesthood, and the holy hour helps to express this fact in daily life. Time may be a problem; but it is usually true to say that the priests who do the most praying also do the most work.

The Priests' Eucharistic League imposes on its members an hour of adoration before the Blessed Sacrament each week. Members must be in major orders and may be either members of religious congregations or diocesan priests. The holy hour may be made at any time, but it should not be spent in fulfilling other duties of worship, such as celebrating Mass or reciting the divine office. As a guide, it is suggested that each quarter of the hour be devoted to one of the four ends of the Mass: adoration, thanksgiving, reparation and intercession. Once a month the plenary indulgence attached to the hour is applied to the deceased members of the League, and it is recommended that priest members offer Mass once a year for the same intention.

In his exhortation to priests, *Menti Nostrae*, Pope Pius XII appealed for daily eucharistic adoration, and an association exists with this object: the Sacerdotal Union of Perpetual Daily Adoration, founded in Italy in 1940.[1] Membership of this Association is restricted to diocesan priests, one of its aims being to promote among secular priests that bond of fraternity which unites and sustains members of religious institutes. Members undertake to make one full hour of adoration each day. The hour may be interrupted by holy Mass, so that a priest who spends three-quarters-of-an-hour in prayer before Mass and makes a quarter-of-an-hour's thanksgiving afterwards fulfils his obligation. The divine office may be recited during the hour's adoration. Seminarists who have received the tonsure are encouraged to join this association but they do not become full members until they renew their application after being ordained.

We may note, finally, in connection with the personal life of the priest, that the rulings of the diocesan synod, or of the bishop personally, are binding in conscience; they are not suggestions, which may be adopted or ignored according to taste, but laws which must be obeyed.

---

[1] *Adoratio Quotidiana et Perpetua Sanctissimi Eucharistiae Sacramenti inter Sacerdotes Cleri Saecularis.* Application for membership of this Association and of the Priests' Eucharistic League may be made to The Blessed Sacrament Fathers, P.O. Box 542, Masaka, Uganda.

Most dioceses have regulations about clerical dress. These vary from place to place, but it is essential that priests should always be recognizable as such, be it only by a small cross in the lapel.

We end this section by printing the prayer which is recited daily by the members of the Apostolic Union. It sums up so much of what we have been trying to say.

Domine Jesu, ego, licet indignus, in sortem sanctissimi ministerii electus, et impulsus Tibi serviendi desiderio, suppliciter peto, ut in conceptis propositis meis usque perseverem, et quotidie magis magisque perficiar in spiritu sanctissimae meae vocationis, scilicet in spiritu fidei, puritatis, humilitatis, paupertatis et obedientiae; in spiritu mortificationis, mundi meique contemptus, caritatis denique, zeli et solidae pietatis, ita ut formeris in me, Christe, et dicere valeam, 'Vivo, iam non ego, vivit vero in me Christus'. O clemens, o pia, o dulcis Virgo Maria, per te fiam votorum meorum compos, donec tecum caelestis gloriae fiam particeps. Sancti Angeli Custodes, Sancte Joseph, orate Cor Jesu pro Unionis Apostolicae dilatatione eiusque fervore. AMEN.

Sancte Pie X, O.P.N., Sancte Joanne Maria, O.P.N.

VOCATIONS

There are still far too few priests of any kind in Africa, and the few that there are mostly come from abroad. In 1963 (latest figures available) there were only 2,624 African priests and in the region of 12,600 foreign missionary priests in the African territories subject to the Congregation of Propaganda. This is clearly an unsatisfactory state of affairs. Missionaries are essentially temporary people, and a Church which is truly established must not rely on them too heavily. On other grounds too it is obvious that an independent Africa needs an independent clergy. So it is that the work of seeking out and training the African priests of the future must be given the very first priority by all those who are working for the Church in Africa today. Any work done for the conversion of the continent will be without long-term fruit unless a numerous and well-trained body of African priests has been created.

The Responsibility of Parish Priests for Vocations

Canon Law places the principal responsibility for encouraging vocations on the shoulders of the parish priest (Can. 1353), and commonsense tells us that the Church must depend on the parish clergy for the uncovering and fostering of vocations to the priesthood and the religious life. There can be no question of force, which would be useless anyway, but there is nothing to prevent a parish priest or curate from suggesting the idea of the priesthood to a suitable boy who has not so far considered it. Vermeersch, among others, understood Can. 1353 in this sense. The confessional is a good place for such a suggestion, and a certain measure of tactful insistence is quite permissible, in the spirit of St. Ignatius' reiterated 'What doth it profit a man...?' to St. Francis Xavier.

There are a number of public ways in which vocations can be encouraged. Four hundred years ago, the Council of Trent urged priests to inspire young boys with a desire for the priesthood during periods of religious instruction. Many parishes have found an annual day of prayer for vocations a useful practice, with special services for schoolchildren and adults. The draft decree *De Institutione Sacerdotali* asks that works of penance be offered for this end. Visits to the local seminary or the Brothers' postulate can be a help for boys, while girls might visit the Sisters' houses of formation. It is particularly useful to keep the idea of vocation before the minds of parents and future parents, and retreats provide obvious opportunities for this.

In practice, it will often be found that the best way of drawing the attention of young people to the priesthood and the religious life will be for the parish priest to speak to the schoolchildren, especially those in the higher classes, twice a year: once at the beginning of the school year and again at the beginning of the final term. He should speak of the different careers open to those who are planning their future, and may insist particularly on the need for vocations. Some dioceses prepare a pamphlet on the subject and distribute it to all schools; this is an excellent practice. Most dioceses too have an annual collection for the seminary; even more important than the money collected is the opportunity which this occasion provides of explaining to the people the supreme importance of the work of training the African clergy, and of their own duties in this matter. The day should be well prepared; African priests might well go round the different parishes during the preceding weeks and preach special sermons.

An admirable practice is to encourage wealthier people to provide scholarships for local students who are studying in the seminary. In some places, the African priests themselves give excellent example by paying the expenses of some of the seminarists.

The Signs of a Vocation

In deciding a vocation, it is sufficient to be sure that there are no notable defects in the candidate; positive proof of a vocation is not required, and is indeed impossible to obtain. The parish priest must himself examine the evidence of a vocation in the boy or girl, but he ought especially to tell the young person to open himself, or herself, fully to his confessor before going any further. Laziness, a disobedient spirit, any strong tendency to scruples or to unchastity, should be carefully looked for; a reasonably careful inspection on such points by the parish priest would have prevented many a boy from turning up at a seminary and having to leave soon afterwards, an experience which can do emotional damage. Parents who refuse to allow their child to follow his vocation commit grave sin; they should be told so. All modern writers teach that a boy is permitted to follow his vocation against the will of his parents, unless his parents or grandparents are in serious want and really need him to provide for them.[1] In cases of doubt, the ordinary is the judge, not the parish priest.

The ability to live a chaste life is clearly of the first importance for anyone who aspires to the priesthood or to the religious life. There must be some sign of such ability in the candidate even before he leaves home; after a certain time in the seminary, he must be morally certain that, in binding himself to a life of chastity, he is not undertaking an obligation which it will be beyond his powers to fulfil. The natural law itself forbids the taking on of any obligations in these circumstances. The best time for making a decision is at the end of the junior seminary course or, at the latest, the last year of philosophy. We have reason to

[1] Can. 542, §2.

believe that this is in accordance with the mind of the Holy See. The confessor will play a key role here, and the public good of the Church, as well as the private welfare of the individual, will largely depend upon his judgement. He will sometimes have the duty of telling his penitent frankly that he has no vocation and, in the case of a seminarian or a postulant, he may even be obliged to make the granting of absolution dependent on his penitent's agreeing to return to the world. Even the occasional confessor may sometimes have to make a decision about a vocation; this is not restricted to the case when the penitent says he prefers not to seek the advice of his regular confessor or spiritual director. If the confessor has no doubt, he must not hesitate to render a great service to his penitent by telling him to leave. He is failing in his duty if he does not do so, and Pius XI in *Ad Catholici Sacerdotii* said that confessors who show weakness in this matter are 'cruel towards the Church'. Parish clergy, retreat preachers and extraordinary confessors all need to remember this. Guidance on the general principles concerning the signs of vocation—piety, docility, chastity and the rest—are best sought from an experienced seminary rector or spiritual director; books of moral theology are not always the clearest guides here. In some dioceses, the bishops give clear, written directives concerning the chastity required to all priests, including the occasional confessor, who are involved in directing future priests, and such a practice is obviously a great help. In cases of difficulty, a year of probation may sometimes be suggested; it has proved a great psychological help to some; one certain, serious fault in this year would be a sign of non-vocation, generally speaking at least, since each soul is an individual.[1]

Looking after Aspirants to the Priesthood

The parish clergy should of course take a special interest in boys who have expressed a desire to enter the seminary. The training in piety that the Code asks the parish clergy to give—*ad pietatem informent*—is best done in the confessional and in personal talks; this is done before the boy goes to the seminary, 'so that', says Pius XI, 'in the seminary may be duly accomplished the work that the parish priest has begun'.

---

[1] VERMEERSCH is outstandingly good on this question—many moralists are brief or vague. See his 'Theologia Moralis', Vol. III, 1935, nos. 34–39. See also M. ZALBA, S.J., *Theologiae Moralis Summa*, Vol. III, p. 498, no. 1029.

They should also be ready to coach older boys in Latin; this may not often be necessary at present, but if really late vocations do begin to show themselves in Africa, as we must hope they will, such tuition by the parish clergy will become a necessity.

There are some subjects on which advice from the local clergy, who are in daily contact with the realities of the pastoral life, will carry more conviction for young aspirants than if it comes from the seminary staff. In particular, from the first day that his vocation is discerned, the future seminarist should be instructed in the evangelical counsel of poverty; the parish priest should make it clear to the young aspirant that in becoming a priest he is taking the Lord, and the Lord alone, for his inheritance. That counsel will be taken to heart in the measure in which the young man sees his parish clergy putting it into practice themselves. The notion that poverty is only for religious is an error to be pointed out at once to anyone who aspires to the priesthood. As a priest, the young man must be told, he will be obliged to seek holiness; whatever the nice distinctions made by theorists in the past between the various states of perfection in the Church, there can be no disputing the secular priest's special obligation to pursue perfection, and he must be taught from the outset first to love and then to practise obedience and chastity, poverty and humility.

A signal pattern of poverty was the diocesan priest Charles Borromeo; he suggested to his clergy this way of facing up to the lure of money: 'Live in such poverty that what you have to give for your churches and the adornment of your altars and other sacred objects may not be merely the overflow of your superfluity but rather savings stolen by mortification from your necessary maintenance.' To this let the African-born priest, and every other, totally pledge himself before he steps forward to the diaconate.

The common practice is to send junior seminarists home for holidays twice a year, where circumstances allow; senior seminaries have each their own regulations, but it is usual for major seminarists to go home at least once or twice during their course. Parish priests will usually receive detailed instructions from the bishop, or from the rector of the seminary, concerning their duties to senior seminarists on holidays; the remarks which follow are meant to apply principally to junior seminarists.

Throughout the holidays of these boys, the priests of the parish should accept special responsibility for their welfare, and the parish priest must send in to the seminary a conscientious report at the end of the holiday period. It is a good plan to gather all the students together one day during the holidays and give them a special instruction. On their first day home, the seminarists come to pay their respects to the parish priest; he must be careful to give them a warm welcome and to spend plenty of time with them. He takes the opportunity of arranging the times of Masses with them, if possible asking them to serve each day, and of fixing the day for the instruction. It is also desirable that either the parish priest or one of the curates make a special point of paying an annual visit to the seminarist's family while the boy is at home. In many places it is also the custom for the priests on the seminary staff to visit the boys during the holidays.

Late vocations, as we have mentioned, are to be encouraged, and special courses should be arranged, either at the junior or the senior seminary, to enable older students to make good any deficiencies there may have been in their education at school.

Finally we must recognize that, in spite of all our efforts, many seminarists will not in fact persevere to the priesthood. This is a normal feature of the Church's life everywhere, although we must always try to increase the proportion of those who do persevere. Ex-seminarists both deserve and need the special interest and love of the clergy, and they should be treated with particular deference. They have made sacrifices for the Church, and the period of re-adjustment to life in the world may be difficult. On the other hand, they have received an excellent religious education, and often turn out to be exemplary Catholic laymen. They must never be allowed to feel that the priests have lost interest or are disappointed in them because God did not see fit to carry them through to the priesthood but had other designs for them. In many parts of Africa, associations of ex-seminarists have been founded, each with its own chaplain, and with special activities, such as an annual visit to their old seminary. This should include a special High Mass, with a suitable sermon, followed by a party in which all the Fathers and students take part.

SEMINARIES

It may be useful to observe that the modernization of these establishments has been one of the more urgent tasks facing the Council. They must be turned into places of real pastoral training, instead of the enclosed gardens which they are so often. The Council draft decree *De Institutione Sacerdotale* requires that the whole of seminary training, spiritual, disciplinary and intellectual be directed to a pastoral end. Cardinal Suenens has put the point succinctly: 'Seminaries, as we know them today, were first founded by the Council of Trent to suit the needs of the time. However, that was four hundred years ago. Today we do not need to develop an opposite idea about them, but a more complete one. From the intellectual and spiritual point of view, they are good, but from the apostolic point of view they are not good enough. What is needed is apostolic practical training—perhaps for only two to three hours a week—to teach the seminarists to become practical apostles: how to speak, how to contact people, how to organize meetings, how to organize Catholic Action movements, and so on. . . . It would not be enough merely to have a seventh pastoral year; the whole six years should be pastoral, the entire seminary training should be practical. Therefore, seminarists must be taught to become apostles not just inside the seminary walls, but outside too. . . . The apostolate is not a danger for piety, if it is really supernatural. It is not a danger for study either, it gives realism to it. Unless piety is apostolic, it is too egocentric, and unless study is practical, it is too closed off from the world's needs.'[1]

One might add that dogma textbooks should be based on the Bible in all theses, and the connection of the tract as a whole with the Bible clearly shown. Links with universities should be close; alas! that may not be possible on any large scale in this continent for many a day. The Council[2] is expected to require that seminarists be given a full pastoral course in the future; it gives detailed instructions concerning the teaching of liturgy.[3] The professor should bear in mind the

---

[1] Quoted in Fides News Service, from 'The Missionary Outlook', in *The Missionary Annals*, Holy Ghost Fathers, Dublin. *Concilium*, Feb. 1965, carries wide-ranging suggestions in its report on the International Congress on Education for the Priesthood, pp. 91–3.

[2] In the schema on priestly training.

[3] *Constitution on the Liturgy*, arts. 15, 16, 17.

liturgical, biblical and catechetical revival, ecumenism, modern pedagogy, psychology, methodology and missionary theology. Surely it should be possible too to give the briefest of training in business methods: a parish priest or curate should be able to type, keep a filing system and simple accounts, and have a sound knowledge of committee procedure. The Council Constitution 'On the Renovation of the Religious Life' will also be necessary reading on the whole of this subject of modernization in the apostolate—and rule, dress and the rest; it is expected to stress that these things are particularly important in the lands of mission.

Seminarists should be led to the practice of contemplative prayer. Their call to this has not been understood. Seminary staffs must not fight shy of it as though it were vague and unpractical mysticism.[1] Is it not a necessary consequence of a sacramental life?

African Nuns and Brothers

Some re-thinking is clearly necessary about the work of nuns, and Cardinal Suenens has done much of it in his book, *The Nun in the World*.[2] He gives a summary of his ideas in the article from which we have just quoted: 'We must encourage nuns to be apostolic. We must obtain from the canonists that the obstacles to nuns' being as apostolic as possible be removed. There are a million religious Sisters in the Church, and if they agree to become fully apostolic, they could do a thousand times more than they are doing now, not only for the old and the sick, but also for guiding young people and for training grown-ups.... We must remember that Edel Quinn, the Legion of Mary's first envoy in Africa, founded 450 Legion *praesidia*. In the countries she visited there were hundreds of nuns. If only they had known how to organize *praesidia*, how much they could have done! ... We must, in fact, give nuns the spirituality of the active life.'[3]

The priest must regard himself as the father of the nuns who are in any way in his charge, and he should be particularly careful to treat each with exactly the same degree of consideration. Jealousy is easily aroused in these circumstances, and the priest must beware of giving any occasion for what might poison the community life of the convent.

[1] See J. Dalrymple, 'The Seminary at Prayer', in *Clergy Review*, April 1964.
[2] Burns & Oates, London, 1961.   [3] 'The Missionary Outlook', *loc. cit.*

The Sisters should be given a weekly conference, if at all possible, and their regular confessor should be well-versed both in the general principles of ascetical theology and in the special character and spirit of the particular congregation concerned. Above all, priests who have anything to do with the direction of nuns must be themselves lovers of perfection, and must set before the Sisters the highest ideals of the spiritual life. There must be no playing down the ideal: they must preach perfection, and preach it with great sincerity and clarity.

Much the same is to be said about the relations between priests and religious Brothers. In many ways their lives are harder than priests' lives; they have narrower interests in their daily life, and their community life is consequently less rich than that of priests. Teaching Brothers particularly can suffer much frustration; their lives are spent with chalk and blackboard and correcting exercise books. The priest can do much to help them by a friendly and sympathetic attitude. We must be understanding and large-minded if teaching Brothers sometimes manifest what seems to us an unduly independent attitude with regard to the clergy; they are experts in their own department and have the right to be recognized as such. There may be occasions when priests are tempted to feel hurt at what they consider the Brothers' critical attitude in their regard. True charity will be slow to take offence, and will readily recognize this for what it often is, a symptom of frustration. Even in our own sphere, in parish schools, for example, we often do well to ask as a favour what we might, in justice, demand as a right. If we have love and respect, it will seldom be necessary for us to use even the authority we undoubtedly possess, much less to require an unreasonable degree of submission. Insistence is a last resort; it comes rarely indeed from a priest who shares Christ's selflessness, Christ's delicate respect for the souls of men.

As we have recommended in Chapter 5, any Brothers or Sisters working in the parish are members of the apostolic team, and the clergy should meet them regularly to discuss the apostolate. They must of course keep their rule, but they should be encouraged not to remain apart from the parish, but to enter into it and share its life. Even those who are busy teaching can do much good, at the week-ends or during holidays, by going round visiting the people, and they should also be invited to share in the giving of instructions, both at the parish church itself and in the outstations. We may perhaps make a special plea for Sisters to be allowed to go out in pairs to visit the people.[1]

Both Brothers and Sisters could co-operate with the public authority by giving lectures on citizenship, domestic science and the like; this is a work commonly undertaken by the wives of Protestant ministers, and it is natural that Catholic Brothers and Sisters should show themselves equally zealous.

We could envisage for the future religious of both sexes who take part in the apostolate not just as a side-line, but as their principal work. The new lay institutes are an excellent example of what can be done; for religious instruction particularly, Brothers and Sisters could do more than most lay apostles.

LAY APOSTLES IN THE PARISH

Lay apostles are an integral part of the parish team, as we have said in the last chapter; the apostolate is the natural activity of the Mystical Body and it is the business of every member of that Body. A parish where there is no active lay apostolate is a parish in a state of suspended animation.

We speak in more detail of the apostolate of the laity in Chapter 20. For the moment we make one or two observations about the relations between lay apostles and the parish clergy. We include catechists under the general heading of lay apostles.

The parish priest is the local representative of the hierarchy, and it is therefore he who directs the lay apostolate in the parish and co-ordinates its various branches. He must beware however of assuming an unduly authoritarian attitude towards lay apostles, and of treating them as if they were his servants; he must also realize that co-operation in supra-parochial forms of the lay apostolate is sometimes necessary.

The greatest danger for the apostolate of the laity is clericalism. If the priest takes too much on himself, and demands of lay apostles no more than passive execution of his wishes, he will soon kill any apostolic zeal that there may be in his parish. Lay people too are often infected with the spirit of clericalism, and may attach an exaggerated importance to

[1] See BISHOP FORD of Maryknoll, 'The Sister and the Direct Apostolate', in *World Mission*, Autumn 1952, pp. 298–302.

the opinions of priests and religious in matters which lie outside their proper sphere. It is for the parish priest to change this. He should be the most zealous anti-clerical in the parish, taking active steps to see that the parish is democratically organized and showing total respect for every parishioner and for his own special competence. The parish priest has certainly the general responsibility for the apostolate of the laity in his parish, but he should delegate as much of that responsibility as possible. Unlettered Christians are often better able than the parish priest to decide what methods of apostolate are the most likely to be effective in the local community; their advice should be sought and followed.

The parish is the normal centre of the lay apostolate, but in some cases inter-parochial organization is preferable. Many of the finest modern forms of the lay apostolate were started at the diocesan or national level, and the clergy must be broad-minded enough to realize that some of their parishioners may do better work for Christ's kingdom outside the parish organization. A parish is not an isolated unit, but part of a Body; the health of the Body as a whole may demand that individual parishioners give their services to the lay apostolate outside the parish, and the parish priest should encourage them to do so. He should have the vision to see that he has a role to play in the diocese, in the nation, and in the whole world, as well as within the boundaries of his own parish.

The laity should be actively apostolic. They should be taught that obedience is an active virtue: it involves taking the initiative, informing Church leaders of what it is essential for them to know, and helping Christ's representatives to take the right decisions. Lay apostles who are simply meek and mild lay curates are of little use when it comes to such a formidable task as setting up the kingdom of God in an indifferent or hostile world.

On the other hand there can be no exaggerated spirit of independence, no laicism; God's people are to recognize that the parish is a community, of which the parish priest is the head, and they should not resent his intervention in their work when direction is genuinely necessary. As members of the parish they are also to remember that priests are human beings, and that, like all human beings, they have their inevitable defects, and need mercy.

A parish where priests, religious and laity are all filled with the apostolic spirit and with a great charity and respect for each other is a strong and healthy cell of the Mystical Body, and its power for good cannot but make itself felt throughout the neighbourhood. If every parish in Africa were of such a kind, the prospects for Christ's kingdom there would be bright indeed.

PART THREE

The Priest's Sacred Activity

9 The Sacraments in General

If THE whole aim of our apostolic activity is the building up of the Mystical Body of Christ in these regions of Africa, the means to be employed will have to be none other than those ordained by Jesus Christ himself. Now all sacred tradition tells us, and St. Thomas resumes the doctrine, that the Church is constituted, built (*fabricata*) by faith and the sacraments of faith. For just as Christ was the sacrament (sign) of God among us, so the Church is the sign of Christ living on in the world and the seven sacraments of the Church are the full expression of that life. Clearly, therefore, the preparation for and administration of the sacraments will have to take first place in pastoral work.

If we are to understand this primacy and the practical consequences drawn from it, we must base our pastoral work on sound theological principles. We state these principles of sacramental theology here as briefly as possible, having in mind the fresh insights that the reflection of contemporary authors offer us. The sacraments are the redemptive acts of Christ himself. By them the Mystical Body of Christ is built up and consolidated.

Refusal of the Sacraments

We discuss in Chapter 13 the withholding of sacramental absolution from a penitent who has not the necessary dispositions. Here we are concerned with the principles governing the refusal of the sacraments in general.

Only those who share in the Church's legislative power have the authority to determine who is to be refused the sacraments; the task of the individual priest is to apply the principles of theology and execute the orders he has received. He is an instrument of the unity of the Mystical Body; if he were to grant or refuse the sacraments according to his own purely personal views, he would be disrupting that unity.

The priest has however the responsibility of exercising the virtue of prudence in applying principles and executing orders. Prudence will teach him how to avoid extreme severity on the one hand and an excessive leniency on the other.

A minimum of good dispositions is required in those who approach the sacraments. They are a means of tending towards perfection, and those who receive them are not expected to be perfect already; but they must not be so imperfect that the sacraments cannot produce their effects. Those without faith, those who are in bad dispositions or those whose lives are destructive of the Christian community cannot receive the sacraments fruitfully, and priests do wrong to expose the holy things of God to invalidity by admitting such persons to the sacraments.

At the same time, the sacraments were instituted for men, and the Church wishes to make the source of divine life accessible to all her children. They should not be denied to Christians, however imperfect, who are capable of benefiting from them. Danger of irreverence is not the same thing as certain invalidity, and is not in itself enough to justify refusal of the sacraments.

When the salvation of a soul is at stake, as in danger of death, priests must do everything except expose the sacraments to certain invalidity, while of course taking the necessary steps to ensure that grave scandal is not given to the faithful.

The sacraments should be refused publicly only to those who are publicly known to be unworthy. The mere fact that a visitor from another parish has no card from his parish priest is not sufficient reason for denying him the sacraments. Even if the priest knows that a Christian has been refused absolution in the confessional, he must still give him Holy Communion if he presents himself at the altar rails. To do otherwise would involve breaking the sacramental seal.

Although the purpose of the sacraments is to sanctify the individual soul, they also have a social purpose, as the *Constitution on the Liturgy* makes clear. It is possible to envisage cases in which building up the Body of Christ will involve refusing the sacraments to individuals, and in such cases the common good must come first. The Church is conferring a doubtful benefit on the individual Christian if she binds him to observe a strict moral code and yet leaves him in a society where this is practically impossible. Withholding the sacraments from an individual who is known to be an imperfect Christian may on occasion be a great help in raising moral standards and so in building up a Christian community. God can give his grace as he wishes, and he will not deny it to a man who is refused the sacraments, for the sake of the community, provided that he does his best.

It will nearly always be up to the bishop to decide which categories of Christians are to be refused the sacraments in these cases.

The Sacraments and Magic

There is evidently a considerable external resemblance between the Christian sacraments and the magic rites of paganism. Both use the language of signs and symbolism, both claim to confer life and power through the performance of outward actions. The differences between them are, firstly, that the sacraments were freely instituted by Christ, as instruments through which he chooses to act, whereas magic claims to have a mechanical, intrinsic efficacy of its own; and, secondly, that whereas magic is wholly exterior, and pretends to operate independently of a man's inner attitudes, the sacraments presuppose right dispositions in those who receive them.

The sacraments are not mechanical formulae, but free acts of Christ, without whom the matter and form are nothing. Christians should be taught not to attach undue importance to the outward signs but to penetrate beyond them with the eye of faith, and see the saviour of mankind coming with love to encounter his brethren, and to offer them his life.

Insistence on the necessity of the personal dispositions of the subject is the most important means of combating the formalism and the 'magic' approach to the sacraments to which many Christians, in Africa and elsewhere, are prone. The sacraments have an intrinsic efficacy, they do act *ex opere operato*, as the ancient practice of infant baptism clearly expresses; but their effectiveness is in proportion to the dispositions of the person receiving them. Counter-Reformation theology was obliged to insist on the *opus operatum* to combat Protestant errors; but this perhaps disturbed the balance of sacramental theology, which must now be restored. Pope Pius XII, twenty years ago, condemned as a 'pernicious error' an excessive trust in the automatic fruitfulness of a correctly administered and validly received sacrament,[1] and Billot remarked, speaking of the holy eucharist, that even though a sacrament is received validly, its good effects may be outweighed by harmful by-effects, if the subject's dispositions, though sufficient for validity, are too defective.[2] When we say that those who receive the sacraments must be in the right dispositions, we do not mean therefore that minimum dispositions are all that we should look for. If the sacraments are really to produce their full effects, they must be received with really living faith and with fervent love. It is not the mere performance of the act that matters; interior dispositions are paramount. It is often said that the old animism has helped the Africans to understand and accept the sacramental system of the Church; this is no doubt true, but if priests do not insist on the essential differences between the two religious systems, African Christians will only too easily regard the sacraments as their fathers did the animistic rites.

The faithful may also be taught the difference between the sacraments and magic by the removal of any unnecessary secrecy in the administration of the sacraments. The mystery will always remain, the mystery of God's love for men; but there must be no artificial mystery-making. The *Constitution on the Liturgy* states that it is 'of the highest importance that the faithful should easily understand the sacramental signs',[3] and this is the main reason why it is so desirable that the sacraments be administered in the vernacular,[4] instead of using a ritual language, such as sorcerers use for their pagan rites. The use of the vernacular is not a concession to priests whose Latin is weak, but a necessary instrument for the solid planting of the Church in Africa. The multiplicity of languages in certain dioceses creates difficulties for a vernacular Mass, but there is much less difficulty in using the vernacular for sacraments to individuals.

The Sacraments as Catechesis

The sacraments make men holy, but their administration also 'contains much instruction for the faithful'.[5] There has been a strong movement in the Church, greatly helped by a document issued by the French hierarchy,[6] to centre instruction to both practising and non-practising

---

[1] A.A.S. (1944), p. 76.   [2] *De Sacramentis Ecclesiae*, I, pp. 569 et seq.
[3] *Constitution on the Liturgy*, art. 33.   [4] Cf. ib., art. 36, §2; art. 63.   [5] Ib., 33.
[6] *Directoire pour la Pastorale des Sacrements à l'usage du clergé*, Paris, 1951.

Christians on a full explanation of the sacraments. All those who ask for the sacraments should be told the meaning of the liturgical ceremonies which accompany their administration. The explanation is given both beforehand and while the rite is being performed; a second priest may sometimes be available for this. This will help lapsed Catholics also, and non-Christians who attend baptisms, weddings or funerals. Provision has now been made by the *Constitution on the Liturgy* for the insertion in the liturgical books of appropriate explanations. The liturgy of the sacraments constitutes a set of perfect visual aids for the teaching of the faith and this wealth must be drawn on to the full.

Since the sacraments are signs of man's dedication to Christ, their administration gives an opportunity to remind the faithful of their responsibility towards Christ's Mystical Body. Each sacrament should be considered as the natural starting-point for renewed zeal for the kingdom of God, for a heightened consciousness of our responsibility as Christians for those who are separated from us. The sacraments are the source of that supernatural duty to bear witness to Christ which is the basis of the whole lay apostolate; they should therefore not only deepen the supernatural life of the individual and instruct him in the faith: they should also increase his apostolic fervour.

Conclusion

A more profound appreciation of the true nature of the sacraments will naturally lead the priest to understand that he has far more to do than simply observe the rubrics in administering the sacraments. He is responsible for instructing the people and for arousing in them the best possible dispositions; his own personal sanctity too will be an important element in the effectiveness of the sacraments which he administers, for although it is true that the efficacy of the sacraments does not depend on the holiness of the minister, yet people will clearly receive them in much better dispositions, and therefore more fruitfully, when they are edified by the priest's perceptible nearness to Christ.

It may be well to conclude with a warning against being too exacting with those who are receiving the sacraments. We must indeed do everything in our power to excite the right dispositions but there may well be occasions, especially in the case of old people and children, when it is impossible to be absolutely sure of the adequacy of their preparation. When the priest has done his best, and the people appear to have done their best, the matter should be humbly committed to God the Son, and his sacraments conferred.

10 Baptism: The Sacrament of Regeneration

BAPTISM is the foundation sacrament, and our Lord's solemn words to Nicodemus have impressed its importance on every generation of Christians: 'No man can enter into the kingdom of God unless birth comes to him from water, and from the Holy Spirit.'[1] Regenerated by the baptismal waters, the neophyte enters into the ranks of the people of God; he becomes a member of Christ's Mystical Body, and is received into the local Christian community. This is the first step in Christian initiation.

In this chapter we speak first of the catechumenate, in which candidates for baptism are prepared, and then of the different categories of people to be baptized. We conclude with some remarks on the actual administration of the sacrament, and some practical points.

The Catechumenate[2]

The catechumenate was part of the ancient discipline of the Church, and it was revived when Catholic missionaries arrived in tropical Africa in the second half of the nineteenth century.

The General Council has now extended to the Universal Church this invaluable heritage from early times: 'The catechumenate for adults is to be restored; it shall comprise several distinct steps, and be taken into use as and when the local Ordinary may see fit. By this means the time of the catechumenate, which is intended as a period of suitable instruction, may be sanctified by sacred rites to be celebrated after successive intervals of time.'[3] These 'successive intervals of time' may be interpreted in the light of a decree of the Congregation of Rites[4] which

[1] John iii. 5.
[2] The Report of the Pan African Study Week, 1964, *Katigondo, Presenting the Christian Message to Africa*, op. cit., is invaluable reading here.
[3] Art. 64.   [4] 16 April 1962.

permitted the baptismal ceremony to be performed in seven separate stages, according to the degree of knowledge of the catechumen.

The catechumenate has often been praised by the popes as a valuable instrument for the instruction and formation of aspirant members of the Church in the countries of mission. It must however be in tune with contemporary conditions.

In many parts of Africa the practice of a four-year catechumenate, introduced in the 1880s, is still maintained. The catechumens are expected to attend regular instructions, usually given by an untrained catechist, and to undergo periodical examinations. In many places, the instruction still consists almost entirely of the catechism and, in addition, the catechumens are required to know certain prayers by heart.[1]

The content of the instruction given to catechumens is now being revolutionized under the impact of the new catechesis and the sooner the revolution is complete the better; but in other ways too the catechumenate needs revision. The old leisurely life of Africa is receding as more men, and even women, enter employment. It is less easy now to summon people to regular instruction several times a week. The mentality and outlook of the people too has changed vastly from that which the first missionaries encountered, and the catechumenate must be adjusted to suit these new people and their different needs.

The length of the catechumenate is much under discussion at present, and we are not equipped to pronounce on a subject which divides the experts. We would only make the obvious point that a common policy is desirable, so that we no longer have the situation, not uncommon at present, where people in one diocese have to wait three or four years before being admitted to baptism, while their neighbours a few miles away are only required to remain in the catechumenate for two years, or less.

As regards admission to the catechumenate, this must be open to all who apply. Even a man who is living in concubinage, or in an irregular marriage situation, may not be refused admittance, provided that he is prepared to put everything right before actually receiving the sacrament of baptism. If enormous numbers apply, so that it is physically impossible to instruct them all, it may be necessary to fix a quota. This

---

[1] An excellent handbook for adult catechumens, *Africa's Way to Life*, has been published by the Department of Education and Catechetics, South African Catholic Bishop's Conference.

however is a special situation, and has nothing to do with the right of the individual candidate; he retains the right to be admitted, but the conditions under which that right may be exercised are wanting.

General Principles Concerning Candidates for Baptism

The *Recueil d'Instructions aux Missionaires du Congo Belge* declared: 'It is a grave duty of charity to confer baptism on those who are sufficiently instructed and disposed. The mere fear of apostasy or public misconduct, when the catechumen shows sufficient guarantee of perseverance, is not a sufficient reason for postponing it.'[1] Baptism is a right, not a reward, for all men have the right to be incorporated into the Mystical Body; therefore a catechumen who has done all that the Church requires must be baptized. It will be the task of the priest and of the catechist to do everything in their power to ensure that catechumens approach the sacrament in the best possible dispositions, but they may not ask more of the catechumen than they do of the baptized Christian.

Canon 752, §1 sums up the matter. After noting that no one may be baptized against his will, it lays down that the candidate must have been sufficiently instructed and that he must have been told of the necessity of contrition.

The Aged and the Handicapped

With old people, one must not try to do the impossible. Belief in the truths of the Incarnation and the Redemption are, according to the usual opinion, necessary for salvation. They should be stressed in instructions to old people, but it is useless to enter upon matters which they will never be able to grasp. In the last resort, it is sufficient that they assent to the essential mysteries in the sense that the priest or the catechist professes them.

Deaf mutes should be baptized if they manifest a desire to be. Those who have received modern expert training will of course be capable of following a more or less normal course of instruction; others may be treated as infants.

Canon 754 gives directions for the baptism of the insane. They may be

[1] No. 80.

treated as infants if their condition is congenital, or if they have never attained the use of reason. Otherwise they should only be baptized during a lucid interval, always supposing that they wish to receive the sacrament. The same principles apply to those suffering from sleeping-sickness or from delirium.

Women and Girls

The dependent status of many women in Africa sometimes makes priests hesitate to baptize them. We suggest the following principles as a guide.

The wife of a pagan husband may not be refused baptism, provided that there is no serious danger of her lapsing from the faith, or of becoming the object of hostility. The same is to be said of the legitimate first wife of a polygamist, even if the validity of the marriage is doubtful; all that matters is that the woman is properly disposed to receive the sacrament.

A well disposed catechumen who is unable or unwilling to marry should be admitted to baptism. It is not part of the priest's task in such cases to interpret what may or may not come to pass in the future.

Pagan children who have reached the age of reason and are sufficiently instructed and wish for baptism have a strict right to it if the parents consent, and even if, after leaving school, they will be exposed to many dangers.[1] Since for baptism they are to be considered as adults (Can. 745, §2) baptism may take place against the will of their parents unless greater evils are feared, for example, *odium ecclesiae*. In this case, baptism is to be postponed, not refused. Indiscriminate and systematic refusal to baptize girls until their marriage, for fear things go wrong, is an injustice: they have a right to baptism without delay.[2] In proximate and grave danger of perversion, a girl to be married to a pagan or polygamist should not be baptized just before her marriage. However, where dispositions are so good that the girl is ready to endure very bad treatment and even death, baptism must be given. A girl who is still young and betrothed to a pagan can be baptized, but only after training and instruction.

[1] *Collectanea* 255, 1293, ad 10.
[2] Reply of the Holy Office, 1949; Denzinger-Schönmetzer (1963), no. 3874.

Separated Christians

In the case of separated Christians who seek admittance to the Church, it must be stressed that their original baptism is to be presumed valid, provided that the matter and form were correct, whatever the private beliefs of the minister may have been.[1]

It is sacrilege to re-baptize such persons indiscriminately and without inquiry. The first step is to make an investigation concerning the original baptism; if this was certainly valid, then the convert is to be received after making an abjuration of error and a profession of faith.

If after due inquiry it is impossible to establish the validity of the earlier baptism, the convert should be baptized conditionally, preferably in private.[2] A good place for this conditional baptism is the sacristy, in the presence of witnesses or sponsors. After baptism, the convert goes to confession, where he receives absolution both from the censure of excommunication and from the sins which he has confessed. In the case of children under fourteen, both the abjuration of error and the absolution from censure are omitted.

We may note in passing that the first confession of a convert can be a difficult and embarrassing experience for him. It should be tactfully explained that he is free to choose any priest as confessor, not necessarily the one who instructed him and who is receiving him. It might be a good plan to suggest that he confess his sins and express his sorrow on the day before his reception into the Church; this will ease his mind, and a simple absolution after baptism will then be all that is required.

With regard to other denominations, it is right to add that some, such as the Salvation Army, have in fact no baptism at all, and the priest should be aware of this.

Those in Danger of Death

We come now to people in danger of death who wish to be baptized. Anyone may, and must, baptize such persons, when a priest or deacon is not available. Canon 742 says that the minister should be chosen, in descending order of preference, thus: subdeacon, cleric, layman, lay

---

[1] Cf. WALTON HANNAH in The Ecumenist, Sept.–Oct. 1963. The ecumenical value of presuming validity is real, but has been overstressed by some. So has the moral certainty of the validity of baptism in certain communions.

[2] Holy Office, 3 June 1908; cf. Can. 759, §2.

woman. The father or mother should not administer baptism to their child if some other minister is available. It is not necessary to go into these details when instructing the faithful, however; it may be wise especially not to mention the recommendation about the father and mother, as this might lead to misunderstanding and result in a child's dying without baptism. Where possible, at least one, and preferably two witnesses should be present at an emergency baptism to give proof of it afterwards (Can. 742, §1).

The obligation to baptize in danger of death must frequently be insisted upon; too often it is neglected, even occasionally by catechists, either out of carelessness or from an unreasonable fear of offending parents and relatives.

People should be taught how to baptize secretly when necessary. A sponge or a piece of cotton-wool is useful for this purpose. Chinese Christians sometimes call baptism the sacrament of the sponge because of the great numbers of dying children who are quietly baptized in this way. All Christians should realize the importance of taking every prudent means of ensuring the eternal salvation of children, and of adults, who are seriously ill (never forgetting the value of perfect contrition either). Practical demonstrations should be given to schoolchildren, and it should often be pointed out that baptism of desire and the desire of baptism are not exactly the same thing.

Even those who refused baptism while they were conscious should nowadays be baptized conditionally if they are dying and unconscious.[1]

A person who appears to be dead should be baptized conditionally unless decomposition has already set in.

If emergency baptism has been conferred on an apparently dying person who later recovers, the sacrament should be repeated, conditionally, if there is any doubt about the validity of the first baptism, provided the person concerned wishes to be baptized.

Infants

'Infants,' says the Code of Canon Law, 'should be baptized as soon as possible. Parish priests and teachers should often remind the faithful of their grave obligation in this matter.'[2]

---

[1] Cf. BISHOP DE REEPER, *The Sacraments on the Missions*, no. 39.   [2] Can. 770.

Private baptism within eight days by a catechist or an instructed Christian is preferable to solemn baptism by a priest with a longer delay. To postpone baptism is particularly serious in Africa, where children must be considered in greater danger of death than in some other parts of the world. The same is to be observed of sick children, who may be in danger of death in Africa when they would not be so considered in Europe or America.

Even if a child's parents do not practise their religion, it should still be baptized, unless it is morally certain that the child will not be brought up as a Catholic.[1] The priest should not demand positive guarantees; it is sufficient that there is no certainty that the child will be brought up as a non-Catholic. Any hope that it will receive a Catholic upbringing is sufficient to justify baptism. Any hope—*si possibilis spes effulgeat*—said the Holy Office.[2]

Illegitimacy is no bar to baptism, nor may the sacrament be refused to the children of parents who have not paid their church dues or who are in an irregular marriage situation. It is a mortal sin to withhold baptism from a child as a way of punishing its parents. Every form of blackmail is of course also to be avoided—'I'll baptize your child once you start coming to Mass.'

If both parents are apostates, or belong to a non-Catholic Christian denomination, the case is rather different from that of non-practising Catholic parents. Children of apostates[3] may only be baptized if the parents or guardians, or one of them, ask for it on the child's behalf and guarantee the child's Catholic upbringing.[4] If only one parent is a Catholic, but both ask and give a guarantee, baptism must be given. If only the Catholic party asks, and the non-Catholic parent does not give a guarantee, it may be wise not to baptize. In doubtful cases, the Ordinary should be consulted. Once again, *possibilis spes* is enough for the guarantee.

[1] Cans. 750–1.   [2] Coll. de Prop. Fide, II, no. 2007.
[3] An apostate is a Catholic who has renounced the faith by some positive and public act; non-practising Catholics and public sinners are not apostates.
[4] Cans. 750–1.

Schoolchildren and Young People

In many dioceses, children in Catholic schools are admitted to baptism, provided that they have been sufficiently instructed and have expressed a desire to receive the sacrament, and their parents have given their consent. It is often wise to obtain this consent either in writing or before witnesses, and it may also be desirable to obtain guarantees concerning the child's religious instruction, his practice of religion and his eventual marriage. The child will naturally be expected to have attended regularly either church or outstation on Sundays. Children will usually receive a week's special preparation before baptism, and it is useful to keep them for a further week, where possible, for a special course of instructions on the sacraments.

Schoolboys who leave school in the middle of their course require special care. They may be baptized one year after leaving school if they live near a parish, or at least near other Christians, provided that the parents are agreeable and suitable godparents can be found. In most places it will also be necessary to make sure that a bride price will be available so that a boy or young man can make a Christian marriage in due course.

The Administration of Baptism

As everyone now recognizes, there are serious defects in the two baptismal rites in the Roman Ritual, and the *Constitution on the Liturgy* directs that these be corrected.[1] The local rituals soon to be produced will no doubt omit, for example, the repeated exhortations addressed by the priest to the infant child, and the successive exorcisms. Of particular interest to the Church in Africa is the suggestion in article 65 that *local initiation rites be adapted to Christian purposes*; there is obvious scope for this both in the catechumenate and in the rite of baptism itself.

Baptism is a community matter, not just the Christian's private business, and it should be carried out with all possible dignity and

[1]Arts. 66–9.

solemnity. It is one way of preaching the Gospel, and as many Christians as possible should be invited to assist at the ceremony, as was the practice in the early Church.

Every church should have a font. Where there happens to be none, the minister of baptism should hand a basin to a by-stander; the baptismal water is caught in this and then poured into the sacrarium. A sacrarium is easily constructed by knocking a hole in the bottom of a pot and sinking it in the ground.

The practice of performing the entire baptismal ceremony at the font is to be discouraged, for it destroys the symbolism of the rite and makes nonsense of many of the words. There are three distinct places for the ceremony: at the church door, at the entrance to the baptistery (or, if there is no baptistery, some feet from the font), and at the font itself.

At times, one priest might explain the rite while another does the actual baptizing. The ceremonies should not however be notably interrupted by this arrangement.[1]

Again, where possible, a short instruction should be given before baptisms are conferred on children. This will aim at instructing the godparents in their duties, and it should also take into account the fact that it could benefit indifferent Christians who might be present.

People who wish to be godparents but are ineligible may be used as witnesses. This is not an officially recognized function, but its invention can prevent people from taking offence. It is not a good thing habitually to use the sacristan or one of the house servants as godparents for anyone who turns up for baptism. The sponsor assumes grave obligations, and the most suitable person will often be a lay apostle who is friendly with the family and who understands what he is doing.

It is better that the priest himself interview the candidates and make the inscriptions in the baptismal register. Even a capable layman may misunderstand the different Latin formulae, and there has sometimes been danger of invalidity, and confusion when the register is consulted later on. If a layman does do this work, let it be carefully checked.

[1] For a detailed scheme, see Fr. C. VAN BERKEL's article in *African Ecclesiastical Review* October 1960, p. 285. Nothing should be done without the approval of the Ordinary.

Some Practical Points

In many places a minimum of literacy is now demanded of adult candidates for baptism. Exceptions however should be easily admitted, and no such demand could be made of the aged.

It is useful to make an annual check to ensure that catechists are baptizing properly. The retreat is the natural time for this.

Nuns and lay apostles should not put pressure on parents to have their children baptized when there is no hope that these children will receive a Catholic upbringing.

All doctors, nurses and midwives should be taught their duties about the baptizing of the foetus, and they should know how to baptize in the womb.

The reception of the further sacraments of confirmation, holy communion, matrimony and holy orders must be noted in the baptismal register of the parish where the Christian was baptized.

To repeat baptism out of a vain scruple or because of a negative doubt is, in itself, sacrilegious, but the sacrament must be repeated conditionally if there is the slightest reasonable doubt.

Catechumens should not be given Christian names before baptism.

A holy picture commemorating baptism, like the pictures for a first communion or for a priest's ordination, might be a pleasant innovation. The people might well treasure such souvenirs all their lives, and they would have at hand a permanent reminder of their privileges and duties as members of the Mystical Body. Many Africans already have the custom of lighting a candle on the anniversary of their baptism, and this is to be encouraged.

11   Confirmation: Full Incorporation into Christ

CONFIRMATION is the second of the three initiation sacraments. By baptism we entered Christ's kingdom; confirmation makes us full, adult citizens of that kingdom. Baptism is the sacrament of Christian birth; confirmation is the sacrament of Christian coming-of-age.

AGE: A THEOLOGICAL DIFFICULTY

In the early Church, confirmation immediately followed baptism; the baptized, confirmed neophyte then proceeded to receive Christ in the holy eucharist. The whole ceremony usually took place during the holy night of the Paschal Vigil. Such was the practice of the universal Church until the twelfth century, and the Eastern Church still preserves it. Spain and Latin America have retained the ancient usage in conferring it immediately after baptism.

Both doctrine and history indicate that confirmation should normally be received before first holy communion. A decree of the Congregation of Sacraments of 30 June 1932, declared that it is both opportune and in conformity with the nature and effects of the sacrament of confirmation, which is the complement of baptism, that confirmation precede first holy communion. The document goes on to say that children who have not been confirmed should not therefore be excluded from making their first communion; but it is clear that the normal order is baptism, confirmation, holy communion.

Confirmation should be received about the age of seven, and holy communion when the child has reached the age of reason and is adequately disposed;[1] this will normally mean very soon after confirmtion. Canon 788 emphasizes that confirmation may be conferred before the age even of seven in special cases, such as danger of death.

[1] Can. 854, §5.

Established custom may justify, temporarily, deferring confirmation to a later age; but it is hard to see why, even in Africa, seven should not be accepted as the normal age. In any world, and in a pagan world particularly, children too have to bear witness to the faith, and they need the help of the divine strengthener. A child of seven has struggles that, in their measure, are heroic. In some places, the sacrament of confirmation has become linked with a 'commitment' ceremony, in which the adolescent solemnly re-affirms his faith and his determination to bear witness to it and to live in accordance with it. A ceremony of this kind is clearly very useful; Anglicans and Lutherans use it with great success; it is in every way fitting that young persons about to embark on an independent life in the world should explicitly renew their dedication to Christ; but it does not seem right to deprive children of the grace of confirmation for several years simply to add greater solemnity to the school-leaving ceremony; this can be made impressive enough by a profession of faith and a renewal of baptismal vows.

The dogmatic treatment of confirmation is rather thin in the standard manuals of theology, and priests may find some difficulty in preparing instructions for those who are to receive the sacrament. Traditionally we tell our people that the Holy Spirit comes into the soul to increase sanctifying grace; he brings with him his seven gifts, and his strength turns the baptized Christian into a soldier of Christ. The tap on the cheek is all that is left of what was originally a kiss; the Council of Trent suggested that it might be considered as a symbol of power to endure, and it could now be explained in this way; strength in adversity is one of the gifts of the Holy Spirit, and it may help people to understand the significance of this gift if we thus explain the ceremonial tap, though its origin lies elsewhere.

The fact remains however that the specific grace of the sacrament of confirmation needs closer definition. The Holy Spirit brings his strength with him whenever he comes: he enters the soul by baptism, and his presence is intensified each time we receive holy communion. We say rightly that confirmation perfects the Christian initiation begun by baptism, but writers on dogmatic theology seem to find it hard to say in what exactly this perfecting consists. No doubt in due time the present discussions concerning confirmation (largely arising from a controversy sparked off by Anglican theologians) will lead to a full theological investigation of the specific grace of the sacrament, perhaps followed by some authoritative pronouncement. Certainly a re-appraisal of the sacrament, inspired by the Bible, the Fathers of the Church and tradition, is necessary. In the meantime, the priest can repeat the traditional teaching, and draw on the text of the confirmation ceremony in the Roman Pontifical. There is no better manual of liturgy than the liturgical texts themselves[1] for, as Pope Pius XI reminded us, the principal organ of the ordinary magisterium is the liturgy.

Dispositions for Receiving the Sacrament of Confirmation

The Church requires that the candidate for confirmation be in a state of grace and that, supposing he has reached the age of reason, he be sufficiently instructed.[1] The priest should advise the person to be confirmed to go to confession beforehand; if he has made his first communion, he will naturally receive the holy eucharist also. Old people, and those who cannot understand or remember the instructions, should not be excluded from confirmation.

Some kind of watch service would be a good way of preparing for confirmation. The all-night vigil has proved popular in some parts of Africa; it belongs to the most ancient traditions of the Church, and as a preparation for confirmation, attended by friends as well as by the candidates themselves, it admirably recalls the novena of our Lady and the apostles in the cenacle.

Confirmation by a Priest

In 1946 the Sacred Congregation of the Sacraments issued the decree *Spiritus Sancti Munera* which gave to parish priests and quasi-parish priests the faculty of confirming people who were seriously ill and in danger of death. This was followed in 1947 by a rescript from Propaganda which granted to all Ordinaries under its jurisdiction the faculty of allowing all their priests in the sacred ministry to confirm the faithful, whether children or adults, who are in danger of death, whether

---

[1] Cf. 'La Signification de la Confirmation', supplement to *La Vie Spirituelle*, no. 29, 15 May 1954. We might add that recent pontifical documents lay no stress on a connection between confirmation and lay apostolate, with, as far as we know, one exception and that attaches the lay apostolate equally to baptism, cf. Pope Pius XI's letter to the Patriarch of Lisbon, 10 November 1933, cited by Fr. P. CAMELOT, O.P., in *La Maison-Dieu*, 54, 1958.

from sickness or from some other cause. Priests teaching in schools and seminaries, but who help with pastoral work, come under the scope of this decree.[1] It is probable that dying separated Christians are not covered by these directives, and they may not therefore be confirmed. In danger of death, however, they could be confirmed conditionally.

Priests who receive this faculty are naturally expected to make use of it, and *habitual* refusal to confirm those in danger of death who ask for the sacrament would constitute grave sin (Can. 785). Confirmation however is not a sacrament necessary for salvation, and grave personal inconvenience, or the obligation to fulfil other necessary or important duties, would justify a priest in not using his faculty to confirm. The faithful should be taught about the priest's power to confirm, and their duty to send for him when necessary, especially in the case of a dying child; catechists or relatives know that they have to send for a priest when an adult is dying, but they may not worry about infants unless we tell them. Christians must not be deprived of the sacrament through negligence; the loss of confirmation means a lower degree of glory in heaven for all eternity, and dying Christians must always be confirmed whenever this is reasonably possible. To use the language of the schools, this sacrament, as St. Thomas says, is not necessary *necessitate medii.*

The Sponsors at Confirmation

If the obligations of baptismal godparents are frequently overlooked, the duties of the sponsors at confirmation are almost universally neglected. Bishops and priests have an obvious obligation to emphasize the sponsor's role, and to prevent its becoming a formality.[2] The Code states that the sponsor is obliged to keep an eye on his godchild throughout life, and to do what he can to ensure that he receives a Catholic upbringing. If the child goes to a Catholic school, it is reasonable to presume that his religious training is being sufficiently catered for; if however the parents entirely neglect the child's religious education at home, and send him to a non-Catholic school, then the sponsor is obliged to make some effort to intervene. Kindness and tact

[1] Cf. L. Buijs, S.J., *Facultates Decennales*, Gregorian University, Rome, 1961, p. 34.
[2] Cf. Decree of the Congregation of Sacraments, 25 November 1925.

are required. The sponsor's interference would be more easily accepted if he had hitherto played the part of an honorary uncle, remembering the child's birthday and visiting him on big feasts. There may well be cases in which the sponsor is helpless, in spite of every good intention; in such cases, he must not torment himself unnecessarily, but simply commend the child to God and pray that he will not be betrayed.

As we have already mentioned in connection with baptism, the best sponsors are lay apostles. The Church directs that each sponsor should normally stand for one or two candidates only, so that he can take a really personal and particular interest in them. If circumstances in Africa are such that sponsors have to stand for large groups of Christians, we might think of the suggestion made by the French hierarchy in their Pastoral Directory that such sponsors should be true representatives and delegates of the parish community, and not simply chance bystanders, nor (especially) wealthier or more influential parishioners who think that they have a traditional right to the office. Another suggestion which has been made is that really worthy sponsors might appoint proxies to stand in for them. In this case the sponsor must himself appoint the proxy; otherwise the sponsorship will be of doubtful validity.[1]

Confirmation of Adults

Adult catechumens should be confirmed as soon as possible after their baptism; ideally, as we have said, before receiving holy communion for the first time. The Code recommends[1] that Catholics should not be married until they have been confirmed, if this is at all possible. If they are reasonably prevented from being confirmed before marriage, they should receive the sacrament as soon as possible afterwards.

Occasionally adult Christians are discovered who have never been confirmed; they are often ashamed to come forward to receive the sacrament with children, but they should be encouraged to do so. Such persons could perhaps be prepared for confirmation in private.

[1] *The Priest*, January, 1953.   [2] Can. 1021, §2.

Conclusion

Article 71 of the Constitution on the Liturgy deals with the sacrament of confirmation. It needs no commentary.

'The rite of confirmation is to be revised; the intimate connection which this sacrament has with the whole process of Christian initiation is to be more clearly set forth; for this reason it is fitting that candidates renew their baptismal promises just before they are confirmed.

'Confirmation may be given within the Mass when convenient; when it is given outside the Mass, the rite that is used should be introduced by a formula to be drawn up for this purpose.'

The faithful should be taught often to invoke the saint whose name they took at confirmation; they are united to him by a special bond, and he has special power with God on their behalf. They might also be encouraged to keep with special fervour the anniversaries of their baptism, confirmation and first communion. Many Africans have the custom of lighting a candle on the anniversary of their baptism. Here is a small but useful way of fulfilling the apostolate of sacramental evangelization, bringing the Gospel to the people of God in ways they love and understand.

12 The Eucharist: the Sacrament of Plenitude

OMNIPOTENT God could not do more: even for infinite love and power the eucharist is the sacrament of plenitude. All the sacraments are acts of Christ, but the eucharist is Christ himself, spring of all grace. The other sacraments overflow with good measure, but they all lead to or follow from the eucharist, which applies afresh all the fruits of the redemption. Christ, present in all the sacraments, (he baptizes, confirms, etc.) is substantially present only in the eucharist.

The sacrament of plenitude is the completion, the term, of the initiation sacraments, baptism and confirmation, it is their term because it effects what it signifies: integral union with Christ, and therefore union of the faithful each with the other through Christ. It is the centre of Christianity in which all spiritual growth and all apostolic activity is joined within itself, because it is joined with Christ, the head. For it is the renewal of the Cross, whence comes all that the Christian can have of good.

The Code of Canon Law sums up well the theology of the eucharist: 'In the most holy eucharist, Christ our Lord is contained, offered and consumed, under the appearances of bread and wine.'[1] We take this concise sentence as the basis of our remarks in this chapter, and discuss, firstly, the Holy Sacrifice (*offertur*), secondly, Holy Communion (*sumitur*) and thirdly, the Real Presence (*continetur*).

THE HOLY SACRIFICE

The redemption of the human race by God-made man is the central fact in the history of mankind. The redeeming act of Calvary is communicated to men by the sacrifice of the Mass. The Mass therefore matters more than anything else that happens on earth.

[1] Can. 801.

The priest is ordained above all to celebrate the Mass; this is his supreme act, and it hardly needs repeating that he should prepare for it by meditation and spend at least fifteen minutes in thanksgiving after it. We come back on the duty of thanksgiving in the following section on holy communion. It is by his Mass that he is judged by his people. The way he says it can be his best sermon.

When all is said and done, the Mass remains an unfathomable mystery. Theologians in every age ponder its nature, revealing some of its many aspects, shedding a little new light, but never adequately explaining, simply because the mysteries of God are too deep ever to be adequately expressed in the language of men. We do not presume to enter deeply into the theology of the Mass; our concern is rather with practical matters, and we speak first of the active participation of the faithful in the holy sacrifice, and then of some material details which it may be useful to have grouped together.

Not as Strangers and Silent Spectators

After all that has been said and written in recent years on the importance of the Mass as a community act, there is no need to defend the thesis that the active participation of the faithful in the Mass is a necessity. It is enough to quote the words of the *Constitution on the Liturgy*: 'Holy Mother Church greatly wishes that all the faithful be brought to that full, conscious and active share in the liturgical celebrations which is required by the very nature of the liturgy itself, and which, by reason of their baptism, is their right and duty as a chosen race, a royal priesthood, a consecrated nation, a people God means to have for himself (1 Peter ii. 9; cf. ibid., 4-5)'[1] From this principle springs the concern of the Council for the dialogue Mass and for the use of the vernacular in the liturgy, and it inspires most of the changes which are now being embodied by the various local hierarchies in the new liturgical books.

All this echoes Pius XII's instruction of September 1958: 'Every effort must be made to ensure that the faithful are present, at low Mass also, not as strangers and silent spectators, but taking that share in it demanded by so great a mystery.'[2]

[1] Art. 14.   [2] Cf. ibid., art. 48.

One excellent way of getting the people used to regarding the holy sacrifice as something in which they have a real and active role is for one priest to explain the Mass and lead the congregation in prayer while another priest celebrates. Once the point has gone home, and the celebrating priest is recognized as truly the leader of the congregation, closely united with all present, this practice will become unnecessary, especially when the celebrant begins to address the people in their own language.

The dialogue Mass has now become the normal practice in many places, and it may be expected to become universal with the introduction of the vernacular. This is as it should be, for it is the natural expression of the social, communal nature of the Mass, and of the priesthood of the laity. It hardly needs to be remarked that the priest who is celebrating must adapt his recitation of the prayers and his whole demeanour to the congregation; he is the president of the sacred assembly, leading the People of God in prayer, as well as the celebrant of the Mass.[1] Experience shows that the two chief dangers for the celebrant are that he should be inaudible or too quick.

The people really do offer the Mass with the priest, though not in the same way, and it might be useful to say something on the rather difficult subject of the priesthood of the laity. This is a reality, with an explicit basis in Scripture, cited by the Council in the passage given above; occasional exaggerations should not be allowed to obscure this reality. We are at least safe in quoting the words of Pius XII on this matter in *Mediator Dei*: 'The unbloody immolation by which, after the words of consecration have been pronounced, Christ is rendered present on the altar in the state of victim is performed by the priest alone, and by the priest in so far as he acts in the name of Christ, not in so far as he represents the faithful. But precisely because the priest places the divine victim on the altar, he presents it as an oblation to God the Father for the glory of the Blessed Trinity and for the benefit of the whole Church. Now, understood in this restricted sense, the oblation is, in their own way, shared by the faithful, and for two reasons: first, because they offer the sacrifice *through* the priest, and, secondly, because, in a certain sense, they offer it with him. And because they have this part in the sacrifice, the people's offering also pertains to liturgical

[1] Cf. 'Dialogue Mass', in *The Clergy Review*, April 1956.

worship.' Clearly, the word 'offer' is analogous, used in one sense for the priest, and in another (quite real) sense for the people.

One way of showing that the people are really sharing in the Mass is to bring the hosts for communion to the altar at the offertory, in procession if some practical method can be devised. It would be an exaggeration to forbid the distribution of hosts which have been consecrated at an earlier Mass, but the Constitution on the Liturgy declares that the practice of consecrating the hosts for communion at the same Mass is a highly commendable practice and results in a more perfect sharing in the Mass on the part of the faithful; they are in this way really sharing in the altar, and the words of the Canon, *ex hac altaris participatione*, acquire real meaning.[1] It is a pity, however, that some have become mildly fanatical about this excellent, but not obligatory, practice.

It is a good thing to vary from time to time the way in which the faithful share in the Mass. The dialogue Mass is not the only possibility: people in Africa especially love to sing, and music has an important part to play in their religious formation. They should be taught hymns suitable for the different parts of the Mass so that, at least occasionally, they can follow the Mass in this way. The catechist's choice of hymns should be watched; they sometimes do not realize what hymns fit in at what part of the Mass.

Some Forgotten Rubrics

Washing facilities should be provided in every sacristy. Washing before prayer is a natural, symbolic thing, practised in several non-Christian religions, and it is prescribed by a rubric in the missal itself.

Nothing should be placed on the altar, either within Mass or outside it, which does not pertain immediately to the sacrifice. Vesting at the altar is a privilege reserved to bishops. When little space is available it is surprising how easily the vestments fit over a chair back.

Oculis dimissis, eyes cast down, to and from the altar; it applies even to parish priests who want to see who's there!

The rubrics of the missal itself prescribe that the missal be marked

[1] Cf. art. 55.

before Mass, so that time does not have to be spent on turning over the pages while the faithful wait for Mass to begin. This is an act of courtesy.

A ciborium which is being consecrated should stand on the altar-stone. If the stone is too small for both chalice and ciborium, then the chalice should be moved aside and replaced by the ciborium during the consecration of the Bread.

When saying Mass without a server, the priests says the *Confiteor* once only, omitting *vobis, fratres* and *vos, fratres*; *nostri* replaces *vestri* in the *Misereatur*, while *de manibus tuis* in the reply to the *Orate, Fratres* becomes *de manibus meis*.

Consecrated hosts should be consumed within a week; if there is no danger of corruption, they may be kept for a fortnight. This does not apply to the *special* European type used in some parts of Africa.

The regulations for the eucharistic fast are now exactly the same for both priest and people, and may be summed up thus:

Water does not break the fast.

Communicants must be fasting for one hour before communion from solid food and alcoholic drinks.[1]

Non-alcoholic drinks may be taken up to one hour before communion.

The sick, even when not confined to bed, may take genuine medicine, even if it contains alcohol, liquid or solid, and non-alcoholic drinks at any time.

We conclude this section on the Holy Sacrifice by recalling that the homily is now compulsory at all public Masses on Sundays and Holy days. It should draw its content mainly from scriptural and liturgical sources.[2]

THE SACRAMENT: HOLY COMMUNION

The sacred banquet is the natural complement of the holy sacrifice; Christ chose to come among us and to offer himself for us under the appearance of food and drink, and food and drink exist to be consumed. The faithful should know that the normal thing is to communicate at every Mass, as far as possible, for their participation in the sacrifice is

---

[1] *Osservatore Romano*, 4 December 1964, which adds that the alcoholic drink must be taken in moderation.

[2] Constitution on the Liturgy, art. 35, §2, 52.

incomplete without communion. Of course those who reasonably ask for holy communion outside Mass may not be refused, but the people should learn to regard this as an exception, and to realize that communion is inextricably linked with the sacrifice. It appears that in the popular mind assistance at Mass and reception of holy communion are felt as two distinct acts of religion, with the latter often regarded as the more important of the two. No doubt this springs largely from an individualistic approach to religion as a private affair between God and men; it will be corrected by a deeper understanding of the doctrine of the Mystical Body and a recognition of the essentially communal nature of the sacrifice and sacrament of the holy eucharist.

After speaking of the effects of holy communion, we discuss in this section some points concerning first communion and the practice of frequent communion, concluding with a note on communion to the sick and on the refusal of communion to public sinners.

The Effects of Holy Communion

If the sacrament of the holy eucharist is to be appreciated as it should be, the priest should himself meditate often on the effects of holy communion and explain them to his people. These effects are usually reduced to four.

Holy communion unites the individual soul with Christ and with all the faithful. The holy eucharist has always been considered as the sign of unity in the Church since, in the words of Pius XII, 'the bread to be consecrated results from the kneading together of many grains of wheat'.[1] In speaking to his people of the holy eucharist, therefore, the priest has yet another opportunity of insisting on the essentially social character of Christianity, and of combating any tendency to a selfish individualism in religion. The physical union between the communicant and the eucharistic Christ symbolizes and effects a spiritual union between the soul and Christ, and all those who are in Christ. For the individual himself, the personal union achieved with Christ is real, intimate, transforming; it is a moral union, achieved by love. This is the first and principal effect of holy communion.

Our Lord insisted that the sacrament of his body was to be truly a

---

[1] *Mystici Corporis Christi*, C.T.S. edition, no. 82.

food; it was to fulfil with regard to the soul the function which food fulfils for the body, that is to sustain and to strengthen. The holy eucharist increases the life of the soul by sanctifying and actual grace, as food increases the life of the body; this is the second effect of holy communion. It brings with it a certain spiritual relish or delight. We can live the life of the spirit, and be truly living and dynamic members of the Mystical Body, only if we continually maintain and renew the life infused into us at baptism; and it is to the holy eucharist above all that we must look for this spiritual food.

We are strengthened against those temptations which come from the material part of our nature. This strengthening against temptation is often called the third effect of holy communion, along with the remission of venial sins, and preservation from mortal sins which cast a shadow over relations between God and the individual. In a particular way, the vehemence of concupiscence is allayed.

In so far as union with God constitutes man's perfection, holy communion gives us a foretaste of heaven; it is thus often called a pledge of eternal life, giving us a special right to the resurrection of the body. Holy communion makes us more like Christ, and so prepares us for that more perfect union with him which we shall enjoy when our bodies, like his, are raised and glorified. 'If anyone eats of this bread, he shall live for ever, and I shall raise him up at the last day'(John vi. 52).

First Communion

A Catholic child may be admitted to holy communion when he has attained the use of reason, and has sufficient knowledge of the blessed sacrament and of the essential truths of the faith. It is idle to ask if the degree of the use of reason required is such that the child is capable of committing mortal sin before it can be admitted to the sacrament; knowledge of doctrine and love of Christ is what matters.

A much higher standard of knowledge is demanded of catechumens, although exceptions are made for old people.

The deaf and dumb may be admitted to holy communion,[1] as may backward children.[2]

---

[1] BISHOP DE REEPER, in *The Sacraments on the Missions*, appendix viii.
[2] *Fiches de pédagogie religieuse*, No. 298.

Frequent Communion

The practice of frequent communion is now well established in the Church, and especially in Africa, which has never known Jansenism; this is something to be grateful for, and the priest must encourage his people to receive their Lord as often as possible.

At the same time, the people must realize that holy communion is a sacred thing, to be approached in a fitting manner. The state of grace is all that is required for the lawful reception of holy communion, but if the sacrament is to be truly fruitful, the communicant must also have the right intention. Such an intention is lacking in one who communicates *merely* out of routine, without making any attempt to realize what he is doing. Routine is of course a permanent danger for all of us, including priests; it cannot perhaps always be wholly avoided, but we are only asked to do our best to combat it. An important way of doing this is to make our preparation and thanksgiving as well as possible It would help the faithful in this matter if the catechist sought to vary the prayers before and after holy communion, instead of mechanically reciting each time a set of standard formulae.

The right intention would also be lacking in one who approached the altar rails *merely* out of a desire to appear pious or respectable in the eyes of others, or *solely* because he feared what others might think or say if he abstained. Such sentiments have evidently nothing to do with religion, and it is an affront to our Lord to use his sacrament for such a wordly purpose as to increase our standing with others. Parents, teachers and lay apostles must be careful not to behave in a manner which may encourage those whom they are guiding to win favour with authority by communicating frequently; when young people communicate daily at a boarding-school, but seldom or never while at home, one may suspect that some purely human motive may be inspiring their apparent piety at school. Priests too should beware of appearing to attach undue importance to the material acts of religion. It is perhaps possible to dragoon large numbers of people into receiving holy communion, but if their communions are not the reflection of a true interior devotion, it is hard to think that they can be very fruitful. This is another aspect of the fight against formalism and exterior religion which has to be waged unceasingly; our concern is to form the minds of the people, to bring them to God by worshipping him in spirit and in truth, and so to lead them to exterior practices which are the genuine expression of interior dispositions.

Yet, *est modus in rebus*: a true balance will exclude Jansenistic rigorism and the opposite error that only the state of grace is necessary. Our Lord does not demand perfection of those who receive him; he requires only a right intention, which St. Pius X defined as a desire to please God and to be more closely united with him by charity, and a wish to seek the divine remedy of holy communion for one's weaknesses and defects.[1] The priest therefore should encourage frequent communion, but he should do this more by expounding the theology of the sacrament and exciting the fervour of the faithful than simply by urging them, without much explanation, to go to communion. A wrong approach may produce record numbers of communions but not do much to foster true religion.

The Dispositions of the Communicant

We have already spoken[2] of the danger of treating the sacraments as mechanical instruments of grace and overlooking the importance of the dispositions of the subject. One way of countering this danger is to insist on preparation, so that the communicant approaches the sacrament really prepared to surrender himself totally to Christ and to the loving demands which he makes on us.

The decree of St. Pius X which promulgated frequent communion insisted on the importance of an adequate period of thanksgiving; priests must themselves give the example in this matter, and encourage the faithful to spend at least some minutes in prayer when possible after the end of the Mass during which they have communicated. The old idea that the sacred species remain in the communicant for a quarter of an hour after reception now seems to be finally discredited; it appears certain that in fact the sacred host is assimilated by the body almost at once, so that Christ remains physically present only for a few seconds after holy communion.[3] This however has nothing whatever to do with

[1] *Sacra Tridentiana*, 20 December 1905.   [2] In Chapter 9.
[3] *Theological Studies*, December, 1960, pp. 617–19.

the duty of thanksgiving. Holy communion is a spiritual experience, and to think that the duty of thanksgiving for Christ's gift varied according to the communicant's metabolism would suggest a strangely material attitude to religion.

Regular instruction therefore on preparation and thanksgiving for communion is very important if the fruits of frequent communion are really to be received. Certainly there are occasions when it is necessary to empty the church immediately after one Mass to make way for the congregation for the next; some effort should be made to remedy this situation, but at least on weekdays no such excuse can be put forward. Those who say that they have to hurry home for other duties often manage to spend five or ten minutes chatting with friends outside the church.

The Ritual too tells the priest to instruct the faithful on the importance of spending some time after communion thanking our Lord for his gift and meditating on his passion; they should be told not to leave the church at once, and not to talk or gaze around them. There is of course no sin here; the time from communion to the end of the Mass amply fulfils strict obligation. But the priest should often speak from the pulpit about thanksgiving after communion. It would however be an exaggeration to advise a person not to communicate because he knows that he will have no time for thanksgiving afterwards.

In schools and junior seminaries, it is always unwise to impose long periods of prayer; it would be better to omit the vocal prayers before Mass rather than curtail the normal fifteen minutes' thanksgiving. It is particularly desirable that seminarists acquire good habits in this matter, for priests look back in later days to their seminary routine as the priestly model. In the same way, Sisters should reduce their vocal prayers before Mass rather than cut down on thanksgiving. The priest should be severe on himself in this matter, forcing himself to give the full quarter of an hour, however wearisome he may find it. Usually he will need a book, and the breviary contains some beautiful prayers suitable for use after celebrating Mass. St. Teresa said of the precious moments after communion that there is no other time when we can so easily enrich our souls with virtues, so quickly climb to perfection.

The Avoidance of Possible Abuses

In religious communities, and especially in boarding institutions for young people, there is an evident danger that those who are conscious of mortal sin may be tempted to make a sacrilegious communion out of fear of revealing their sin to others. An Instruction from the Holy See, dated 8 December 1938, dealt with this problem and suggested three remedies: instruction, ample facilities for confession before Mass, and the abolition of undesirable customs, such as approaching the holy table in order of precedence, and general communion days.

In their instructions, preachers and confessors should encourage frequent communion, but they should make it clear that there is no question of any obligation to communicate every day. Superiors must find ways of letting their subjects know that they do not think any less of those who communicate less frequently than others, and they should stress liberty and delicacy of conscience. If the superior considers it prudent to speak on this subject at all, he must confine himself to general exhortations, and never give advice to individuals: that is the task of the confessor.

The gravity of a sacrilegious communion must not be exaggerated, and certainly must never be compared to the treason of Judas. There are worse sins, and it is wrong to frighten the young and sensitive by usurping the place of God and passing harsh judgement. We should make it plain that only *certain* unconfessed mortal sin is a barrier to holy communion. There must be no exaggeration, and above all no cruelty to the young.

No one is obliged to abstain from holy communion if his reputation will be seriously damaged thereby; Can. 856 expressly states that in cases of urgent necessity, and where facilities for confession are lacking, a person conscious of mortal sin may communicate after making an act of perfect contrition (although in practice it is obvious that it is often possible to find simple ways out of this dilemma). It may perhaps be objected that facilities for confession are lacking when one has a great repugnance to the available confessor because, for example, he will certainly recognize our voice, and one has daily dealings with him outside the confessional. This will often be the case with priests who are teaching in a school or seminary.

In seminaries and colleges it might be considered unwise for the rector always to say the community Mass, and members of communities and of school staffs should be forbidden to discuss who went to holy communion and who did not. Most writers disapprove of encouraging the innocent to abstain from holy communion occasionally with a view to making things easier for those who are obliged to abstain. Sodality communion days must be understood as invitations, not as rules, and solemn communion days, when all are expected to communicate, and are shepherded to the altar rails in ordered droves, are forbidden. Clearly the wearing of special insignia by communicants, and still more the giving of prizes to individuals or groups who communicate frequently, is an intolerable practice. No priest or teacher should quiz schoolchildren on Monday morning about who went to communion the previous day. Membership of parish sodalities and the like should not depend on regular reception of holy communion, and on general communion days, again understood as invitations, no attempt should be made to record the number of communicants (Can. 859). If parents reproach their children with their infrequent communions, the children have only to say: 'My confessor says that people go to holy communion only when they want to.' Even the Easter duty may be lawfully postponed on the advice of the confessor.[1]

The most important way of rendering more remote the possibility of sacrilegious communions is to provide facilities for confession as the Holy See commands; where there is frequent and daily communion, there must also be frequent and daily facilities for confession. The best thing is for the priest to sit in the confessional, for some people are too sensitive to ask directly for confession. Communities of nuns and schoolgirls who are wholly dependent on visiting chaplains should be treated with special delicacy in this matter; it is desirable that every priest who says Mass for such a community should automatically receive facilities to hear the confessions of those for whom he celebrates Mass; here too he should make a habit of sitting in the confessional for some minutes each morning before Mass, whether anyone comes or

---

[1] The parish aspects of this matter are well treated by Fr. F. J. McCONNELL, C.SS.R. 'Holy Communion through Coercion', in *American Ecclesiastical Record*, March 1944. For institutions, see 'De Probatione ante S. Communionem', in *Periodica*, IV, 1926 (unsigned article, almost certainly by VERMEERSCH), cited by CANON MAHONEY, 'A Roman Instruction', in *The Clergy Review*, August 1939.

not. Quite apart from the danger of sacrilegious communions, it is important that those who are striving after perfection in any form of college or seminary should have easy access to confession; immediate confession after a sudden fall, following a long period of resistance and success, prevents discouragement; a fall in these circumstances has, psychologically, the danger of several subsequent falls if confession is delayed.

Communion to the Sick

In communities and boarding establishments, holy communion should only be taken to the sick when they ask for it. Those concerned must be taught that they will only be brought holy communion if the initiative comes from them, unprompted. In all cases, the sick person should be asked by the priest if he wishes to go to confession before communicating.

Common law requires that the blessed sacrament be carried publicly to the sick, but in most parts of Africa, and indeed in most places in the world nowadays, circumstances will excuse one from this regulation, and the priest will carry the holy eucharist privately to the sick person. He carries the pyx, suspended from a cord round his neck, in an inside pocket, and he should wear a white stole[1] under his outer garment; if possible, he should be accompanied by a lay person, and be met outside the house by one of the family with a lighted candle. The priest should inculcate respect for the blessed sacrament by refusing to take part in general conversation while he has the sacred host on his person. When a priest is taking communion to a sick person in some out-of-the-way place, the Ordinary may allow him to give communion to others also. It is not permitted to carry the blessed sacrament beyond the length of a day's journey; if he has to travel far, the priest should take a portable altar and celebrate Mass on the following morning.

Refusal of Holy Communion to Public Sinners

It hardly needs saying that anyone who presents himself at the altar rails must be given holy communion, unless he is already publicly known as a sinner. Even if the priest knows that the person is in fact in

[1] Coll. no. 345.

an unworthy state, he has no right to destroy a reputation by passing over someone who is generally regarded as a good Christian. We speak only of those who have no reputation to lose.

In general, public and notorious sinners may not be admitted to holy communion until their repentance and reform is known and the public scandal or harm that they have given has been repaired. If the sinner has gone openly to confession and renounced a notorious occasion of sin, such as concubinage, then he may be considered to have repented publicly; as far as possible, any harm done should be repaired before the penitent receives holy communion.

Difficulties may arise in the case of those who have caused damage which is irreparable; one may think of a man who has spread error about the truth, or paid or accepted a dowry for an invalid marriage union, or encouraged or tolerated trial marriages. If it is really impossible to undo the harm that has been done, then the sinner may be admitted to holy communion once he has repented, made his confession, and publicly retracted what he has done, as far as possible. The worst sin is not beyond the scope of God's mercy, not even the sin of selling one's daughter into concubinage, and God does not require any man to repair the irreparable. The Ordinary may decide for the common good in special cases to impose a public penance, with a view to emphasizing the serious nature of the sin, and to remove any possible scandal by publishing in this way the reform of a notorious sinner; but no one may be excluded from holy communion once he has really repented, even though he is still performing a penance of this kind.[1]

THE REAL PRESENCE

The heart of the sacrament of Christ's love is to be sought in the sacrifice of the Mass, and in the holy communion which completes that sacrifice; it is true also that the practice of reserving the sacred species outside Mass is a comparatively recent development; nevertheless this practice is a perfectly legitimate development, and it is an impious error and contrary to the mind of the contemporary Church to suggest that devotion to Christ in the tabernacle is in some way an aberration because it was unknown in the early Church. The eucharistic presence

[1] Cans. 853 and 855.

of Christ in the churches of the world symbolizes Christ's presence in the Church, and it reflects too the unity of the faithful among themselves, everywhere gathered together round the same Christ. The faithful are to be encouraged frequently to renew their faith in Christ's presence in the tabernacle and to visit him there. They will be helped in this by the priest's own reverent behaviour in church, and by his insistence on recollected behaviour from others, especially perhaps on the occasion of a baptism or a wedding, when the congregation is apt to include persons whose acquaintance with the church, and with the kind of conduct suitable in church, is not extensive. Good Catholics themselves often give the Blessed Sacrament little respect on these occasions. There is a strange view abroad among a few of the clergy that these things do not matter—they are in their Father's house. . . . All the more reason for respecting their Father; if they do not learn respect for him from the priest, from whom will they learn it? The material, the outward seeming, does matter to simple folk. In suitable places, devotion to the real presence may be encouraged by instituting perpetual adoration without exposition; it is surprising how popular this apparently heroic practice can become. Night vigils have also been surprisingly popular in some parts of Africa (without perpetual adoration or exposition of the Blessed Sacrament). The priest should take great pains to know and to follow the prescriptions concerning the eucharistic reservation, which is confided to him as a most sacred trust. We mention here a few rubrics which are sometimes forgotten; their careful observance should be a reflection of our veneration for the gift of God.

The tabernacle should be immovable, i.e., very difficult to move (*moraliter immovibile*), and it should be covered with a veil which hangs down on all four sides, like a tent. The word 'canopaeum', like 'tabernacle' itself, means 'tent', recalling the carrying of the Ark of the Covenant across the desert by the Israelites; the memory is well preserved by keeping the correct shape of the veil. There should be no veils on the tabernacles of side-altars, and a purple veil should be used for the high altar tabernacle during requiem Masses. Black veils are forbidden. Note that the sure sign of presence of the Blessed Sacrament, apart from the burning lamp, is the veil.

The sanctuary lamp should be kept burning night and day, and the faithful may be taught that the lamp is the sign that they are with Christ in the tabernacle in spirit, though their duty obliges them to be physically elsewhere. In Africa, where it may be difficult to provide a light, Ordinaries are empowered to allow their priests to dispense with the sanctuary lamp where genuinely necessary. Otherwise, an interruption of twenty-four hours is usually considered grave.

Apart from the Blessed Sacrament itself, nothing whatever, not even empty sacred vessels, may be kept in the tabernacle.

The custody of the tabernacle key has been the subject of very severe regulations, and a priest whose negligence in this matter leads to desecration of the tabernacle is liable to heavy penalties; the facts of the case must be forwarded to the Congregation of the Sacraments. The key should be kept in a locked drawer or safe, of which the key is kept in the priest's house or on his person. It is wise to have a duplicate tabernacle key, to avoid ever having to force or pick the lock of the tabernacle. The key may never be left on the altar or in the lock, even during the hours when services are being held. In convents of Sisters only the chaplain may keep the tabernacle key and he may not keep it inside the convent. The Sisters are permitted to keep a duplicate key of the drawer or safe in which the tabernacle key is kept.[1]

Where missionaries have not yet a safe church in which to reserve the Blessed Sacrament, they should reserve it in their house, for the benefit of the sick;[2] if there is danger of sacrilege, the Ordinary may permit the reservation to be made in some decent place in the house, without a burning lamp.

Benediction of the Blessed Sacrament, like the reservation itself, is a comparatively recent practice, but one which has a great attraction for all; and it is one of the most touching ceremonies of the Church, and an excellent way of expressing devotion to Christ and thanking him for his gift. Six wax candles are required by common law for Benediction; in Africa the Ordinary may allow Benediction to be given with two lights of any kind. In religious communities, the permission of the Ordinary, the authors say, is probably not required for Benediction with the monstrance, if the doors of the chapel are closed, since this is

---

[1] Instruction of the Sacred Congregation of the Sacraments, 26 May 1933. Penalties include removal from the parish.

[2] Coll. no. 1079, ad 2.

not then public Benediction. No permission is required for Benediction with the ciborium.

The Benediction Host should not be left in the lunula without a cover.

Most parish churches have a monthly Holy Hour, and this should be made an interesting and attractive service. The people should not be kept in church beyond the hour, and there should be no long reading of prayers by the priest, even if they are intelligible. The hour should be carefully planned, and it is wise to vary the formula from month to month; it will generally be useful to divide the hour into the four quarters, but there is no reason why a full-length sermon should not occasionally be introduced. The people should see the priest, and this means using the pulpit. Long silences are out of place, but there could be short moments of silent prayer; the priest should always explain carefully what is coming next, and when inviting the people to pray silently, he should first let them know when he is going to start talking again. If the choir sings a Latin hymn, by way of exception, the priest would do well first to read a translation to the people. Brief readings, explanations, hymns and prayers should comfortably fill each quarter. As in all church services, the people must be encouraged to play an active part; the liturgy itself will be our model here.[1] Careful preparation by the priest is essential; if he wanders off into a series of haphazard and disconnected ideas, he can hardly hope to prevent the people's attention from wandering. A good plan is to have a key word for each quarter; for example, the four ends of sacrifice can sometimes be a useful general guide.

To acquire the right technique, many have tried listening to a broadcast of a Catholic service of this kind. This will be all the more helpful if it has been 'tailored' by the radio corporation's team of experts. They sustain the listener's interest throughout, explain what is coming next and make sure that more than one voice is heard during the service; and they keep to a pre-arranged time-table. We ourselves must always have a clear time-table prepared, and must finish exactly within the hour. Mark beforehand what may be omitted should time run out. Variety is the highly developed technique of those whose bread and butter depends upon sustaining the interest of their listeners; if we

[1] 'The Holy Hour', in *Worship*, 30 October 1938.

imitate their skill, the people will begin to look forward to the monthly Holy Hour, instead of finding it something of an ordeal.

A last word concerning the private Holy Hour, which was spread so zealously by the late Father Matteo Crawley. The faithful can, of course, always make private Holy Hours before the Blessed Sacrament. (They would do well to join the People's Eucharistic League; full information can be obtained from the Blessed Sacrament Fathers, P.O. Box 542, Masaka, Uganda.) But what Father Crawley did so much to popularize was an hour of prayer at home, and this might attract the old and sick, and those who live in outstations.

In seeking to increase his people's faith in, and love for, the holy eucharist, the priest should realize that the decisive factor will always be his own interior attitude. If, in spite of much weariness of spirit, he is genuinely trying to deepen his own interior life, to make the Mass the focal point of each day, and to form his people into a truly Christian community, his own spirit will infallibly communicate itself to his people and, almost without his noticing it, a deep appreciation of Christ's gift will grow up all around him. Here perhaps is the heaviest responsibility of the priesthood: for better or worse, the priest can never live his own spiritual life in isolation; only a eucharistic priest can form a eucharistic people.

13 Penance: the Sacrament of Reconciliation

THE hardest of the priest's tasks, the sacrament of reconciliation, in many ways brings the best returns. In his other work he may sow painfully and water the land; here God gives the superabundant increase. That was why St. Pius V said he knew no better way of reforming Catholics than by giving them good confessors. And because the task is at once so difficult and so fruitful, it is, as St. John Baptist de Rossi used to say, the priest's shortest road to heaven.

Our masters in theology tell us that the confessor fulfils three roles: he is father, judge and physician. The first implies kindness, the second knowledge, the third prudence, with skill.

THE CONFESSOR AS FATHER

Thou Art My Father, He Shall Cry Out to Me

As father, the confessor strives to imitate God in whom all paternity is named. Christ instituted this sacrament for mercy, in order to show the divine Fatherhood, not to exercise inexorable justice. The priest's power, conferred upon him by Christ, is as boundless as that of the divine mercy itself: *misericordia absque ullo termino*, as St. Thomas says. Only the heart of a father can dispense mercy such as that. Sinners are easily discouraged, but at a father's word they get up and shoulder their burden again.

Each soul has to be treated as an individual; how difficult that can be! If the penitent shows fear or has been away long, a word of encouragement at the beginning can work wonders. Inaudibility, lack of preparation, and scrupulosity, complete silence, ignorance of the most essentia truths, rudeness, the numbness of repetition, the strain of dealing with such large numbers—only the charity of a father can support these things. One sign of tired nerves and perhaps no further sin will be confessed; the penitent leaves having made a sacrilegious confession, determined perhaps never to come back. Men in particular resent confession; they look at it as a humuliation and they suffer from human respect. A child confessing something materially or formally serious for the first time will be afraid: the slighest suspicion, real or imaginary, of harshness, and that may be the last time for years or even for ever that that sin will be confessed.

Latecomers can be trying, and yet . . . so small a thing as the priest looking at his watch because he is being kept late for another engagement can be misunderstood even by the intelligent and devout. Poor Father; he continues for hours, nerves on edge, straining to catch whispers, attuning his ear to one voice after another, constantly aware that any sign of weariness may be misinterpreted. But he can only forget his own burden and live again in himself the inexhaustible charity of Christ.

LOVE JUSTICE, YOU THAT ARE THE JUDGES OF THE EARTH

A judge without love and knowledge of the law is worse than useless. St. Alphonsus said that a confessor without the requisite knowledge is in *statu damnationis*. It is not possible to have the requisite knowledge without study after ordination. The priest is like the doctor, lawyer, or scientist—he has to revise his books and keep abreast of new thought. It is too easy to forget, and when he goes back to his books, the priest is surprised to see how many important things he has overlooked or not properly understood. Every priest should subscribe to at least one good theological review, such as the *African Ecclesiastical Review*, the *Nouvelle Révue Ecclésiastique* or the *Clergy Monthly* (of India).

The Duty of Interrogating

As judge the confessor must usually believe what the penitent says. If he has extra-confessional knowledge which gives him reason to doubt what is said, he must still give the penitent the benefit of the doubt.

If he is certain that what the penitent says is not true, he cannot believe him and must act accordingly—tact will be necessary here. The Ritual and all the authors insist that it is unwise to interrupt while a penitent is telling his sins, even though this might mean that the priest will forget some serious sins about which he is bound to ask questions. The old tip about numbering major points on one's fingers has helped some. Often people keep serious sins to the end; if interrupted they may never reach this point.

The species, circumstances and number of all serious sins have to be confessed, but at the same time anything that would make confession odious must be avoided. This last is one of the chief obligations of a confessor, excusing him from many things which would otherwise be obligatory. Then, too, any form of imprudent questioning exposes him to talk outside the confessional. It is of course strictly forbidden to ask the name of an accomplice. Unless it is obviously necessary, it is always wise to ask when the penitent has finished if there is anything else he wants to tell. Sometimes it is good to say: 'People of your state of life and age often commit such and such a sin; do you think you have done so? Don't be afraid, I will help you.'

Contrition More Important than Integrity

As judge the confessor has also to decide upon the three parts of confession: the complete confession of serious sin or, if there is no serious sin, sufficiency of matter, the giving or withholding of absolution and the imposing of a fitting penance. A word, first, about contrition before we go on to absolution and the penance. It is possible to forget that contrition is more important than integrity. No one can doubt that some confessions are invalid for the want of it. Some people might come, for example, solely because of heavy moral pressure from relations or friends. True sorrow for having offended God and a firm purpose of amendment may be absent when the penitent enters the confessional but the confessor can in most cases dispose the penitent sufficiently well by speaking of the motives for contrition. One way is to go through each part of the act of contrition and explain it.

Here again it is worth saying that perfect contrition is not difficult for ordinary folk. Our Christians often live far from a priest; it is therefore necessary in these regions of Africa, where so many die without the last sacraments, that they should be well instructed in what perfect contrition is and how to make the act of it.

The Refusal of Absolution

The question of refusing absolution is an anxious one,[1] but it should be said that if the confessor errs at all in this matter it should be on the side of leniency; the penitent must always be given the benefit of the doubt. There will be many occasions when the confessor will be quite unable to come to a firm decision about the penitent's state; broad moral certainty that he is fit to receive absolution must often suffice, or, failing this, conditional absolution must be given.

It may be that the Ordinary has made special regulations about withholding absolution, and these of course must be carefully observed. There are cases where absolution may be deferred, for the penitent's good (not for more than a fortnight, and better still for only a day or an hour); and this should only be done when the penitent agrees, and when it is certain that he will return. If the penitent is ignorant of necessary truths, *necessitate medii*, absolution would be invalid, but the confessor should be able to instruct him on the spot. He would, of course, have to promise to attend the instruction classes.

In general, there will be only four cases in which an otherwise well-disposed penitent will be unable to receive absolution validly and must therefore be sent away without it:

(1) if he lives in a habit of mortal sin and makes no attempt to get out of it;

(2) if he lives in a proximate occasion of mortal sin and refuses to give it up, though he could easily do so;

(3) if he nurses a bitter hatred against another person and refuses to be reconciled with him;

(4) if he refuses to make restitution when he could easily do so.

In these circumstances, the penitent is incapable of receiving absolution validly and the priest must therefore withhold it.

Normally a penitent who promises to make the necessary restitution

[1] Cf. Chapter 9.

must be absolved. There may however be occasions when the confessor has good reason to feel sure that the restitution will not in fact be made, and he may be obliged to defer absolution until it has been made. This will of course only apply when the obligation to make restitution is a serious one. It is, in general, hard to understand the strange notion that in practice absolution can always be given, whatever the circumstances.

A special problem concerns those who, over a long period, only come to Mass and the sacraments once a year, in the Easter duty period. In old Catholic countries, it may well be that, in spite of every effort to instruct him, the penitent has never really grasped that the obligation of Sunday Mass is a serious one; he may therefore be judged guiltless of grave sin and absolved. This will hardly be the case in countries of minority Catholicism such as Africa, however, and a Christian who, after several warnings, never comes near a church except for the annual visit for the Easter duties can hardly be truly contrite and must therefore be denied absolution; but even here it may be that the confessor judges that, in spite of his past record, the penitent now seriously intends to come to Mass every Sunday.[1]

It is evident that a public sinner who is properly disposed and who has done what he reasonably can to repair any scandal or harm he has caused must be given absolution.

Refusal of Absolution for Non-Payment of Church Dues[2]

Christians are under an obligation to give material support to the Church. This obligation, which is connected with justice as well as with religion, is in itself a grave one, but most authors consider that in practice failure to meet it will seldom be a mortal sin. Fr. J. Génicot, S.J., writing for India, which has problems not unlike our own, declared that a parish priest is offending against both charity and justice if he refuses to exercise the sacred ministry in favour of those who do not fulfil their obligations of supporting the Church.[3]

[1] This solution is excellently set out by the French hierarchy, in *Directoire pour la pastorale des sacrements*, 1951, no. 53.

[2] Cf. Chapter 6 above, pp. 57–8.

[3] *Clergy Monthly*, 1949, p. 12. He quotes the decree of Propaganda Fide, 13 May 1816 (Coll. I, 713, ad 4) in support of his view. See also Father E. DE BEKKER, in *African Ecclesiastical Review*, April 1963. For the case for refusing absolution, see BISHOP DE REEPER, 'The Problem of Church Tax in the Missions', in ibid., January 1959.

One at least of the national hierarchies of Africa has declared that the obligation to pay church tax could not be considered a grave one, and that defaulters could not justly be refused absolution, except in the rare case of formal contempt; it is unlikely that anyone with dispositions of formal contempt would approach the confessional anyway.

It seems to follow that it would always be wrong, in England or America for example, to refuse absolution to a Christian who failed to support the Church. In Africa, the only situation in which a case might be made out for refusal would be where the Church is in such dire need that the common good urgently requires that this severe sanction be brought into operation. In other words, refusal would be urged as justifiable not *per se*, but *per accidens*. An additional argument here would be that sanctions of this kind are in the line of African cultural patterns (witness the too strong sanctions of lay parish committees). A bishop may therefore, in the last resort, issue a ruling to this effect. Nevertheless it is hard to envisage circumstances in which this could be said to be a wise policy. In places where it has been applied, the money has certainly come in, but there has also been an increase in the number of lapsed Christians. To leave souls in mortal sin for the sake of better and more numerous ecclesiastical buildings is too bitter a price. The public image of the Church also suffers when there is too much insistence on this duty of material support. As education spreads in Africa, anti-clericalism is also spreading, and continual talk about money and harsh measures to extract it will reinforce this attitude.

What the common good certainly demands, as we have observed in Chapter 6, is that the people be educated in this matter. This is a long-term policy, and it can be expected to show its full fruit only after a number of generations, as more than one African-born bishop has insisted. It takes a long time to build up a new mentality and new habits, and the necessarily paternalistic attitude of missionaries for so many years has created an ingrained conviction in the minds of many Africans that the material side of the Church is the priest's responsibility. For the moment, patience seems to be the best policy. People are more important than buildings, and it is better to have a mud-and-wattle church with a fervent congregation than a splendid edifice with a critical community, some of whom are perhaps excluded from the sacraments.

We have avoided in this discussion reference to remarks made in the past by Secretaries of Propaganda or Apostolic Delegates. The sum value of these might be that if an Ordinary, rightly or wrongly, is convinced that absolution should be refused in his diocese, the Sacred Congregation would not, despite its own standing prohibition, demur.

One practical point about Church tax in general. Why, in some places, should all children of school age have to pay? Equity seems to require that a family with eight school-age children should pay no more than a family with one.

The Imposition of Penance

The third part of the sacrament, the imposition of a penance, is the last of the confessor's duties as judge. The priest is obliged to impose a penance in proportion to the number and gravity of the sins confessed. The bishops of the Congo pointed out that a confessor who imposes a light penance for a grave sin 'diminishes in the eyes of the penitent the gravity of mortal sin, and the sinner will see in the sacrament of penance only a cheap way of paying off an enormous debt against divine justice'. The priest's obligation in the case of grave sin, is *per se*, grave. At the same time, the penance must not be of such a kind as to require exceptional exertion or humiliation, nor must it make confession distasteful to the penitent or to others. In general, in our countries, it is unwise to impose a penance which cannot be completed immediately.

Public penances may not be imposed for secret sins, since this would amount to breaking the seal of the confessional. The common good may however suggest, or even require, that public penances be imposed for public and notorious sins, though only with the Ordinary's approval. Public scandal demands public reparation. It is however for the confessor alone to decide what penance to give, though the parish priest is within his rights in suggesting to a curate what he considers to be a suitable penance for a notorious sinner who has previously announced his intention of seeking confession.

All prayers and good works enjoined in confession have a sacramental value superior to any other penitential exercise; for this reason Father Vermeersch was in the habit of suggesting to devout penitents that they ask for a big penance, especially if there has been much serious sin in their lives. The same priest would also say occasionally: 'Whatever good works you do in the next two days will be your penance.'

This approach is in fact suggested by the Church herself, for many theologians think that it is her intention, in the prayer 'Passio Domini Nostri Jesu Christi', to raise to the dignity of sacramental efficacy all the penitent's good works and sufferings until the satisfaction due to the sins which he has just confessed has been made. For this reason, Noldin and others recommend that, although a reasonable cause excuses the priest from saying this prayer, it should be at least recited secretly as the penitent leaves the confessional. Some of our priests, however, are so overwhelmed with confessions that they might not be able to do even this.

THE CONFESSOR AS PHYSICIAN

To Heal the Contrite of Heart

'The spirit of the Lord is upon me . . . he hath sent me to heal the contrite of heart' (Luke iv. 18). The confessor is not only father and judge, he is a physician of souls. As a physician has to heal the wounds of sin. For this he needs prudence and skill. It is as physician that he persuades and instructs, disposes the reluctant and unprepared, leads souls to perfection. He knows that, as St. Philip Neri used to say, the big fish come by at awkward times; sometimes, like Nicodemus they come at night. The physician of their souls welcomes them, careless of his own inconvenience, for he knows that if he demurs he may never again be in a position to heal their wounds.

He must, of course, be a realist, and often he cannot hope to achieve more than the minimum dispositions necessary for the valid reception of the sacrament. Nevertheless, even in cases where he must concentrate on essentials, the priest should try not to omit the short admonition, if at all possible; a priest who has, say, to hear three hundred confessions in five hours or less every Saturday morning cannot do this, nor can he do quite a number of other things not required for validity that we have mentioned in this book. 'Concentrate on the nouns, and forget the verbs', one priest said to his newly ordained curate. There are indeed some who would include the admonition as belonging to the bare essentials, for it is God's plan to guide men to heaven through the ministry of their brethren, and without this kind of direct, personal dialogue, progress in the spiritual life is not normally possible. The confessor must not allow himself to be distracted by the thought of how many more penitents are waiting outside; he must give his whole attention to the person actually in confession and allow him all the time he needs. St. Francis Xavier even went as far as to say that it is better to hear a few people well than many negligently. It is evident that a few words, addressed to the individual, and adapted as far as possible to his special needs, can be far more effective than any sermon. The admonition should seldom last for more than a minute or so; long talks are out of place, as the Capuchin realized when, after addressing a lengthy discourse to a child, he discovered that his penitent had absent-mindedly knotted the venerable beard round the holes of the grill.

Spiritual Director

Some priests of course are called upon to act as spiritual directors outside the confessional; this is a specialized and exacting task. The essential qualifications are personal holiness and a good knowledge of ascetical theology, along with a spirit which is docile to the workings of grace. The spiritual director does not seek to evade responsibility, but he is careful to respect the individual vocation of each of the souls he is called upon to direct, and never attempts to impose his own purely private views. He should perhaps bear in mind especially that he is not called upon to teach his penitents self-improvement for its own sake, but to lead them to Christ, above all through charity and apostolic work; they are to look outward to God rather than inward to themselves. Never should he hold back a generous soul by limited views of perfection or excessive prudence: God in everything, God alone.

THE CONFESSIONAL SEAL

Everyone knows that the confessor is bound to secrecy with regard to what passes in the confessional, but the law may be repeated here for the sake of completeness. He may not reveal, either directly or indirectly, the sins of a penitent, nor may he use any knowledge gained in the confessional in a way which would offend either the penitent or other people. This means that he is even prevented from consulting another priest on some technical point of moral theology if he cannot do so without revealing a penitent's identity. In practice, the only safe rule is to keep completely silent about all one's experiences in the confessional. Lay people, however intelligent and broad-minded, feel uncomfortable if the priest refers to such experiences, even if only to comment, say, on the lack of preparation in the children who confessed that day.

SOME SPECIAL CATEGORIES OF PENITENTS

Priests

No priest can guide himself; to obtain forgiveness of his sins, he must, like every other man, humble himself before one of his fellow-creatures. The admonition will clearly not be omitted when hearing a priest's confession; he is not so different from other men, and it is more than likely that what he needs above all is encouragement. Wounds must be probed with skill and charity.

Religious

The confessor is, at least in part, also the spiritual director of the nuns and Brothers who come to him for confession. In spite of all their spiritual readings and conferences, for them too there is nothing like the individual word. They should be encouraged in their difficulties, and, week by week, guided to Christian perfection.

Children

It is very important that children be well trained for their first confession; otherwise confession may be a burden to them, and to their confessors, throughout their lives. The priest will always need the greatest patience with young children, but his task will be greatly eased if they have been well taught, and realize the necessity of contrition and of sufficient matter.

There are some modern thinkers who recommend the abolition of the custom of making first confession before first holy communion; they argue that a child of six or seven, while capable of recognizing the sacred character of the Blessed Sacrament, is not able to commit mortal sin, so that frequent confession by very young children not only exposes the sacrament to invalidity through lack of matter and of true contrition, but also induces bad habits regarding confession which can persist throughout life. It happens only too often that adults never outgrow the approach to confession which they were taught as children, and which is quite unsuitable to mature and responsible adults. The linking of confession and communion also gives rise to the false idea, found in so many adults, that it is forbidden to receive holy communion without having gone to confession immediately beforehand. We would prefer not to comment at all on this opinion. But there will be occasions when the priest will judge that a child is incapable of receiving the sacrament. In these cases, the child should be dismissed with a simple blessing (once the confessor has made sure that conditional absolution is not the answer), though even here the priest should always seek to arouse contrition and love of God, since, as Frassinetti remarks, this is the moment when the needs of their souls may be met. The same applies to totally uninstructed adults.

Children must always be told to tell their parents or teachers if someone is attempting to lead them into serious sin. Whatever the social consequences, those who corrupt the young must be exposed; our Lord's remark about those who scandalize his little ones is clear enough.

Children who confess faults against purity for the first time must be treated with the greatest tenderness and delicacy. A discreet but straightforward instruction at this stage may prevent the formation of disastrous habits, and some tactful questioning may be useful if the priest has reason to think that the penitent is holding something back.

For all who have not reached puberty, but particularly for the older ones, the confessor should watch for serious matter; bad habits, especially solitary sins, are often contracted at this period: though they may not always be formal sins, they are serious matter, and can lead to a permanent habit of formal sin later. A child of this age can be put off by the slightest thing in the confessional, and may never mention the trouble again until puberty is reached, and perhaps not even then.

Among older schoolgirls the confessor should tactfully ask concerning the existence of sins, alone or with others.

Habitual Sinners

If the penitent is living in an occasion of sin, the confessor must exact a formal promise that he will avoid any voluntary, proximate occasion, and in the next confession the priest should ask if this promise has been kept. This applies to habitual sinners and to recidivists (*consuetudinarii* and *recidivi*); our people do not always realize this. Hemp or other drug smokers are one of many examples that could be cited. Experience has shown that it is necessary to require that superstitious objects be destroyed; if they are only thrown away, they may too easily be retrieved under strong temptation. Of habitual sinners especially, it must be repeated that the confessor judges only on present dispositions, and not on his estimate of what is likely to happen in the future.

Men and Boys

A monitum of the Holy Office of 15 July 1961 condemned the excessive stress on lack of culpability which is common in contemporary psychoanalysis; it was believed that it was principally solitary sin that the document had in mind. The literature on this subject written by doctors and psychoanalysts, not excluding Catholic doctors and psychoanalysts, is sometimes disturbing. Thus, one book carrying an episcopal imprimatur contains the statement that the author had not met a case in which he thought the subjective elements required for mortal sin were present; this can only be excused on the supposition that the writer was drawing on consulting-room experience, i.e. unusual and unbalanced cases.

These errors do not invalidate certain cases on which the sound school of contemporary psychoanalysis has thrown light. There is the person, for example, who constantly suffers the martyrdom of being unable to get to sleep because for an hour or so he is tortured by temptation; the case is hardly verifiable except for the devout. There is little doubt that the act by which this long struggle, after much prayer, is sometimes ended, will be either partly or wholly reflex, doubtful therefore or certainly non-sinful. There is here a lack, or at least a hampering, of the choice of the will. Less commonly these acts can occur after an almost momentary period of temptation; and there is the much more difficult and questionable case about which we have to be so guarded, of sin with others. More often than not, when even a well-instructed and devout person honestly believes that he did not act deliberately, we must decide that nothing is certain, and that the judgement can only be left to God.

Some contemporary theologians say that when the confessor judges that there has been no grave subjective guilt in the case of the long, protracted struggle before sleep, he should tell the penitent so; but they exclude external occasions and lapses (after no long struggle as we have described) due to a strong habit. Others would exclude all cases (except the too obvious one of acts when waking up from sleep). We have to guard against letting people persuade themselves they are not committing sins when they are. But there seems good reason that when we are sure there is no doubt we should say so; even, but only in a completely suitable subject, we might possibly be justified in saying this of *some* acts due to long habit. Only the confessor can judge of the last two cases; he may decide in particular cases that silence about complete certainty of lack of guilt is best. When genuinely doubtful it is unwise to advise a devout penitent to abstain from communion.

These considerations affect questioning in the confessional. If the penitent's confession contains other serious matter or shows proof of neglect of the ordinary means of avoiding sin, it should ordinarily be presumed that sins of this kind were serious. But if there are signs that the penitent is trying hard and has not other species of mortal sin, he should be asked: 'Do you think that what you did was deliberate or only partly deliberate or not deliberate at all?' Unless he replies 'fully deliberate', he should be instructed to say in future confessions that he acted only partly deliberately, or not deliberately at all, or that he is doubtful. Good can be done in this way by the confessor: the penitent might otherwise give way to despair, or because of one doubtful act commit fully deliberate acts afterwards before coming to confession because he wrongly believes he has already committed one mortal sin. It indeed is wrong to take every statement as 'I did a bad action!' as indicating serious sin, especially in an early adolescent who may never have been instructed on the conditions required to constitute mortal sin.[1]

The Seriously Ill and Dying

The suggestions that follow are taken from Aertyns' *Theologia Pastoralis Complectens Practicam Institutionem Confessarii.*

When summoned to a dying person, the priest should find out from others if the penitent would prefer another confessor; he should also try and find out from others something of the dying man's spiritual background, especially concerning restitution and the harbouring of hatred towards others. He might also ask if the dying man has made a will. As far as possible, the priest should do his questioning of the dying man outside confession, for he may have to withhold anointing and he would be unable to do this if he had obtained the information in the confession itself. The penitent must make restitution at once if possible, and ask pardon of all whom he has injured. He should be tactfully asked if he had ever made a bad confession.

A small penance only should be imposed on the seriously ill but, if convenient, a larger one may be added, to be performed if and when they recover. The priest should evidently do everything to keep away from a dying man anyone who might arouse evil passions, such as hatred, in him during his last hours. Worldly affairs should be settled as soon as possible, so that the sick man can put this world out of his mind and turn wholly to God.

SOME PRACTICAL POINTS

Before feast-days, when the church is full of penitents, it may save time to close the doors and help all the penitents to prepare in common for confession by an examination of conscience and, above all, by exciting true contrition.

If it is impossible to recite the whole of the formula for confession (*Misereatur, Indulgentiam,* and *Passio Domini*), it is sometimes recommended that the whole formula be said at least for the first

---

[1] J. J. FARAHER, S.J., 'Notes on Moral Theology', in *Theological Studies,* December 1960.

penitent. We have already spoken of the concluding prayer, *Passio Domini*, in connection with the sacramental penance.

There should always be a screen between priest and penitent. When travelling, the priest may make use of a table or chair. He can hardly be expected to carry a screen about with him everywhere.

Confessions should not be heard outside a church except in cases of necessity. Confessions of nuns by a priest with only common jurisdiction, and apart from cases of necessity, are invalid if heard outside a church or semi-public oratory, or a place approved by the Ordinary.

The deaf should be heard in the sacristy, or in some other place apart from others, to avoid their being overheard.

It is recommended to leave the door ajar when hearing the confession of a sick woman. In general it is better to hear confessions in view of other people, and not, for example, inside a hut. Women should not be heard in the dark, not even in church, unless others are present.

When hearing confessions before Mass, the priest should break off to allow the Mass to begin on time. It is better to hear as many of the confessions on the previous day as possible.

General confessions may be recommended (though not for the scrupulous) on certain big occasions in life: before marriage or religious profession, or before entering upon a worldly career.

Arrangements should be made from time to time for an outside confessor to come to a parish. This is appreciated by the people, and it should not be difficult for parishes to exchange priests for confessions before big feasts.

All priests who have received faculties from their Ordinary, or from the ordinary of the port of embarkation, have special faculties for voyages by sea.[1] The Ordinary of any port of call may also give the necessary approval. Voyages on the Great Lakes of East and Central Africa are included in this category, but river trips are not. The jurisdiction extends from the moment the journey actually begins to the time of arrival in port. The priest should not hesitate on such occasions to hear the confessions even of those whose language is completely unknown to him, for he may always act, if they ask for confession, as though they were in grave need. If possible, some way

---

[1] *Acta Apostolicae Sedis*, January 1948, p. 17, extends these faculties to journeys by aeroplane.

should be found of conveying to them their obligation of repeating any grave matter in the next confession they make to a priest who understands their language.

There should be no hesitation either about using the 'common error' of Can. 209; this applies whenever the faithful reasonably, but in fact wrongly, assume that the priest has jurisdiction to hear their confessions, and the priest can assume that they are in grave need.

14   Christian Marriage[1]

IN SEEKING to bring Christ to Africa, the Church is interested in every department of African society, public and private; but above all she is interested in the family, the basic cell of all society, and in marriage, on which the family is founded. For only out of truly Christian families can a Christian society be constructed. Whatever else the Church may achieve in Africa, she cannot be said to be truly planted until the Christian ideal of family life and the Christian notion of marriage has taken root among the people. All priests in Africa, therefore, but especially priests who are themselves Africans, must make it one of their first pastoral preoccupations to transform traditional African attitudes to marriage, in so far as the service of Christ requires such a transformation. This must be especially the task of African priests for, once again, the Church has no desire, and no mandate, to import Western forms of society into Africa for their own sake, and the Catholic priest from Europe or America may sometimes find it difficult to distinguish, in the family life which he has known, those elements which are Christian in inspiration and those which stem from the secular tradition and cultural development of Europe. The question facing the Church is not, 'How can African family life be changed into European Christian family life?' but 'How can Christ be brought into the African family?'

We do not presume in this chapter to give an adequate answer to this question, which demands a very deep understanding of African family traditions;[2] we simply make some remarks which may help those better equipped, in the course of time, to re-fashion African family life according to the mind of Christ. We offer some simple suggestions concerning the preliminaries to marriage, and add some remarks on the marriage ceremony, bride-price, polygamy and contraception.

[1] In addition to the usual manuals, we recommend to the reader interested in the moral and canonical aspects of marriage two books by BISHOP DE REEPER: *The Sacraments on the Missions* and *A Missionary Companion*.

[2] J. ROBINSON, *The Family Apostolate and Africa* has good material here.

147

The Preliminaries to Marriage

African Christians need in the first place careful instruction about marriage. At present such instruction to those intending marriage is often very difficult, since everything is concluded so quickly; not infrequently, a young man chooses a girl almost at random, her father gives permission, the couple meet, become engaged and are married, all in the space of a week or two. Courtship is not part of the African tradition, but commonsense demands that the young couple should know each other well before plunging into marriage. However, it is commonly agreed that, with the exception of the educated classes, the time for this has not yet come. Some dioceses have sought to inculcate the necessity of due preparation by performing marriages only at certain fixed periods—perhaps the week after Christmas, the week after Easter, a week in August and one in November. In one diocese at least, marriages were at one time performed only once a year. Young men should be instructed that choosing a wife is a serious affair which needs time, and parents might be told to withhold consent until they can be reasonably sure that the couple are properly prepared for marriage. Fathers are often to blame for suddenly announcing permission and letting their son choose, wed and bed his bride in the twinkling of an eye. This should be pointed out in the pulpit and privately. But the father's rights against the pressure of the clan are to be vindicated.

In present circumstances, it may often be possible merely to give an instruction on the day before the wedding, and this is clearly the absolute minimum. The ideal arrangement would be one instruction a week for three months; an immediate aim might be to require three weeks' notice before performing a wedding, and to give one instruction in each of those weeks.

Instructions should be based on holy Scripture and on African thought, making as much use as possible of common local proverbs; but sometimes it may be necessary to refer to the old sayings for the purpose of pointing out their incompatibility with Christianity. Pulpit preaching on marriage should be positive, with stress on the nature of marriage as love, contract and sacrament; the duties of husband and wife really to love each other and their children should be often spoken of, in order to extinguish the too common idea that marriage is no more than a physical union to satisfy the man's desires and to have plenty of children. A negative or casuistical approach to marriage questions must be avoided. Godparents should be encouraged to take an active interest in the marriage of their godchildren, and parental instruction must not be omitted. The teaching of domestic science and domestic economy fosters happy marriages, and special boarding schools with courses for prospective brides have done well in Congo-Leo. Marriage retreats and Pre-Cana days (as well as Cana Days after marriage) have been found useful too.

Prenuptial Inquiries

The priest has a serious obligation to investigate the canonical situation of the bride and groom, even if there is no special reason to suspect that there is an impediment to their marriage. It is usually best to question each of the parties separately, and alone; the parents of neither party should be allowed to attend. It may also be useful to have the couple's statements confirmed afterwards by two reputable witnesses. The oath required by Can. 1031 (§1, 1°) is usually omitted in African dioceses.

On the occasion of these interrogations, the priest should explain the different canonical impediments to marriage, and ask the couple if any are involved in the marriage they are proposing to contract. It is always good to suggest that each of the parties tell the priest in confession that they are getting married; this not only helps the confessor to notice impediments and use the powers which he has for the internal forum, but it also provides him with the opportunity of giving a brief marriage instruction.

Parents in Africa sometimes exert undue pressure on their children in the choice of a marriage partner, and the priest would do well to take particular care in investigating free consent, and to make it clear, for example, that a widow cannot be forced to marry her brother-in-law. The free consent of the parents must be sought where possible (free in the sense that the parents should not yield to unreasonable pressure from the clan), but the Church has always insisted that young men and women must be free to marry even without the consent of their parents; in the case of minors who wish to marry without parental consent, however, the priest must consult the Ordinary before agreeing to bless their marriage.[1]

If Catholic sinners are unwilling to go to confession before marriage, the parish priest has no right to insist.

Dispensations granted by the Ordinary must always be noted both in the marriage register and in the baptismal register of each of the parties. The inscription of marriage in the baptismal register is particularly important, as a safeguard against attempted bigamy; deaths also are noted in the baptismal register in some dioceses.

When a dispensation, for example from the impediment of mixed religion, requires guarantees (*cautiones*), divine law itself demands that there be moral certainty that these will be honoured.[2] Whatever canonical reasons may be found for the granting of a dispensation, it cannot be given if there is real danger to the faith of the Catholic party or to that of any child to be born of the marriage. The situation must be such that men in general would reasonably think that there is no probable danger to faith; there must be that broad moral certitude which, as St. Thomas says, embraces the truth in most cases but in a very few fails to do so. Experience has shown that the faith of the Catholic partner is in greater danger in marriage with a separated Christian than in marriage with a non-Christian, and this should be taken into account in assessing the degree of certainty.

In seeking dispensations, the priest should bear in mind that the common good comes before the private good. It is not enough to ask whether the granting of a dispensation is for the good of the parties concerned; the priest must also consider what effect the granting of the dispensation is likely to have on his parish as a whole. It may be that the common good in a certain area will demand the refusal of a dispensation from *mixta religio*, even though the grounds are in themselves sufficient and the dispensation would have been granted elsewhere. On the other hand, a dispensation from, for example, consanguinity, may be given for reasons which would usually be considered insufficient, if this will remove grave scandal or heal quarrels or put an end to a public concubinage.

---

[1] Can. 1034.

[2] Pending guidance from authority, we reserve any comment on recent claims that this moral certainty is not required by divine law.

The Ordinary is the judge of what is good for his diocese in the matter of dispensations, and it is not true to say that because the Code or a Roman Congregation permits them, therefore he must also. He is perfectly entitled to have his own rules for the refusal of a dispensation even when a clear canonical reason is to hand.

With regard to mixed marriages, we may recall the words of the Code: *Severissime Ecclesia ubique prohibet* (Can. 1060). Greater leniency may be required in certain places or at certain times, but there is no gainsaying the fact that mixed marriages are often unhappy for the husband and wife and that they are responsible for loss of faith among great numbers of Catholics. Even if the children of a mixed marriage persevere in the faith, too often *their* children lapse eventually. We are writing before the completion of the final session of the Council, which may have something to say on this painful subject. Some rethinking is perhaps necessary, and no one wishes to give offence to our separated brethren; but it remains hard to see how the Church can ever allow her children seriously to endanger their faith by giving wholesale permission for mixed marriages.

The Marriage Ceremony

To underline the sacred character of marriage, it is good to give as much external solemnity as possible to the marriage ceremony itself. The ceremony should be so prepared that the dignity, piety and meaning of the rite may shine out and all who take part, but especially the bride and groom, should take an active part. The church might be decorated, may we suggest, and the bride and groom should enter and leave the church together; during the Nuptial Mass let them kneel together in the sanctuary, coming up to the altar steps for the two blessings. Hymns should be sung and bells and drums used, and local cries of joy encouraged in the church itself; the *Constitution on the Liturgy* encourages the local hierarchies to retain or devise suitable marriage ceremonies, and there is plenty of scope for initiative in this matter in Africa, where marriage is so often surrounded with a wealth of traditional ceremonies. It is in accordance with the African spirit of welcome to allow the bridegroom to act as host, waiting for the bride at the church door and conducting her to her place in the sanctuary. The ring is not an African custom, but some Africans like it, and there are advantages in always wearing this external sign that one is married. The groom as well as the bride could be given a ring during the ceremony. The symbolic handing over of gold and silver comes from the old Sarum rite and is still observed in England; some African priests find this attractive, and it might be introduced. The gold and silver would usually be represented by two or three silver coins.

The *Constitution on the Liturgy* directs that marriage be normally celebrated within Mass, after the Gospel and the homily. When giving the homily, the priest should bear in mind that he probably has a rare opportunity of addressing non-Christians and careless Catholics; any non-Christian parents should always be invited to attend the marriage, and for a grave reason a non-Catholic witness may be admitted in a mixed marriage. The Conciliar Constitution allows the prayer for the bride (to be amended 'to remind both spouses of their equal obligations to remain faithful to each other') to be said in the vernacular, and advantage will no doubt be taken of this in Africa. If a wedding is celebrated without Nuptial Mass, the Epistle and Gospel from that Mass are to be read as an introduction to the marriage ceremony, and the couple should always be given a blessing.

Marriages rightly take place in the bride's parish church, but the priest should not make difficulties if the couple wish to be married elsewhere, in the groom's parish, for example, or in some other church.[1]

Everything possible should be done to emphasize the sanctity of marriage. The homily and the revised form of the nuptial blessing will help here, and in addition any suitable local marriage custom should be brought into the Church and made holy. A blessing of the marriage bed might be considered a useful innovation in some places.

Bride Price

An almost universal custom in Africa obliges a suitor to hand over a considerable amount of property to the family of his prospective bride; this property, known as the bride price, has its roots in the economic system of traditional Africa. When the clan lost a woman by marriage, it lost not only a worker but also a source of future workers, and it

---

[1] VERMEERSCH, *op. cit.*, 3rd edn., vol. III, p. 676.

demanded compensation. This was certainly one important reason for the system, which it is false to regard as a crude and brutal trade in women. The bride price helped to maintain the stability of marriage as an institution, since the wife could only obtain a divorce by returning the bride price to her husband; it also gave a measure of security to children, for the bride price was distributed among a large number of the wife's relations, all of whom therefore took an interest in, and felt responsibility for, the children.

With the introduction of a money economy into Africa and the growing independence of the individual, the reason for the bride price has been largely eliminated, and there is reason to believe that the system will die out. In the meantime, however, abuses have crept in, sometimes enormous abuses; unscrupulous parents in some places really do seem to be selling their daughters to the highest bidders; this can result in an inflation of the bride price to a point where only the rich can afford to marry, and the majority of young men are unable to find a wife and so resort to concubinage. Archbishop Zoa, in a strongly worded article in the *African Ecclesiastical Review* for July 1962, said that in the Cameroons a bride price of $1000 was not rare.

Clearly the Church must do everything in her power to put an end to such abuses, which degrade the status of women and lead to widespread immorality. It is not perhaps yet possible, nor even desirable, to suppress the bride price system completely; it is so ingrained in the minds of many people that a marriage is not considered permanent without it; but priests should insist in their preaching on the essential dignity of women and on the freedom of young people of both sexes to marry the partner of their choice. It is also desirable to obtain a maximum legal bride price of reasonable proportions, say a month or two's wages for an ordinary labourer, or the equivalent in cattle. It is often wise to refuse to marry a couple until the whole of the bride price has been handed over and all obligations to the wife's parents met; one might even demand a written certificate to this effect from the wife's father.

There can be no doubt that under present conditions the system of the bride price does constitute a real threat to public morality. Time however is surely working towards its abolition, and one may believe that the new governments of Africa are anxious to see it disappear.

It would be good to fix an age of legal maturity for girls, not lower than eighteen, on attaining which they could marry without the consent of their parents. The Church must aim at assisting this trend, while refraining from any wholesale condemnations; the bride price is certainly a danger, and it has largely lost its *raison d'être*; but it cannot be said to be intrinsically immoral, any more than the dowry among the middle classes in Europe, which is only just dying out. As a schoolman would say, it is in itself (*per se*) not evil, but in particular circumstances (*per accidens*) it can be evil. The Cameroons bride price was in the latter class and was therefore forbidden under pain of grave sin.

The Conquest of Polygamy

Traditional African society was nearly everywhere polygamous, usually in the sense that one man could have several legal wives. Very rich or powerful men could acquire hundreds of wives, while ordinary men might have two or three. The numerical balance between the sexes of course made it impossible for every man to have more than one wife, and in fact most households were monogamous; but legally there was nothing to prevent any man from having several wives, and circumstances often led him to take a second wife: the sterility of the first wife, for example, or her lack of skill as a housekeeper, and taboos against intercourse, especially during the lactation period, which lasted for two to three years or even longer. The system could be socially beneficial, for it meant that no woman was left to fend for herself; single women were unknown, and widows were catered for by being at once taken into the household of a brother-in-law; but there can be little doubt that polygamy as practised in Africa was based above all on the idea of the inferior status of women. The marriage contract was unequal, for while it obliged the woman to remain with one husband, it left the husband free to take other wives.

Like the bride price, polygamy is disappearing in Africa, and several states have already declared it illegal. Under the old economic system, a man might really need several wives to do the work of his household, and an important man, who did much entertaining, needed many wives to prepare food; it is thus at least an over-simplification to say that polygamy was invented to satisfy the lust of men. A money economy makes the individual independent of the group and enables him to pay employees, or use machines, to do the work traditionally performed by women in Africa; further, the idea of the equality of the sexes has been accepted by educated Africans in general, so that on all counts polygamy may be considered doomed.

The Church of course must teach the revealed doctrine that God's plan for the human race is one man, one wife; she is utterly opposed to polygamy and is anxious to secure its abolition. Priests should support especially the efforts now being made to have African children weaned after about nine months. The priest should also do everything possible to promote the abolition of the taboos on intercourse at traditional times.

At the same time, Africans living in polygamy, like those living in concubinage, are often in situations from which it is difficult for them to extricate themselves, even if they wish to adopt the Christian code. The Church cannot abandon them. Such people may not be baptized, but they can be welcomed as 'Friends of Christianity', and treated, if they wish it, as intimate associates of a Church in which they cannot for the moment be accepted as children.[1] It would be necessary to make quite clear that they were not full members of the Church; should this step result in indifference to further progress, it would have to be dropped.

Married Life

It is important to teach people that marriage is not designed simply to satisfy the man's physical desires, and that the marriage act must be inspired by mutual and unselfish love, an act holy in itself as the expression of the highest love between two human beings, and made more holy by the institution of matrimony as a sacrament. People should be taught that intercourse should be the result of mutual consent; women in Africa frequently complain of exaggerated requests by husbands. Real married love is a communion of persons, characterized by deep affection, and expressed in physical union. Husband and wife must understand each other's physical and emotional needs, and find in each other the strength that comes from mutual confidence.

[1] Suggested by the meeting in Rome, May, 1962, of *Présence Africaine*.

Wives must indeed be told that they have a grave obligation to accede to their husbands' reasonable requests for intercourse; but husbands too must be taught that consideration is a duty, and that a wife needs above all to feel that she is loved and prized for herself, and not treated simply as an instrument of physical pleasure.

Such instruction cannot be given in the confessional, and indeed can hardly be given by priests at all, for Africans would be shocked to hear a priest speaking of the intimacies of married life. A suitable layman is in the best position to give advice, and especially a Catholic doctor, who might take the opportunity of giving some instruction on the occasion of a pre-marriage medical examination; he might even be invited to give an address to Christians who are taking part in a marriage retreat. A suitable catechist could also give advice, and a trained woman would be useful for wives. In a special case, as when a priest is lecturing in a Teachers' Training College, he might give instruction on married life if he judges that he can do so without giving scandal. Marriage Guidance Councils, made up of a priest, a psychiatrist and a doctor, are most useful institutions; a humble start might be made in towns by the combined work of a priest and a doctor.

The traditional, semi-public announcement of the successful consummation of a marriage after the first night is to be discouraged as indelicate, and as frequently involving customs which are sinful. Experiments before marriage to see if the couple are both capable of the act are not uncommon in Africa; they are of course utterly at variance with the Christian code of morality and must be forbidden. Let those intending to marry go instead to a doctor for examination.

Contraception

Contraception is still practically unknown in the African countryside, but it is already practised in towns, particularly by the educated, and may be expected to spread. Most priests in Africa have not yet been obliged to deal with this question, but as they will no doubt meet it in the future it may be useful to indicate the Church's position in a general way.

Conception may be frustrated either by *coitus interruptus* or by the use of a mechanical device during the performance of the marriage act.

Spermicides are also used. The teaching of Pius XI and Pius XII is that both the *coitus interruptus* and the use of mechanical or chemical contraceptives are sinful because opposed to natural law. Another way of preventing conception is to restrict intercourse to those days in the month when the woman is unfertile. This is called the rhythm or the safe period, and all theologians agree that good reasons, such as grave difficulty in providing for the needs of future children, or even lack of accommodation in a town, or to foster mutual love, justify a Catholic couple in restricting intercourse to the safe periods.

In recent years scientists have produced pills, not yet perfected, which can postpone or otherwise regulate ovulation and so make conception predictable. The use of such pills would enable a Catholic couple to know exactly when conception would result from intercourse, and so allow them to plan their family with certainty. There is still much discussion on the morality of using these pills—there are different kinds —and obviously we can make no pronouncement on the subject here. It is expected that the Holy Father will make a statement on the subject fairly soon. A pill which is purely and simply a sterilizing agent would appear to come under the heading of direct contraceptives and to be immoral. Whatever His Holiness may ultimately decide, it seems clear that there can never be any question of the Church's allowing wholesale contraception. Until the law has been clarified, the priest must teach his people that any method of birth control except the safe period is forbidden; at the same time, he must show great sympathy and understanding towards Catholic couples who are in difficulties in this matter. The critics are right in this: in presenting the Church's teaching we need a more positive approach to the theology of love.

Although the use of contraceptives in the strict sense is sinful, it should be remembered that the wife may be allowed to co-operate passively in contraceptive intercourse if she would otherwise expose herself to serious physical harm.[1] In the *coitus interruptus* in particular, which begins as a completely natural act, the wife may co-operate normally, and need not show her disapproval on each occasion if doing

[1] In the condomistic approach, can the wife ever act passively because of an exceptionally grave, non-physical threat? A reviewer of competence, Mgr. L. R. McReavy, has found one author, Fuchs, who would admit as an excusing cause, real danger of divorce, combined with either the removal of the children or the loss of subsistence for the woman. See 'Cooperatio in Copula Condomistica', in *The Clergy Review* February, 1963.

so would involve her in danger of serious harm. This is one of the occasions where the husband may be left in good faith, for sufficient reasons, e.g., if there is reason to fear that he would seek association with other women if his wife refused her co-operation, or if serious quarrels would ensue.

15   The Anointing of the Sick

By THE sacrament of the sick, our Lord continues the ministry which occupied so much of his time and attention while he was walking the earth. In the early days of Christianity, this sacrament was considered simply as the Church's bodily medicine, the *oleum sanitatis*, or simply the *medicina Ecclesiae*. The idea of its being a preparation for death, along with the name extreme unction, only came in in the twelfth century, and the succeeding centuries saw a new stress on the spiritual effects of the sacrament, as opposed to its bodily healing.

Rethinking Its Theology

The *Constitution on the Liturgy* has furthered the former notion of this sacrament as a medicine rather than as a proximate preparation for death. '*Extreme unction,* which may also and more fittingly be called *the anointing of the sick,* is not a sacrament reserved for those who are at the point of death. Hence, as soon as any one of the faithful begins to be in danger of death from sickness or old age, the most fitting time for him to receive this sacrament has, beyond all doubt, arrived.'[1] (Note that probable danger of death is required for validity; no other view can be followed in practice.) The original schema submitted to the Council contained the words 'grave illness', but the majority of the Fathers preferred the expression 'danger of death', and this was therefore substituted. Nevertheless, there has clearly been a development of the Church's understanding of this sacrament, which is now seen to be connected with illness rather than with death; as the years go by, and

[1] Art. 73. The Council's decision, disciplinary, not doctrinal, does not preclude further discussion on the nature of the sacrament. We cannot ignore pre-Tridentine pastoral practice; the text of the Ritual says nothing about a strengthening against death, and Trent's clause on danger of death is considered by some as disciplinary only and aimed at current superstitious uses. Trent, while stressing its important role for the dying, may be said to have left its wider efficacy intact.

the theology of the anointing evolves, it will perhaps be in this same direction, and the idea that this is one of the last sacraments may disappear altogether.[1]

The Time of Administration

The sacrament of the sick is not a miraculous interference with the laws of nature; it co-operates with and strengthens natural forces, and it can only achieve its object of bodily cure, normally speaking at least, if given in reasonably good time. It should not as a rule be associated with imminent death, and should be given at the beginning rather than at the end of a grave illness. The last rites of the Church are holy viaticum and the last blessing; ideally the anointing will take place separately and earlier. At the same time, there will naturally be cases of sudden dangerous illness where everything has to be done at once, and here again the *Constitution on the Liturgy* has restored a more logical order of things by directing that confession should come first and be followed by the anointing. The holy viaticum comes at the very end. This replaces the previous custom of leaving the anointing to the end, and restores the real sense of viaticum as a preparation for a journey; the faithful soul about to embark on the last, momentous journey from time to eternity is comforted and strengthened by the Body of Christ himself.

The Church has now made it clear that the anointing should not be delayed out of fear that the sick person will fall into fresh sins in the period between the reception of the sacrament and the moment of death; if a Christian should have the misfortune to sin after having been anointed, sacramental absolution is the remedy.

The cures effected by our Lord during the public ministry were nearly always associated with the faith of the sick person, or of the one who petitioned on his behalf; Christians should therefore be told to receive the sacrament of the sick with great faith in the power of Christ,

---

[1] Cf. 'Le Sacrement des malades' in *La Vie Spirituelle*, October, 1944, p. 334; 'l'extrême onction est-elle le sacrement de la dernière maladie', in ibid., March 1955, p. 242; and L'Onction des malades', in *La liturgie des malades, La Maison-Dieu*, 15, p. 91, 1948; 'L'effetto corporale dell'estrema onzione', in *Gregorianum*, 98, p. 385, 1957. See also C. DAVIS, *The Study of Theology*, London and New York, 1962, chapters XIX and XX; and, *Studies in Pastoral Liturgy* (articles collected from *The Furrow*) Dublin, 1963.

for only thus will its most fruitful effects be realized, if such be the loving will of God. The friends and relatives of the sick person should be encouraged to pray and to make acts of faith in the healing power of Christ, which operates now in this sacrament. The Ritual suggests that the litany of the saints or the seven penitential psalms be recited by the bystanders while a sick person is being anointed; simpler prayers, such as the rosary, may of course be said instead if they are considered more suitable, and this will often be the case in Africa.

The Subject of the Sacrament

All sick Christians should be anointed, including the newly baptized, provided that they have reached the age of reason and are in danger of death. The principles, understandably, are the same as those for giving or denying penance. The danger of death should be real, but no doubt this is to be interpreted broadly. It is impossible to assess areas of danger, and the priest should always anoint, at least conditionally, if he is in any doubt.

There is no necessity to have made one's first communion before being anointed. However, at least at the present stage of theological thought, it is necessary to have reached the age of reason (and therefore be capable of committing at least venial sin) and evidently where at all possible the sick person should be instructed in the meaning of the sacrament he is about to receive. The age of reason is thought to be necessary because of the association of this sacrament in recent centuries with the remission of sins; it could be, however, that with the restored emphasis on the medicinal object of the sacrament, it will in time be accepted that even infants can be validly anointed. Needless to say, it would be completely wrong for any priest to do this at the present moment.

Only living people can receive the sacraments. The moment of death however is very often uncertain, and priests may take the view that in most cases the only certain sign of death is putrefaction; the anointing may therefore, strictly speaking, be given up to the time of the appearance of that condition. It is rightly and commonly taught that in practice the anointing must be given up to half-an-hour after apparent death, and up to two or three hours afterwards in the case of sudden death, except of course in the case of some terrible accident which so destroys the body that real and apparent death coincide. It may be useful to explain to bystanders, when anointing after apparent death, that it is possible that the soul has not yet been separated from the body.

With regard to separated Christians, it is important to realize that they are probably capable of validly receiving the sacrament of the sick, which should therefore be given to them. Formal heretics or schismatics, being in a state of formal sin, may not receive the sacrament, but almost all separated Christians are good people, following the truth as they see it, and since they belong in some way to the Mystical Body by virtue of their baptism, they should not be deprived of the sacramental anointing which Christ instituted for the benefit of his sick brethren. In practice, many theologians teach nowadays that almost any unconscious, dying person may be anointed, at least conditionally (*si capax est*, not *si dispositus est*), and the French hierarchy commended this view to their priests in their 1951 *Directoire des Sacrements*. The anointing must of course be preceded by baptism, absolute or conditional, if there is any reason to believe that the person concerned has not been validly baptized.

Priests to whom the care of souls is entrusted are obliged in justice to anoint those of their people who are sick and in some danger of death. The anointing is one of the divinely-appointed channels of grace; it is Christ's gift to his sick brethren, and it must be made available to them. There may even be very rare cases where a priest would be obliged to endanger his life in order to anoint a Christian whose eternal salvation would otherwise be in jeopardy. We discuss the ministry to the sick and dying more fully in a later chapter.[1]

The Administration of the Sacrament

The anointing of the sick is a holy thing, and it must clearly be surrounded with all possible dignity and cleanliness; the priest's reverence and care for the externals of the sacrament will help the people to an understanding of its sacred character. People should be taught how to prepare the material things necessary for the anointing; where possible, there should be a table, covered with a white cloth,

[1] See below, Chapter 19.

with a crucifix, a clean dish to receive the cotton-wool, and bread[1] for purifying the priest's fingers; there should also be at least one candle burning on the table. *Oleum infirmorum* which has been blessed for more than a year may only be used for anointing in cases of necessity. If the priest has brought the wrong oil by mistake (oil of catechumens or chrism), he should perform the anointing conditionally with these, if the matter is urgent, and then return later with the correct oil and re-anoint conditionally (*si nondum est inunctus*).

One may increase one's supply of holy oil by adding a smaller quantity of unblessed oil. This should only be done in cases of necessity; one should not add fresh oil immediately the newly-blessed oil arrives on Holy Thursday.

Conditional absolution should be given before anointing an unconscious person, unless he appears to be at the point of death, in which case anoint first.

The *Constitution on the Liturgy* directs that 'the number of the anointings is to be adapted to the occasion',[2] and the practical application of this directive will be embodied in due course in local rituals. For the present, the anointings should be performed according to the Roman Ritual, omitting the anointing of the feet for any good reason. The short formula, with a single anointing, is clearly sufficient for the valid reception of the sacrament, but, as things are at present, the priest who uses this form in urgent cases is obliged to supply the individual anointings later, if possible; this obligation lapses after about an hour.

After anointing a parishioner, the fact should be noted in the parish register; when anointing outside one's own parish, one should inform the parish priest of the person concerned, so as to avoid exposing the sacrament to invalidity by repetition. Normally the sacrament may not be repeated during the same illness, but it is an approved practice to anoint every month or so a sick person who seems neither better nor worse, whatever his age.[3]

---

[1] If unobtainable, use meal, a food paste or cotton wool.

[2] Art. 75.   [3] H. DAVIS S.J., *Moral and Pastoral Theology*, 3rd ed., Vol. IV, p. 8.

16   Christian Burial

EVEN in pagan religions, dead bodies are treated with respect and surrounded with religious rites. It was thus with the Greeks long ago, and it is so with the animists of Africa today. The almost universal instinct of mankind prompts men to see a connection between religion and the mystery of death, and to view with religious awe the remains of a man who has passed from time into eternity.

The dead body of a Christian is a holy thing. The Church pays great respect to it, for it once housed the Blessed Trinity, and it is destined to share the glory of the Risen Christ. It is to be carried into the church, there to lie before the crucifix and the tabernacle; the minister of Christ is to offer the holy sacrifice in its presence, cleanse it with the blessed water and honour it with incense. By the graveside, the Church speaks of the future glory of these poor earthly remains, when the Son of Man shall send his angels with a trumpet and a great voice, and they that are in the grave shall live. Even before the body is brought into the church, the Ritual directs that it be laid out in a seemly manner, with a crucifix in the hands and a light about it, while those who are present should pray for the repose of the dead person's soul. And it asks that the body be not kept too long in the place of death, lest people lose respect for it.

What is Possible in Africa?

The *Constitution on the Liturgy* directs that 'the rite for the burial of the dead should express more clearly the paschal character of Christian death, and should correspond more closely to the circumstances and traditions found among the peoples in different parts of the world'.[1] The death of a Christian should be seen as his triumphant entry into eternal joy, his sharing in the joy of the Resurrection of the Lord; exaggerated grief, as in Africa, and an excessive dwelling on the terrors

[1] Art. 81.

of the Judgement, such as has crept into parts of the Latin liturgy, are really incompatible with the Christian spirit, and the new rites to be drawn up should reflect that joyful attitude to death which is natural to the Christian. Christ has conquered death and hell; they hold no terror for the faithful soul.

Ecclesiastical burial means carrying the corpse to the church, performing there the prescribed funeral rites, and interring the body in a place set apart for the burial of the faithful. In Africa it is seldom possible to carry out this full rite. The shortage of priests means that usually a catechist conducts the funeral service alone, while the climate often makes it necessary to bury the body so soon after death that a Requiem Mass with the corpse present is not possible. Nevertheless, everything possible should be done to encourage the natural reverence for the dead which many Africans feel very strongly, though there must be no element of fear. Cemeteries should be solemnly blessed and kept in good order. It is desirable to have a cemetery attached to each station, perhaps surrounded by a living hedge, and kept in order and free of weeds by the local Christians. It would usually be in sight of the church, so that those going to and from the church would be reminded to pray for the dead.

There is danger of premature burial in the tropics. It is sometimes suggested that it should be made a rule never to bury a body until twenty-four hours have elapsed since death, except where decomposition has already set in, or where for other reasons there can be no doubt that death has really taken place.

Baptized infants may be buried in a special corner of the cemetery, and their funeral could be marked by sounding joyful bells or drums; a pleasant custom of crowning the little body with flowers or herbs is mentioned by the Roman Ritual. The present rite for the burial of infants is unsatisfactory from many points of view; the *Constitution on the Liturgy* recognizes this, and states that it is to be revised.

Panegyrics for important persons may sometimes be unavoidable, but they should be temperately phrased, and care taken not to arouse jealousy among those whose relatives received no such public tribute. A few words of sympathy, with a reminder of the duty of praying for the dead, and perhaps a reference to the inevitability of death for us all, would always be in place. The faithful should be encouraged to visit the graves of their friends and relatives, especially on their anniversaries, and to pray there for the repose of their souls.

The priest who performs the burial should enter in a register the name and age of the deceased person, with the date of death and burial; it would be useful in many places to add the names of the dead person's parents, and of the wife or husband in the case of a married person. The sacraments received before death may also be noted.

A word on wake-keeping. The National Liturgical Commission of Ghana has some useful remarks here. The non-Christian ritual, if not fetish, should be allowed, and the priest, when possible, should be present at the beginning. There might be Bible readings, prayers at the washing of the body, the lying in state, the placing of the body in the coffin. Catechists should not forbid non-Catholics who wish to take part and Catholics should be allowed to attend the wake, for example, of a Methodist.[1]

Refusal of Ecclesiastical Burial

A refusal to bury someone can lead to bitterness between the priest and the dead person's relations. Nevertheless, there are times when such a refusal is a duty.

Christians have a right to ecclesiastical burial, and this right may be denied only to those whom the Church has declared to be unworthy. Those who are not baptized are not of course members of the Church and are not buried by her; catechumens, however, and those who have lived as Catholics, but have remained unbaptized through no fault of their own, are friends of the Church and may receive her funeral rites. Canon Law excludes from ecclesiastical burial the following persons, unless they have shown some sign of repentance before death: notorious apostates, heretics and schismatics; members of masonic or similar societies; those who have been excommunicated or placed under an interdict by name; deliberate suicides; duellists who die from a wound received in a duel; and those who gave orders for their bodies to be cremated and persisted in this intention.[2] As regards this last category

[1] Report of meeting held at Opoku-ware College, 29 July 1964. The report cites as full of excellent suggestions *La Mort Chrétienne*, published by the Centre of Pastoral Liturgy, Paris, 1960.
[2] Can. 1240.

of persons, there are signs that the Church's attitude is changing, since cremation no longer suggests the denial of the resurrection of the body with which it was once associated. The list concludes with sinners who died apparently unrepentant after a notoriously sinful life, or in the act of serious sin, or who obstinately and before witnesses refused the sacraments in their last illness.

All doubts should be resolved in favour of the dead person, provided there is no danger of scandal. A person guilty of a secret crime, or one who had incurred a hidden censure, might be buried in consecrated ground; but such burial would have to be denied, for example, to a murderer known to have been killed in the act of attacking his victim. No one should be refused burial simply because he did not make his Easter duty. In case of doubt, the Ordinary should be consulted. It may help a parish priest who has to live with possibly embittered relations if he can say that he is simply obeying the bishop's instructions.

A classic predicament concerns the burial of an unbaptized infant of devout parents. In Africa the question of interment in a family grave will seldom arise, so that one source of much disappointment in Europe is absent. The funeral rites cannot be performed, but there is nothing to prevent the priest from going to the house of the bereaved parents and saying prayers of his own choosing over the child. The body should be buried in unconsecrated ground, but again the priest could go to the cemetery and recite the rosary or similar prayers. He should not however give the impression that he is officiating at an ecclesiastical burial in the strict sense; one suggested way to do this is that he should not wear cotta or stole. The Ordinary may approve or forbid this as he sees fit.[1]

In the case of the apparently unrepentant sinner, there must often be doubt, and church burial will therefore be permitted. If there is danger of scandal, this may be removed by a word from the pulpit, or in private conversation. Any sign of repentance will justify priest or catechist in burying a notorious sinner; often it will be enough if it is known that the priest came when the man was dying. In those rare cases where there has been absolutely no sign of repentance, and where the deceased's apparently sinful state was a matter of notoriety, the priest must do his duty and refuse burial; but he must at the same time go to all lengths to show charity and sympathy to the relatives.

[1] 'Christian Burial', in *Clergy Review*, January, 1956, p. 36.

17   The Sacred Liturgy

HAVING discussed the priest's sacramental work in relation to each of the sacraments, we come now to the sacred liturgy, wherein above all the Church fulfils her supreme task of worshipping God. In this work of worship, the priest of course has a vital role to play, and we offer in this chapter some general remarks about liturgy and paraliturgy, in the hope that the principles we outline will inspire the whole of the sacred activity of the priest in Africa.

The spearhead of the contemporary renewal which is changing the face of the Church is the liturgical revival. Sixty years ago, St. Pius X foresaw that the liturgical revival would gradually become the hope and the rallying cry of the spiritual forces of mankind, and there are signs that the doctrinal renewal and the transformation of popular piety which we are now witnessing in the Church are bringing this prophecy to fulfilment. The liturgical revival has a vital part to play in informing the world with the spirit of Christ, and it is in every way appropriate that the first document to be produced by the Second Vatican Council should be that of the Church at prayer, the *Constitution on the Liturgy*. In his *Motu Proprio* of 25 January, 1964, *Sacram Liturgiam*, Pope Paul VI declared that it was his dearest wish that the faithful, and especially priests, should study the *Constitution* and make every effort to carry out its provisions in due course. It is indeed clear that the liturgical education of the faithful, so urgently needed if the revitalization of the Church's worship is to produce all its fruit, requires new knowledge, and this is to be found above all in the introduction and first chapter of the *Constitution* (articles 1–46), where the nature of the liturgy is carefully explained and the general principles behind the liturgical revival are set forth with compelling clarity. Now that the Council has made its mind clear in so vigorous a fashion, we should perhaps no longer speak of the liturgical movement, as if this were something in which we were free to take an interest or not, according to taste; the liturgical revival is now officially part of the life of the contemporary Church, and the liturgical apostolate must be one of the principal preoccupations of priest and lay apostle.

Sharing in Christ's Worship of the Father

We mean by the liturgy the worship paid by the Mystical Body of Christ, both head and members, to God the Father. It is expressed in the system of prayers and ceremonies which tradition has gradually developed as the Church's own worship, and which are embodied in official, liturgical books. Now that the principle of local rituals has been accepted by the Council, these books will of course become much more numerous and diverse.

St. Pius X stated that the liturgy is 'the foremost and indispensable fount of the Christian spirit', and the *Constitution* expresses the same sentiment: 'the liturgy moves the faithful, filled with the paschal sacraments, to be one in holiness; it prays that they may hold fast in their lives to what they have grasped by their faith; the renewal in the eucharist of the covenant between God and man draws the faithful into the compelling love of Christ and sets them on fire. From the liturgy, therefore, and especially from the eucharist, as from a fount, grace is poured forth upon us; and the sanctification of men in Christ and the glorification of God, to which all other activities of the Church are directed as towards their end, is achieved in the most efficacious way possible.'[1] Let us add that it is above all in the liturgy that individual souls will find the first answer to their intimate need for closer union with the spiritual and the divine.

The object of the liturgy is the worship of God. It is wrong to think that the liturgical revival is concerned only with the trappings of worship, such as the use of the vernacular, vestments, the dialogue Mass, Mass facing the people, reform of the rubrics and similar current changes; it is interested in these things only because they seem to express with greater fidelity the heavenly mystery which is the liturgy itself.[2]

[1] Art. 10.

[2] *Instructio ad Exsecutionem Constitutionis de Sacra Liturgia Recte Ordinandam*, 26 September 1964, art. 5. This instruction came into force on the first Sunday of Lent, 7 March 1965. It adds to, but does not take away from, the directives of the *Constitution on the Liturgy*. Cf. J. D. CRICHTON, *Changes in the Liturgy*, London, 1965.

The liturgy is directed first of all to the sacrifice of the Mass and to the sacred banquet of the holy eucharist; next it is concerned with the other six sacraments; then with the word of God in the Bible, which, as we shall have occasion to notice when speaking of catechetics, is closely connected with the liturgy in the life of the Church; only last of all is the liturgy directed towards the details of the liturgy which are set out in the rubrics.

In due time, the liturgical revival is bound to have a profound influence on popular piety. Among other things, it involves re-thinking the theology of the holy eucharist, and already people are coming more fully to realize that adoration of the real presence, a most beautiful and admirable devotion, is not to be equated in importance as a eucharistic practice with assisting at the holy sacrifice and receiving the Body of the Lord.

The liturgy presents Christ to us as a divine person; the Church, guided by the Holy Spirit, brings us to Christ in his various mysteries so that we may make supernatural contact with him. These mysteries, the birth, resurrection, ascension and the rest, presented to us in the various feasts of Christ throughout the liturgical year, are not only given to us as examples; they are sources of grace. Each mystery represents a state of his sacred humanity and brings us the particular grace of that particular mystery; this is a special sharing in the divinity. We do not celebrate the mysteries only to praise and thank him for them. This recognition of Christ as a divine person is important, for although he is our model, we cannot imitate him simply by natural efforts, as we would a great human personage. No, if our imitation of Christ is to be a true imitation, it must be of the supernatural order. Now, only the Holy Spirit, the finger of God's right hand, can trace upon our souls the supernatural, the true likeness of the Son in his mysteries, for that likeness can only be achieved by grace, by that supernatural faith and love which comes to us through sacramental contact with the divinity in the liturgy. We can be saints only in the measure in which the life, the mysteries of Jesus, live in us.[1]

[1] Cf. DOM MARMION, *Christ in His Mysteries*, pp. 20–6.

Africa and the Liturgy

In our third chapter on adaptation, we have already referred to the importance of Africanizing the liturgy. More than anything else, a truly African liturgy can see the Church in Africa safely through the present critical stage, for, as the *Constitution* says so clearly, it is the liturgy which 'daily builds up those who are within into a holy temple of the Lord', while at the same time 'it marvellously strengthens their power to preach Christ, and thus shows forth the Church, to those who are outside, as a sign lifted up among the nations under which the scattered children of God may be gathered together until there is one sheepfold and one shepherd'.[1] If the new Christians of Africa are given the full liturgy, and the opportunity to take an active part in it, they can acquire the spirit and enthusiasm of the first Christians of the Roman Empire. The first golden age of Christianity drew its inspiration above all from the holy sacrifice and the eucharistic banquet; if we are to witness a second such age which will transform the world, it is to the same source that we must look for inspiration. No instruction can so enlighten the mind and so move the heart as the story of Christ's mysteries unfolded in the liturgy day by day before our eyes, and a parish based on a truly African liturgy will be a Christian parish indeed, firmly rooted in the faith and filled with the apostolic spirit.

Hitherto the chief emphasis in the African apostolate has been on primary schools and on works of charity. Now things have changed. We cannot tell when our schools may be lost; when that day comes, if it does come, the only remaining stronghold of the faith will be the parish, and those parishes will have to be strong parishes, firmly based on the liturgy and on the ministry of the word, for there will be no other medium for giving Christian instruction. There must of course be a living link between the liturgy and preaching; the Council has helped greatly in making this possible, by insisting on the importance of the homily, which, from 16 February 1964, has been obligatory at all public Masses on Sundays and solemn feast-days.[2] The liturgy has a

[1] Art. 2.
[2] 'It should draw its content mainly from scriptural and liturgical sources, and should be a proclamation of God's wonderful works in the history of salvation' (Art. 35).

natural appeal for the African, as the contemplative life has for the Asian. The idea of public worship is firmly embedded in the traditional culture of Africa, and the old ritual life is providentially adapted to the Catholic liturgy. The heart of the Bantu philosophy, for example, as Father Tempels has pointed out, is a belief in a vital force coming to people from God through their ancestors, and Africans easily grasp the sacramental grace of Christianity. They have a natural feeling for the mysterious and sacred, and understand the deeper meanings of worship in common. All this means that the liturgy is the most natural way for the Africans to come to Christ.

Liturgy, in Africa and elsewhere, must mean active participation, as did the traditional rites: animism *acted*, rather than looked at or thought, and an African Christian liturgy demands the same character. It must also be a truly African worship—is an African to be less an African because he is a Christian? The Church is willing to change Western ways for African ways; her priests must be the same, if they are to be faithful to their stewardship. The Council has made it abundantly clear that it wishes to see the liturgy adapted to national traditions and different cultures. 'Even in the liturgy, the Church has no wish to impose a rigid uniformity in matters which do not implicate the faith or the good of the whole community; rather does she respect and foster the genius and talents of the various races and nations. Anything in these peoples' way of life which is not indissolubly bound up with superstition and error she studies with sympathy and, if possible, preserves intact. Sometimes she even admits such things into the liturgy itself, so long as they harmonize with its true and authentic spirit.'[1] If Africa's priests can make their own the outlook of the *Constitution on the Liturgy*, it will not be long before the continent at last evolves a truly African Christianity, a place where an African is not less, but more African because he is a Christian.

One of the most interesting unofficial papers circulated to the African bishops during the Second Session of the Council contained a suggestion that experiments might be made with an Oriental rather than the Latin rite in Africa. The author was a religious superior with missionary experience in Pakistan and Israel, and he was thinking especially of the two Eastern rites which already exist in Africa, the Ethiopian and the

[1] Art. 37.

Coptic; his own preference was for the Coptic rite. This was of course only a suggestion, but it was useful as a reminder that the Latin rite is not the only possible liturgy for this continent. The first meeting of the superiors of contemplative orders of Africa and Madagascar at Bouake, Ivory Coast, in May 1964, came to the same conclusion (without, unless I am mistaken, naming a particular form of Oriental liturgy). They added that the rhythm of the year and the African seasons (no European four seasons here) necessitated changes in the African liturgy; only in ways such as this could the reinterpretation of the African patrimony be envisaged.[1]

All the existing rites, both Latin and Eastern, grew up over a period of centuries, and this is the ideal way for any liturgy to develop. Does the pace at which Africa is changing, however, make it impossible to wait for a slow, spontaneous development? It is surely useful to raise the question about the possibility of adapting an Eastern rite to the special needs and personality of the African Church.[2]

Some New Regulations

Most of the changes contained in the *Constitution* will by now have been embodied in local rituals, so we omit them here. It may help, however, if we list certain changes which actually came into operation on 16 February 1964, three weeks after Pope Paul VI's *Motu Proprio*, *Sacram Liturgiam*.

Each diocese must have a special committee to promote the liturgy, and knowledge of the liturgy, though several dioceses may combine to set up one committee to serve them all. There should also be a committee for sacred music and another for sacred art serving each diocese.

As far as possible, the hours of the office should be prayed at the appropriate hour of the day. Thus lauds should be regarded as the morning prayer, and vespers as the evening prayer; these two hours, says the *Constitution*, are the two hinges on which the daily office turns. In his *Motu Proprio* of 25 January, 1964 Pope Paul put into operation two of the recommendations of the *Constitution*: prime can be

[1] *Informations Catholiques Internationales*, 1 July 1964, pp. 11 and 12.
[2] Art. 40, nos. 1 and 2, of the *Constitution* allows restricted and preliminary experiments in 'an even more radical adaptation' than that envisaged in art. 38.

omitted, in private recitation, and any one of the remaining three little hours can now be recited, according to the time of day.

Priests who live together are urged to pray at least part of the office in common, to underline the public character of the divine office, which is the whole Mystical Body publicly praising God. The *Constitution* also recommends to parish priests that the chief hours especially be sung, where possible, and that the laity too be encouraged to pray the office, either with priests, or among themselves, or even individually.

Bishops may dispense their priests, wholly or in part, from the obligation of the divine office, or substitute for it some other prayer. Religious other than priests who recite, as part of their rule, either part of the divine office, or some other smaller office modelled on the divine office, are taking part in the public prayer of the Church.

Church Music

Pius XII in his encyclical *Musicae Sacrae Disciplina*, the first encyclical to deal with sacred music, speaks amply on music as a form of the missionary apostolate. He makes clear his understanding of the difficulties concerning sacred music in mission territories where the number of Christians is not sufficiently great, where churches and schools have to be built, where priests are few. Yet, in spite of these difficulties, the Pope exhorts 'apostolic workers who are labouring strenuously in these extensive parts of the Lord's vineyard to pay careful attention to this matter as one of the serious problems of their ministry'. He points out that many of the mission peoples have a great love of music and use religious music in their pagan worship; therefore he asks missionaries to use this love of music (which is often highly admired in older civilizations) and compose Christian music and hymns in the tongue and to the melodies and rhythms that the people know.

Concerning Gregorian chant, he notes that from the earliest times, missionaries have introduced the Gregorian chant; missionaries should remember this and follow their example. 'Baptizing' indigenous melodies is therefore to be commended, provided always that the association of a non-Christian melody is not undesirable, as will sometimes be the case. The *Constitution on the Liturgy* speaks in the same strain and permits musical instruments other than the pipe organ. It adds that the clergy

should be competent to promote the traditional music of their people,[1]
which as Fr. Gelineau says, in Africa gives musical expression to the
communal sense to a degree not common in other societies.

The answer to the search for African Church music lies with the
African priest and layman. There are wide differences between Gregorian chant and African chant, but there is an affinity of mode and in fact
Africans sing Gregorian well. Why not have some Gregorian in the vernacular? And why not sing psalms in the vernacular to African melodies?
There seems to be some agreement among experts that every European
hymn which does not appeal to our Christians should be removed from
African hymn books unless it has high religious, literary and musical
value and is already well known in Africa, such as *Adeste Fideles*.

Recent ethnological discoveries have shown that music is a much
more essential factor in the life of many races in the lands of mission,
including Africa, than it is in the West. The African's music is of the
stuff of all the actions of his life: it is almost his soul. He is born, lives
and dies to the clamour of the drum.

To those interested in further reading, we commend Father
Hofinger's *Worship, The Life of the Missions*, part IV, which has three
chapters on this subject. Among many review articles are two in
World Mission: 'Music should be native too' (Winter, 1957, vol. 8,
no. 4), and 'The Dilemma of Church Music in Africa' (Fall, 1959,
vol. 10, no. 3). This last pleads among other things for the establishment
of a school of sacred music for missionaries and Africans while the first
pleads rather for courses in established music departments in our
Catholic educational organization. These, we suggest, could work
under, or as part of the diocesan commissions for sacred music required
by the *Constitution on the Liturgy* (art. 46).

Paraliturgy

By paraliturgical ceremonies we mean public acts of worship,
approved by the competent ecclesiastical authorities, but not contained
in the official liturgical books of the Church. Thus a catechist's service
on Sunday in place of Mass belongs to paraliturgy.

Paraliturgical ceremonies are very useful, especially in Africa, where

[1] Art. 119.

they can incorporate traditional forms of worship. It is necessary however that they be controlled by the Ordinary if abuses are to be avoided. Experience has shown that it is not safe to leave the devising of such services wholly to the initiative and taste of the individual priest.

There are numerous occasions when a special service in church would help the people to connect religion with their daily life. Blessing of seeds and fields at the beginning of the sowing season; a rogation service at the proper time, that is when the crops are beginning to grow; blessing of the first fruits at the beginning of the harvest, and a harvest festival at the end; a solemn blessing of children, perhaps on the feast of the Holy Family; a blessing of houses; a blessing of tools:[1] all these are obvious examples of how the Church's sacramental principle can be extended to influence the whole of life with the spirit of Christianity. Any appropriate customs which are dear to the people would be included in the service, but care must be taken to avoid anything which is incompatible with Christianity.

The only paraliturgical service mentioned directly by the *Constitution on the Liturgy* is the Bible service. This is to be encouraged on the vigils of the more solemn feasts, on weekdays in Lent and Advent, and on Sundays and feast days. 'They are particularly to be recommended in places where no priest is available; when this is so, a deacon or some other person authorized by the bishop should preside over the celebration.'[2]

A special need in Africa is for a more or less standard Sunday service for the benefit of those many people who, because of the shortage of priests, are unable to hear Mass on Sundays. The ideal would be to have an annual scheme for a whole country, so that travelling Christians, of whom there are so many now, could feel at home wherever they were, either at the Sunday Mass, or at a familiar paraliturgical service. The studies of Father Hofinger on this subject are particularly useful.[3] Opinion is against the so-called 'Dry Mass', that is, the recitation of the prayers of the Mass, minus the consecration; the consecration is the heart of the Mass, and without it the sacrificial prayers lack relevance. The general structure of the Mass, however—a catechetical part followed by a prayer part—provides an ideal pattern for the Sunday

[1] Some blessings of course are liturgical, others are paraliturgical.   [2] Art. 35, 4.
[3] *Worship: the Life of the Missions*, Part III, esp. pp. 114 and 150.

service. The ministry of the word should centre on the Gospel of the day, and there should be a homily based on it.

We are glad to say that this widely held view now has the authority of the Commission for the implementation of the *Constitution on the Liturgy*. 'Let the method of this celebration be practically the same as the method employed in the liturgy of the word in the Mass; generally the Epistle and Gospel of the day, preceded and interspersed with singing, especially from the psalms. . . . The whole celebration is to be concluded with the *oratio communis* (prayers of the faithful) and the Lord's prayer.'[1]

[1] *Instruction for the Implementation of the Constitution of the Sacred Liturgy*, art. 37.

PART FOUR

The Priest's Apostolic Activity

The Christian priest has two broad areas of activity: as an ordained minister he is responsible for leading the Christian community in worship and for dispensing Christ's sacraments to his brethren; as a pastor of souls he instructs Christian people and seeks in every way to build up the Mystical Body. We have discussed some aspects of the priest's sacramental and ritual work in Part Three; it remains to consider his role as an apostle, dedicated to strengthening those within the Church, and to manifesting the Church as perfectly as possible to those scattered children of God who are outside it.

18   The Ministry of the Word: Modern Catechesis[1]

FAITH comes by hearing, and oral instruction in Christian truth is an important part of the apostolate. Christ is the great teacher of men, and the Church continues his work of teaching, as she also rules and sanctifies men in his name. She is under divine protection, so that the Christian message will never be lost; but her founder wishes her to use human means to ensure that the good tidings he brought to earth will be passed on to the succeeding generations of men until the end of time.

We speak in this chapter of modern catechesis, but what we say applies also to preaching, as generally understood. A distinction is sometimes drawn between catechesis, which is for children and converts, and preaching, which is directed towards adult Christians. We feel that the distinction may not be of great importance anywhere, and certainly not in Africa. No Christian is ever perfectly instructed in the faith, and we prefer to group, under the general term of catechesis, instruction to all members of the Church, whether perfect, baptized members, or inchoate, unbaptized members. The same principles apply, no matter to whom the Christian message is addressed.

In recent years, the teaching of religion has been subjected to very critical scrutiny throughout the Christian world. As a result, the whole approach to catechetics has been overhauled. No specifically African catechetic has yet been developed,[2] but the general principles of the new catechesis are as valuable in Africa as anywhere else, and they deserve our attention here.

---

[1] Two books, important and fundamental, on modern catechetics are: J. A. JUNGMANN, *Handing on the Faith*, New York; J. HOFINGER, *The Art of Teaching Christian Doctrine*, Notre-Dame.

[2] But see LEDOGAR (ed.), *Katigondo, Presenting the Christian Message to Africa*, London 1965.

The Reformation forced the Church into a defensive posture, and for four centuries her teaching was based on apologetics. When the faith was being attacked on all sides, the Church sought to prepare her children by showing them the reasonableness of the faith, and by providing them with the answers to Protestant objections.

The post-Reformation era is now coming to a close, and the importance of apologetics has diminished. Modern religious instruction is positive rather than negative, it seeks to construct rather than to defend. No doubt the new catechesis has not yet assumed its final shape; it is still in the course of formation, and it would be foolish to think that we could say anything like the last word on the subject in a short chapter of this book. We shall try, however, firstly to explain the inspiration of the catechetical revival, and then to sketch some of its principal features.

The Origins of the Catechetical Revival

Every society or movement with an idealistic basis must be continually returning to the sources of its initial inspiration if it is not to degenerate into formalism. We may illustrate this principle from the history of religious congregations in the Church. One day a saintly man makes his appearance, with a new, vital understanding of how the principles of Christianity are to be applied to the contemporary world. Inevitably, he attracts disciples. They seek to embody his teaching for all time in the written word in the form of a rule. The day comes when all those who knew the founder are dead. His latter-day disciples tend to seek him exclusively in the rule which he inspired; it is regarded now as something of value in its own right, instead of simply as the expression of an ideal. If the ideal is lost, minute observance of the rule can become formalism. So it is that the task of religious superiors in every generation is to go back to the sources of their congregation to keep alive the flame enkindled by the founder.

The Church is under the special protection of her divine founder. She can never wholly lose the truth, can never officially teach false doctrine. At the same time, she remains a society of men. As in the religious congregation, so in the Church as a whole, formalism is a danger, and can be avoided only by a never-ending study of the origins of Christianity. Hence the importance in every age of the study of holy Scripture and of the Fathers of the Church, those early Christian writers who were in touch with the apostolic age.

The catechetical revival in the twentieth century is a return to the sources, a rediscovery of the initial Christian inspiration. It was felt that the doctrines of Christianity, at least in the way they were often presented at the popular level, had ceased to be an inspiration for life, and were in danger of becoming sterile formulae. Let us get behind the words in which doctrine is expressed, say the reformers now, and rediscover the spirit. How were the apostles able to present Christ's teaching in a way that drew immediate and enthusiastic response from thousands of people? How can we, in our age, re-invest Catholic teaching with its primitive urgency and converting power? The catechetical revival has therefore been accompanied by a revival of interest in the apostolic, and the immediately post-apostolic, Church. It is there that we are to seek the spirit of Christianity; and the spirit must be preserved at all costs, for without it the letter brings death.

Now a counter-Reformation theology was necessary in its day. It was an age of intellectual discussion, and in defending the truth the Church adopted the philosophical language in which the reformers' objections were couched. Eighteenth-century rationalism demanded a similar philosophical approach, so that by the beginning of the twentieth century Catholic teaching had become very largely intellectual; there was a tendency to forget that religion is addressed to the whole man, to his heart and will as well as to his intellect.

A result of this over-intellectual approach to Christian doctrine was that ordinary people no longer felt its appeal. The Christian life seemed to have been reduced, in part at least, to learning a collection of dogmatic formulae and observing a legalistic moral code. There was danger of formalism.

The defection of the masses from the Church in the last hundred years was the immediate inspiration, we may believe, of the catechetical revival. At length it was realized that the intellectual content of religion had been stressed at the expense of other, equally important, elements, and modern catechists are now seeking to redress the balance.

SOME CHARACTERISTICS OF MODERN CATECHETICS

The Kerygma

The first Christian sermon was preached by St. Peter on the day of Pentecost. His message was simple: Jesus Christ is the divine messenger, and he has, as you see, poured out the Holy Spirit on us according to his promise. The apostles did not subject their disciples to a course of complicated instruction: they just proclaimed Jesus Christ the Lord and saviour of mankind. They felt this truth deeply, and communicated their enthusiasm to others. People who accepted the message were baptized.

We mean by the kerygmatic approach to catechetics just this same, urgent proclamation of the personal, the essential message that Christ is Lord and saviour. Kerygma is the Greek word for message; the apostle has a message and is possessed by urgency to communicate it. The catechist is filled with this truth and bears witness to it by his words and by his whole life. He is himself deeply involved; he is not simply a professional teacher, but a man with a vital message from God. He does not seek to pass on the message in sophisticated formulae: he proclaims it in vibrant tones, and leaves it to do its own work. He does not rely in the first place on his own persuasive powers; he regards himself as an instrument of Christ, who is addressing mankind through him, using him to deepen the spiritual lives of his brethren. Modern catechesis thus helps the teacher as well as the taught, for it brings him nearer to Christ, whose mouthpiece, however unworthy, he recognizes himself to be. He is not an employee of the Church; he is Christ's friend and messenger. Religion, we say, is not taught but caught, and the catechist communicates his own spirit to his pupils, inspiring them with that same urgent desire to bear witness to Christ with which he is himself filled. He seeks not to impart instruction for its own sake, but to bring life to souls; our Lord came on earth for the same purpose—'that they may have life, and have it more abundantly' (John x: 10). The catechist is continuing the work of his master. His approach is Christ-centred, not man-centred.

Conversion, not instruction, is the aim of the catechist. The catechumen receives the message, and responds by a change of heart which is translated into a life of faith, hope and charity, a life of obedience to Christ's commandments, not out of fear, but out of love. He becomes aware that the earth is the Lord's and all that is in it; he feels himself quickened by the apostolic spirit, impelled to pass on his faith with others and to do what he can to sanctify the temporal order; he recognizes that Christ is counting on him to do his share in assuring the extension and the welfare of God's kingdom on earth.

The Catechist's Message

The message which the catechist proclaims is a simple one: it is the apostolic message—Christ is our saviour, and we have in heaven a loving and merciful Father. God is not an abstract idea, not a logical conclusion, not a silent first principle: he is a living person, the almighty creator certainly, but also our loving Father. Under his guidance, and in spite of sin, the world is moving towards the day when there will be a new heaven and a new earth, with all men living in an imperishable union with the Father who dwells in them. The message is Christ-centred, because it is in Christ and through Christ that the Father achieves his plan of love; it is Christ who teaches us of the Father and of the Holy Spirit, it is Christ who brings us the good tidings, and it is Christ who, by his death, resurrection and ascension, saves us from sin. Hs is the dominant figure in God's historical plan for mankind; the Old Testament looks forward to him and he is the centre of the New Testament, which measures the progress of the Holy Spirit towards the Parousia of the Lord, when the glorious Christ shall gather together the People of God who await the day of the Lord, and cleanse them and give them life, bringing them to all truth.

The message shows too how Christ continues to live and work in his Church, through the Holy Spirit and by the ministry of his shepherds. This he does principally through the sacraments. He unites all the members with himself, their head, and with each other, for by the one bread many are made one. The members of the Church are God's chosen race, a royal priesthood, God's family, and to each of them he gives a particular task; the Church is God's home on earth, the city set on a hill, lit by the light of Christ.

The Bible

The modern catechetic, we have said, is essentially a return to the sources of Christianity, and it rests on the twin pillars of holy Scripture and the liturgy.

The Bible is God's word, and it tells the story of his dealings with the human race from creation down to the end of time; for we are living now in the last days. The crucial importance of the Bible as the great book of truth and of life was obscured in the sixteenth and succeeding centuries, for Catholic teachers were taken up with the urgent task of defending the faith against the Protestant teaching that the Bible was the sole source of salvation. It is through the Church in the first place that Christ saves and sanctifies his brethren; but for a long time the truth that God's word in the Bible had a unique place within the Church seemed to remain in the background.

The Bible is God's book, *the* book. It must be the catechist's handbook *par excellence*. The disciple of Christ learns to understand his master and his teaching above all through God's own word. There he reads how the chosen people were prepared for Christ and his teaching, there too he meets the 'irresistibly majestic figure of the historical Jesus, risen and glorious, the centre of mankind's long story and the only hope for its future earthly career, as well as for the final destiny of eternal joy which he came to confirm'.[1] The Bible also shows the catechist the methods to employ in handing on his message. He finds that our Lord taught above all through stories, stories of wonderful simplicity and directness, and he adopts the same method himself.

In the past, the tendency has been to use the Bible to illustrate abstract principles; modern catechesis moves in the opposite direction, taking the Bible as the starting-point and seeking to uncover the principles which it teaches. It is God's living word; it has a sacramental power; independently of us it will pierce the hearts of Christians more than any two-edged sword.

[1] F. H. DRINKWATER, 'Handing on the Faith', in *The Way*, January 1964.

The Liturgy

The second great pillar of modern catechetics is the liturgy. The renewed interest in the official worship of the Church is another feature of that return to sources which characterize the life of the Church today. We have noted in a previous chapter[1] that in the early Church systematic presentation of doctrine was unknown; it was through the liturgy that the faithful were brought into contact with the mystery of Christ, a contact that wonderfully enriched and deepened their spiritual lives.

There is a strong didactic element in the liturgy; it seems indeed that it was realized from the beginning that organized worship is one of the most efficacious ways of communicating the Christian message.[2] The liturgy proclaims the mystery of the redemption through the words of the Bible; it expresses that mystery in prayers and hymns and sacred signs, and renders it sacramentally present to the worshippers. The Mass of the catechumens is expressly designed to instruct candidates for baptism in the mystery of Christ, through readings from the Bible, prayers and the creed. The use of what has become an unknown language for this portion of the Mass has obscured its didactic purpose, and this is why renewed interest in catechetics has been accompanied by a strong plea for the use of the vernacular in the liturgy.

There is hardly a mystery of the faith which is not contained in the liturgy, said Pius XII. When the Church celebrates her mysteries, she assembles God's holy People and worships him; Christ is in her midst, and she is filled with the Holy Spirit. The people hear the good tidings in the Mass of the catechumens, they are taken up into Christ's redeeming sacrifice by the sacramental celebration, they are filled with strength to proclaim the word without fear.

Such a realization of what we are doing when we take part in the Church's liturgy reinforces Christian conviction, and deepens attachment to Christ and to his Church: and these are precisely the objects of catechesis.

[1] Chapter 2, p. 19.   [2] Cf. *Constitution on the Liturgy*, art. 33.

Systematic Catechism

The Christian witness of the catechist, the Bible, and the liturgy are three ingredients of modern catechetics. A fourth ingredient is systematic teaching, based on the Church's creeds and catechisms. This is not the whole of catechesis, and all now agree that there was something seriously wrong when it was considered sufficient for the catechumen to commit to memory a series of more or less understood catechism answers; nevertheless, the intellectual element in religion remains essential, and modern reactions against past deficiencies must not be allowed to obscure this truth. Otherwise we are in danger of basing religion on sentiment. Development of doctrine is a fact; and it is untrue to say that we can find the whole of Christian revelation in the Bible. Worship is the supreme act of religion, but it must have a sound theological foundation.

We accept the necessity of some kind of catechism, but the old methods of teaching it must be changed. Firstly, nothing must be committed to memory which has not first been understood. Secondly, it is not enough simply to know stock answers, even if they are understood. Catechesis is aimed at the whole man, and must seek to extract a real, and not just a notional, assent to the Christian faith. Even when he is teaching dogmatic truths, the catechist cannot forget that he must relate religion and life. Enlightened religious instruction must help Christians to solve all the problems of daily living in the light of the faith, must furnish them with the intellectual basis of faith; but at the same time it must inspire them with a longing to grow into living witnesses of Christ, able and anxious to explain their faith in an intelligible and attractive form to those who are looking for the truth.

Opinions are still divided about the utility of learning catechism answers at all. We may simply note that most writers seem to feel that, at most, it is useful to learn a few, key answers, and that only in the later stages of primary education.

The General Aims and Methods of Catechesis

A sound catechesis for adults will aim at deepening conviction, and at training them for living the Christian life. There must be no outworn controversy, no scholastic subtlety. What people need are the great truths of the faith, which are to be presented to them simply and directly: Christ's mission, the redemption, the Church. Christianity corresponds to all that is good in human nature, and the catechist will make full use of whatever is valuable in old non-Christian beliefs and customs.

Well-instructed Catholics will recognize their responsibility for the religious education of their children; when we have a properly-catechized community, we shall no longer see children from devout families turning up to prepare for their first holy communion unable to make the sign of the cross. This only happens when parents think that the religious education of their children is the responsibility of priests, teachers and catechists.

The new catechesis should form adults who recognize that fraternal charity is the first of the virtues, and the distinguishing mark of the Christian, and who also see that the apostolate is the responsibility of every Christian, since to work for the conversion of others is the highest form of fraternal charity. The catechist must stress that the apostolic spirit is essential to true Christianity, and that the lay apostolate means working for the growth as well as for the protection of the Church. The life of a good Catholic, of a fervent Christian community, is the best apostolate of all; not only does it nourish the faith of Christians themselves, but it is also the normal way by which non-Christians are led to Christ and to the Church; whereas the un-Christian life of many Christians is the chief obstacle to the conversion of Africa.

Different categories of people of course need a different approach and in most places it will be found convenient to divide those under instruction into five groups: adult Christians; adult non-Christians; Christian children before their first holy communion; Christian school-children; and non-Christian schoolchildren. The schoolchildren will of course be divided up into their various classes, and those in Catholic schools will be separated from those in undenominational schools.

In many parts of Africa it is important to insist on the special importance of giving religious instruction in Government secondary schools. All the available periods must be made use of.

Good catechesis aims finally at introducing the catechumen into a living Christian community, and at making him an active member thereof. The first Christian communities remain models for those of all ages: 'There was one heart and soul in all the company of believers; none of them called any of his possessions his own, everything was shared in common' (Acts iv. 32). Modern economic conditions prevent these apostolic practices from being imitated literally today; but the spirit behind them must animate every Christian community. As for the Christians themselves, their instruction should lead them to embrace and heartily to welcome the newly-baptized. The neophyte must be made to feel at home, must be supported and encouraged in his faith. Only in the Christian community can he discover Christ's full message, and experience the bonds of charity which unite all men in Christ.

The New Pedagogy

The catechetical renewal has coincided with a pedagogical revolution in the whole world of education. In all departments of education, teaching-methods are being changed, and catechesis, while insisting that the message itself is more important than any amount of technique, naturally seeks to make use of the new methods. Audio-visual aids, pictures, dramatization, drawing, memory work: all these can be a great help to the dedicated catechist. If he is not dedicated, nothing is of any use. We have listed five teaching aids: there are many more, of course: the Eichstätt Mission Catechetics Study Week, 1960, listed fifty, then wisely went on to say that they only help if they are used in the right way.

Audio-visual aids and ordinary pictures used in Africa should depict the local people; it would be unfortunate if the African child unconsciously absorbed the idea that the white race alone populated heaven—or hell. In general, pictures should be used to illustrate and recapitulate what has already been explained verbally. Dramatization is perhaps especially valuable in Africa, where people are less inhibited than they are in Europe; children naturally express themselves in actions as well as in words, and they should be encouraged to do so in religious classes as well as elsewhere. Drawing can be useful for the teacher as well as for the pupils. Psychologists attach great importance to the spontaneous drawings of children, and they can provide the catechist with valuable suggestions about how to present Christian truth in a way that will appeal to his pupils.

Memory work plays a necessary part in all education. Children learn by heart easily, and this facility should be exploited by the teacher of religion. Whether or not we consider it useful to learn catechism answers by heart, it is certainly desirable that children learn by heart prayers, rhymes and songs, and above all the words of Christ, and of the Bible generally. It should be recognized that ideas and principles of action are much more suitable for memory work than doctrinal formulae.

We have spoken of the absolute necessity for the catechist to be a convinced and committed Christian, a man of true humility, who knows that he stands before his pupils as one whose task is to minister, and not to be ministered unto. This is his essential qualification. But, given this qualification, he must make full use of human means for his work. He should, as the Eichstätt Congress insisted, prepare his instructions carefully by study and reflection and written notes, as well as by prayer. He should ask himself before each lesson: what is my message today to these brethren of Christ? How can I best express it in a way that will lead my hearers to living faith? What Bible story would be best suited for this purpose? Basically, this method of teaching will always be the same: a simple tale, fully adapted to the mentality of his hearers, with the moral clearly drawn out. Anything like a philosophical discourse is out of place. If he is giving an instruction on sin, for example, he might very well start by telling the story of the Prodigal Son; if he wishes to speak about the duty of thanksgiving, he might tell the story of the ten lepers. Like all good teachers, he must do everything possible to keep his lessons interesting and varied. He might often insert brief, spontaneous prayer in his instructions; his pupils will be more effectively formed in habits of prayer by seeing the catechist pray himself, than by hearing him talk about prayer. So after speaking of the ten lepers, he might invite his pupils to say with him a simple prayer: 'I thank you, God, for all that you have done for me; help me not to forget you as the nine lepers did.'

The priest's role in catechesis will vary from place to place. Usually the regular instructions will be left to the catechist, but it is important that the priest's presence be felt, at least in the background. It is a good plan for the priest himself to give a period of religious instruction once a month to primary school children and perhaps once a fortnight to those in non-Catholic schools. (This would not be enough in countries where the Church is long established, but what more can a single-handed priest do when he has, say, ten to twenty schools and six to forty thousand Christians, not to mention the non-Christians, all round him?) His aim on these occasions will not be to introduce new matter, but simply to go over what the children have been learning since his last visit. This will encourage the teacher, and help him to take very seriously his duties as a catechist; the greatest dignity of the human voice, he must be reminded, is that it should be the organ of God.

Conclusion

It may be objected that the new catechesis which we have outlined in the chapter is the work of dreamers, of men hopelessly out of touch with reality, men who know nothing of the type of people who actually make up the membership of the Church. All catechists are not saints, neither are all priests; it is Utopian (it may be said) to imagine that they will ever become so, or that the ordinary Christian will ever develop into a fervent apostle, aflame with zeal and charity.

The answer to this is clear. The Holy Spirit is at work in the Church, and the upsurge of interest in catechetics nowadays is the result of his promptings. Every priest and catechist has a plain duty to make himself familiar with the catechetical revolution, under pain of being unfaithful to the divine light. We live by faith, not by canny calculations of what is humanly possible. If we enter robustly into the life of the contemporary Church, our part is done. The results we can leave to God, who alone can change the hearts of men.[1]

---

[1] We have based our remarks in this chapter as far as possible on the Pan-African Congress at Katigondo, 1964. This Congress in turn assumed and reinforced the teachings of the Eichstätt Study Week of 1960.

19   The Pastor and His Flock

THE priest sanctifies his people by giving them the life of Christ in the sacraments, and he feeds them with God's word. He has also to tend Christ's sheep, and we discuss in this chapter his work with some of the classes of people who go to make up the Christian community. A concluding section deals with parish retreats and missions.

The Family

We have spoken earlier of the importance of the family in the life of the Church; we repeat here that a holy community can only be built up through holy families, and much of the priest's effort to sanctify the community is therefore concentrated on individual families.

The family apostolate has always been exercised in the Church in the form of pastoral visitation by the parish clergy; nothing can replace this work, irksome though it be. If only there were more priests to do it. Parish visitation by the clergy is not however enough; Christians themselves must realize that their families provide them with the most important field for their own apostolic activity. There is something very inadequate about the outlook of a lay apostle who is prepared to work zealously enough for the spiritual welfare of the community, but fails to recognize that his first duty as a baptized apostle is to sanctify the members of his own household. The Christian life is to be practised in the first place in the family; adult education schemes and the Christian Family Movement should be used to drive this point home.

Christian worship in the home is important everywhere, but it is especially important in Africa, where it must replace a pagan cult which was largely domestic in character, a true *lares et penates* centred on the great family events of birth, marriage and death. The father of the family was usually the minister of the pagan worship, and the Christian father should retain this priestly character in the home. The principle of substitution urgently requires the development of a Christian domestic cult in Africa.

Parents and children should be advised to go to Mass and to receive the sacraments as a family. On important family occasions, the father might ask the priest, when possible, to say Mass, with the whole family attending, and there might be special prayers in the home. Full use should be made of sacramentals to sanctify the details of domestic life; Christians should know and seek the blessings for a pregnant mother, a sick child or adult, and a house, and there should be extensive use of paraliturgy in blessing such things as seeds, cattle, first fruits and the marriage-bed.[1] The enthronement of the Sacred Heart in the home is a powerful form of the apostolate. The picture or statue of the Sacred Heart, after the house has been consecrated, is the focal point of the home, and all the family devotions can be performed before it. If a member of the family receives the anointing of the sick, or if the priest comes to assist at a death, the whole household should gather round and pray. There should be holy water in every Catholic home, with a candle blessed on Candlemas Day, and a blessed palm. The faithful could be reminded from time to time that the sign of the cross is a sacramental, and should frequently be made; a pleasant custom is to sign oneself on leaving or entering one's home.

The most important family prayers are those recited in the morning and at night; the father should lead, and the whole family should be united on these occasions. This may be difficult in the mornings, but it should be the rule at night. The family rosary may also be said occasionally, perhaps for a special intention, and a common grace before and after meals is a venerable Christian tradition. It is hard to exaggerate the importance of family prayer for a child's Christian development; where there is an authentic and enlightened religious atmosphere in a happy home, religion enters into the child's mind and heart, and he is unlikely ever to fall away from the practice of the faith. It should be added however that family prayers must be adapted to a child's powers of concentration; if he is required to take part in long prayers, religion becomes burdensome and boring, and the child may react in later life by abandoning it altogether.

Many Christian families are ruined by drunkenness. There are a

[1] See above, Chapter 17.

number of total abstinence organizations, including the Pioneer Movement, and the parish priest may very well decide to introduce one of them into his parish.[1]

Youth Work

Children need special help in the years immediately after they leave school, when they have left the security of regular school life but are not yet fully integrated in the adult world. Young people must encounter the Church when they leave school if they are not to drift into secularism, and the successful establishment of Christian communities depends to a very large extent on the religious formation of youth. At present most African children leave school after their primary education, and the ideal solution to much of the current social unrest would be the setting up of institutes where they could receive a further two years of training in handicrafts and agriculture and reach permanent literacy through a course of guided reading, while at the same time consolidating their moral and religious convictions. Shortage of money will probably make it impossible to realize this ideal completely, but we should seek to work towards it as far as possible. There are many youth organizations which can help: sodalities of various kinds with a religious aim; clubs which provide training in agriculture for boys and in domestic science for girls; Boy Scouts and Girl Guides are particularly useful in that membership begun in school can be continued afterwards; the Young Christian Workers, the Young Christian Students, and the Legion of Mary provide young people with excellent outlets for their apostolic zeal. Schoolchildren should be encouraged to belong to such groups as the Xaverians, the Boy Scouts or the Girl Guides; membership of these organizations makes them sociable and club-minded, so that they naturally join Christian youth associations later on.

Young Farmers' Associations are particularly valuable. They should provide recreational facilities and some religious instruction as well as actual training in agriculture. There might be weekly meetings, with perhaps an annual exhibition of work to encourage both the members themselves and the people of the district. In many places it would

[1] Cf. *African Ecclesiastical Review*, June 1964.

probably be wise to admit non-Catholics to membership of the Young Farmers; these associations should evidently not be too 'churchy', but should have as their main object to help farmers in general and to raise agricultural standards.

Many young Africans of the present generation will be appointed to high positions without having passed through the bottom rungs of employment; it is therefore important to provide training in leadership both in schools and in youth organizations, which should be natural breeding-grounds for leaders. All teachers' training colleges and secondary schools should have flourishing lay apostolate organizations; the Legion of Mary and the Young Catholic Students are particularly suitable in such places.

If we could turn every Catholic schoolboy and schoolgirl into an apostle, the conversion of Africa would not be far off. No doubt we cannot hope, humanly speaking, totally to succeed in this aim, but we must keep it in view, and seek to include as many as possible in the lay apostolate organizations. As we have already remarked, it is a serious error to think that these are only for an élite; many a careless Christian has been transformed by work as a lay apostle.

We must of course train our young people to be not only good Christians but also good citizens, and they must be urged to fulfil all their civic duties with conscientiousness. Youth organizations under Church patronage should seek to co-operate at the diocesan and national levels with similar organizations run by other Christian bodies. The question of collaboration with state youth organizations, and with the youth wings of political parties, is a difficult one and needs the advice of the Ordinary. Some African states require all young people to belong to the national youth movement; it is evidently desirable to introduce a Christian element into these organizations. It is not at present easy to see how this can be done.

Later in this chapter we shall discuss the question of the leakage among the young.

The Educated Classes, Leaders of Their Country

Africa in the second half of the twentieth century is in a state of emergency, and in these conditions any leader is better than none. If good leaders are not provided, bad ones will certainly take over. Hence the importance of the Church's work among the educated classes. In former days, the Church sought to win over the chiefs, so that they in turn might influence their people; the educated are in this sense the chiefs of modern Africa, and if the continent is to receive a Christian stamp, it can only be through these men.

The priest must seek at all costs to deepen the spiritual lives of educated people, and this can only be done by personal contact. He should show these people the respect which they look for and to which they are entitled. It may indeed be that their education has been deficient in certain respects, but if we treat them with deference, and as social equals, we are at the same time educating them and winning ourselves friends for life. In most parishes, the educated are still a small minority; they should have their own local associations, and they should be grouped in special lay apostolate organizations. Special retreats might also be arranged for them.

As long as the Church has its own schools and colleges, they must be used to train young people for life in the world, that is, life in a parish. Too often Catholic boarding schools and colleges model themselves on seminaries, or even on religious novitiates; as a result, young people receive an excellent religious training in an enclosed garden, but it is a training which is often quite unrelated to the life they will be leading as adults. This is a matter that needs attention. We do not consider ourselves competent to examine it here in detail, but we may observe in passing that compulsory daily Mass in these colleges seems unwise.

All Africans have a strong sense of their obligations to their immediate family and to the clan, but their loyalties seldom extend further than this. Priests, and Christian leaders generally, should seek to build up in educated people a sense of their obligations to the nation, and indeed to the whole human family. Teachers particularly need broad horizons and large loyalties, and their religious education should keep step with their secular culture. We may refer here to the paragraph on secularism in the first chapter of this book, and underline once more the urgency of providing educated Christians with the weapons they need to fight this most dangerous of the enemies of Christianity in Africa.

Some dioceses require the parish priest to provide all the teachers in the parish with a monthly conference. Here he has an opportunity of developing their religious culture, and so providing Africa with committed and zealous Christian leaders.

Women

A nation's youth is formed above all in the nation's families, and the key role in the family is played by the mother. Lenin knew what he was talking about when he said that the success of a revolution depends on the degree of participation by the women. Mankind's moral conscience is being increasingly formed by women. Their new role opens up an unprecedented era in the history of mankind.[1] The priest's and the layman's work for women will have far-reaching effects.

Parents' associations and women's clubs of different kinds can seek to teach mothers how to bring up their children as good Christians. Africans love their children, and this is no doubt the most important factor in a child's home education, but the need for discipline should be insisted on too, and parents should be helped to teach their children how to occupy themselves in their spare time. A great object will have been achieved if mothers can be brought to realize that the moral and religious education of their children is not primarily the responsibility of priests and teachers, but their own. There are still children in Africa who never attend school, and the special obligations of mothers in these cases must be pointed out. Too many parents allow their young daughters to drift to the towns without knowing or caring where they are going.

Social work for women should include courses in citizenship and in the various branches of domestic science, including light crafts. The provision of such courses will be the responsibility of the lay apostle, but the priest's encouragement and advice will often be necessary. Where the government provides these facilities, the clergy should give

[1] Cf. CARDINAL SUENENS, in *The Nun in the World*, ch. II, p. 16.

full co-operation. It is all to the good if women's clubs offer an occasional opportunity for giving a spiritual and apostolic talk. The difference between the number of boys and the number of girls in Catholic schools is painful Until education becomes a universal obligation, we can only make up the lack by these courses.

We have spoken in Chapter 14 of the difficulty of giving adequate marriage instruction in the present circumstances in Africa. Women's clubs may provide the framework within which to give suitable talks to girls contemplating marriage; a full course could do much to meet the pastoral difficulties so often encountered in connection with marriage. Subjects to be treated would naturally include the unity and sanctity of marriage, the wife's obligations to her husband, the duty of giving example to children and of educating them in a Christian manner.[1]

Women must be brought to realize that they have apostolic duties in the community at large as well as in the home, and special women's groups of the lay apostolate should be formed. Women catechists might receive their training in the Confraternity of Christian Doctrine; the programme might be drawn up and supervised by the parish council, or by a full-time catechist. Women catechists are very valuable; they are often more religious than men, and they can approach other women and children more easily. There is today a wide realization that the raising of the status of women in Africa is an urgent task, and that to have a woman catechist in the village is a help towards its fulfilment.

The Sick

In the Gospel story there do not seem to be any people to whom our Lord paid more attention than the sick. He spent the three years of his public life helping them and his chief miracles were worked for them. *Circumibat curans omnem languorem et omnem infirmitatem.* And before he left the world, he bequeathed the care of them to his apostles: *in quamcumque civitatem intraveritis curate infirmos qui in illa sunt.*

There is a long chapter in the Roman Ritual on the visitation of the

---

[1] Two useful handbooks on this subject have been produced by the Catholic Centre in Ottawa: *Course of Preparation for Marriage* and *Fundamentals of Marriage.* Both would require adaptation by an African priest.

sick which is a good guide to the attitude of the Christian pastor towards the sick; it would make good reading, say, during a retreat. The priest should not wait to be called, but should pay a visit to a sick parishioner as soon as he hears of the illness. His visits should be short and frequent, rather than rare and long. He should continue to visit the sick person as long as the latter needs him. It is usually well to suggest confession to a well-disposed sick person on the first visit, even though he is not seriously ill. The priest should try to explain the value of Christian suffering when it is willingly accepted. There is nothing more uplifting than to visit a sick person, whom one expects to find depressed, and find him full of gaiety. The sick should be shown what a wonderful field of apostolic example is open to them.

Sick people are particularly susceptible to religion, and many a man has received the grace of conversion on a sick bed. The family of a sick person are also often deeply affected, and the priest should remember that God may have sent this visitation in order to draw the whole household to himself.

Sick priests of course receive every attention, but they should be urged to receive the sacraments in good time. It is well known that many priests die without profiting from Christ's sacramental gifts, partly because of distances, and partly because they do not realize the state they are in.

Prayers and exhortations may be whispered into the ear of an unconscious person, for it is not possible to say how far he may not still be able to hear and understand.

The Aged

Old people in Africa are probably better looked after than old people in some North Atlantic countries, for they occupy a place of honour, and are usually surrounded by their family; nevertheless they have their own special problems, and old women particularly can suffer a great deal.

Old age has its special mentality, and it has to be understood. The old do not like change, and they feel deeply the tendency of the young and active to ignore them as being hopelessly out of touch with life. They feel dependent and often unwanted; others seldom understand the extent of their physical miseries. Their sense of loneliness may cause them to become embittered and oversensitive, so that they lapse from the practice of the faith even while they are still able to get to church.

The priest should seek to meet the old with loving understanding, and try to develop in them the special virtues of the old; self-forgetfulness, a willingness to adapt, and a great love for the young. Old people usually like to meet the young; young and old lay apostles should be encouraged to visit them. When the priest is in the pulpit, he should remember that he almost certainly has some old people among the congregation, and he might drop occasional reminders of the Christian's duty of resignation to the will of God, might speak too of the apostolate of prayer and of the value of suffering which is united with the passion of our Lord. The enforced and often unwelcome leisure of the old gives them opportunities of practising the apostolate of prayer.

A social centre can be a help for the old, especially perhaps in towns, where they are more likely to be left out of things than they are in the country. Little is needed in the way of entertainment, and there is hardly any expense; all the old people want is a change from home and the opportunity of a chat with their contemporaries. Sick old women fare worse in our countries than sick old men. They get their food, then they are left. In the towns and settlements the Christians should do more for them than they do now.

Holy Viaticum

Those in danger of death, whether from sickness or from any other cause, should receive the Body of the Lord to accompany them on their journey. Children who have reached the age of reason but who have uot yet made their first communion, as well as newly-baptized converts, should be given holy viaticum when in danger of death; it is enough that they know that in receiving the consecrated host they are receiving the Lord. *Unconscious* dying Christians should also receive viaticum, if there is no danger of irreverence; it is sometimes suggested that an unconsecrated host be given first to see if it can be assimilated. St. Thomas's teaching in the similar case of the dying insane, as also the practice of the early Church in giving holy communion to newly baptized infants, is the justification here. The Church does not allow the administration of viaticum to non-Catholics.

The Dying

Dying people need the priest more than anyone else. We do not know exactly how God judges men, but it is a venerable tradition in the Church that the moments before the passage from time to eternity are critical for determining a man's fate in the next world and the priest should do everything in his power to ensure that his people are full of the love of God at the moment of death. There is no sense in allowing a Christian to think that he is going to get better when he is obviously dying; he will be glad to be reminded of God, and to be prepared for the imminent meeting face to face. It matters even more to tell him that he is dying if he is a careless Christian. Of course dying people are not to be badgered with theology; their powers of attention are diminished, and it is sometimes enough to hold out the crucifix for them to gaze upon, and to say some simple prayers. The family or bystanders, even if daily communicants, often fail to help the dying man to pray, and do not pray themselves. They should show him the crucifix from time to time, bless him with holy water, and whisper easy little prayers to him. Priests and lay apostles should tell them this when they visit the sick and dying. The dying man's salvation and degree of glory in heaven are affected by these last hours. It is most regrettable that relations and friends hide from him the fact that he is dying.

The Priest's Obligations to the Sick and the Dying

Priests engaged in the pastoral ministry are under an obligation to ensure that their people do not die without first receiving the ministrations of the Church. This obligation is well recognized, and priests usually go far beyond their strict duty in this matter. It might be useful here, in view of the exacting conditions in this continent, to try to determine the limits of a priest's obligation to answer a summons to a dying person.

Evidently if he can attend the sick person without inconvenience, the priest is under a grave obligation to do so. In Africa however, where priests are scarce, it is important to realize that there will be many cases where the priest is fully excused from going out to minister to the sick;

there will even be cases where prudence forbids him to go; the common good comes before the good of the individual, and it would be wrong to run a serious risk of depriving a whole community of a priest for the sake of individuals.

In normal circumstances, a priest may not endanger his life or his health for the sake of an individual Christian; certainly he can never be obliged to do so, again under normal circumstances. One might imagine situations in which a refusal to minister to the dying would involve serious scandal; thus in times of civil disturbance, a priest might feel it a duty to endanger his life as a profession of faith, or for the honour of the priesthood; but such situations are rare indeed.

To ease consciences, the Congo bishops issued a ruling which has been adopted in many parts of Africa. A priest is not obliged to go on a sick call which entails a walk of four hours in daylight, or a walk of two hours at night. Several dioceses in Zambia, and perhaps in other countries have added that a priest is not obliged to go to a dying person by car or motor-bicycle if the total journey would take more than one hour and a half. It will often be wise to keep to these rules, although a priest would be at liberty to travel longer distances if he is sure that he would not damage either his health or his general apostolic work by doing so.

The above rules are suggested for priests who are in good health and who are otherwise free to answer the sick call; a priest in poor health, or one who was engaged in important work which cannot be omitted or postponed, would be excused from even shorter journeys. It would be wrong to undertake a sick call which would mean depriving Christians of Mass on a Sunday, or on several consecutive week-days. A priest who is busy administering baptisms or making urgent marriage inquiries would likewise be under no obligation to leave such work to go on a sick call. In general, commonsense and sound judgement will be the guide. If a priest is alone in the presbytery, and to leave the house would expose the parish (a poor one) to theft; or if his presence is required to supervise building operations which are urgently needed for the good of the Church, then he may justly consider himself excused from undertaking a sick call.

It is clear therefore that, at least in Africa, there will be many occasions when a priest is obliged in conscience not to go on a sick call.

It goes without saying that any priest will be anxious to undertake this important ministry, even at great inconvenience, if he can do so without detriment to the common good.[1]

Ministering to Dying Non-Catholics

If a dying non-Catholic sends for the priest, there should be no hesitation about anointing and absolving if the sick person is unconscious when the priest arrives. Any bystanders could be informed that the person concerned has asked for the priest; this would avoid giving the impression that the priest thinks one religion is as good as another.

If the sick person is conscious, he may be asked if he wishes to become a Catholic; if he says he does, he should be briefly instructed in the essential truths of Christianity so that he can make an act of faith; these essential truths may be reduced to the existence of God as rewarder, the blessed Trinity, the incarnation and redemption, and the effects of baptism; more instruction may be imparted if this can be done easily, but for the rest implicit faith in the Church and her teaching is sufficient. This constitutes a probable, therefore a usable, opinion. It applies even to those who belong to a communion that formally denies any or all of the three sacraments (baptism, penance and eucharist). It is clear that good faith must not be disturbed at such a time. The sick man should be helped to express sorrow for sin and a desire for the sacraments, which he can then receive unconditionally.

In the case of a dying non-Catholic who is unconscious, and who has shown no leaning towards the Church, the priest can only give conditional absolution, and this will often have to be given secretly to avoid scandal. Always, when absolutely everything else fails, teach the dying the act of perfect contrition.

If a dying non-Catholic has asked for the priest, but says that he does not wish to become a Catholic, the priest should try to get him to accept the essential truths; if he says that he is willing to do all that Christ asks in order to reach the heaven which is promised to those who believe, the priest may interpret this as an implicit request for absolu-

---

[1] See BISHOP DE REEPER, *The Sacraments on the Missions*, p. 434, for details of the Congo bishop's rules, together with his own additions and comments.

tion. The sick man has the right intention, and after helping him to make acts of faith, hope, charity and contrition, the priest may, secretly, give conditional absolution.[1]

Baptism of course is the essential sacrament, and the priest must do everything possible to ensure that every dying person with whom he comes in contact is baptized. It may be however that baptism cannot be conferred without doing harm to the general good of the Church; in such cases the individual must be left to the mercy of God. When conditional baptism has been conferred on an unconscious person, it must be repeated, again conditionally, if he recovers, and wishes to become a Catholic. Dying babies and children who have not reached the use of reason should be baptized, secretly if necessary, but if the common good of the Church is imperilled, leave them to the un-covenanted mercy of God.

Hospital Work

Visiting hospitals can be a trying task, but it is one of the most fruitful of the priestly ministry. Visits should be short and frequent, and where possible a kind word should be addressed to every patient in the ward. It is important too to be on good terms with the staff, for the priests and lay apostles will often need their goodwill. When dealing with the nursing staff, care should be taken not to arouse jealousy by spending too much time with the younger members.

The priest should try to ensure that all who are to undergo an operation first receive the sacraments of penance and holy eucharist; the day before the operation would usually be the best for this purpose. Where the operation to be performed is in opposition to God's law, the priest may leave both patient and medical staff in whatever good faith they may have, if he is *sure* that he can do no good by revealing the truth and provided his silence will not injure the common good. Otherwise he must state the truth very plainly.

Hospital chaplains need to be well versed in medical ethics, and particularly in the principles governing the complicated situations which can arise in connection with childbirth. While knowing the

[1] We have drawn, here in particular, on Mgr L. L. McREAVY, 'Ministering to non-Catholics', in *The Clergy Review*, February 1955.

Church's teaching, however, the chaplain should also understand the meaning of discretion, and realize that there are occasions when it is better to keep silent than to speak.

Tubercular Patients

There is such a thing as the psychology of the tubercular patient. He is liable to depression because, although his mind is clear, he has nothing to do and his cure can take a very long time. Moreover the toxic effect of the bacillus reacts on the nervous system and makes him excitable. It happens too that an exaggerated sensibility makes chastity difficult. The priest concerned should know all these factors and do what he can to counteract them. His first step should be to boost the patient's morale in general and then to exhort him to receive the sacraments often and so get courage from God.

There is sometimes more difficulty than usual with regard to giving the anointing and viaticum to these patients: even devout Catholic staff who in a general hospital would certainly call the priest may fail to do so in a sanatorium in their anxiety to avoid depressing the patient.

The Deaf

Deafness is sometimes considered a worse affliction than blindness, and certainly it cuts the Christian off more completely from the community. The deaf never hear a sermon, and they may have received no instruction in childhood; they can find employment only with great difficulty, and are unable to take part in social life. They have therefore a special right to considerate attention.

Modern methods have achieved remarkable success in enabling the deaf to communicate both with each other and with normal people, and it is desirable that institutes for the deaf be established in Africa when possible. If the government is unable to act, the Church might herself take the initiative. Deaf children should be admitted as soon as possible to special schools, which are probably best run by religious.

One priest estimated that in his parish two-thirds of the deaf Christians no longer practised their religion, largely no doubt because they could not achieve a sense of belonging to the parish community. It is evident that something must be done for these lonely and unfortunate people. Perhaps meetings could be held every month in a special hall, with confessions, and a sermon in sign language. There would be Mass too, or at least Benediction, followed by some kind of social entertainment with refreshments. Anything which will draw the deaf out of their isolation and provide them with a measure of social life should be attempted as a work of Christian charity, and priests and Sisters who are specially interested should be encouraged to learn the sign language.

The Mentally Sick

The priest's ministry to the mentally sick must take into account the results of modern research. Sound psychiatry and religion are complementary, and the priest and the mental specialist should seek to work together. There are many cases where the ministry of the priest can alleviate the condition of people suffering from guilt neuroses. Each patient will of course need individual study and guidance by the priest, and it is certainly not every priest who is fitted for this exacting ministry. The great object of the chaplain to a mental hospital is the same as that of any priest: to spread about him the kindness of Christ in every way that suggests itself to him, and to draw souls to Christ.

Migrant Catholics

Wandering Christians, whether they are seasonal workers or more or less permanent immigrants, are everywhere a problem. Very often they are social misfits, and they fall away from the Church in large numbers.

In Africa, where opportunities for employment are so scarce, men move about a great deal, and many towns consist principally of rootless workers, who have no sense of community and whose instability and frustration are sometimes a menace to social peace and public order. The priest's task in such conditions must be to minister to the individual Catholic and seek to bring him fully into the life of the Church, and at the same time to work for social justice at the level of the community.

One difficulty is that of language. Even educated people often have misconceptions about confession, and fear to approach the sacrament because they do not know the formulae for the various prayers in the local language. The priest should take pains to assure them that they can say their prayers in any language they like, and that, even in confessing their sins, all that God asks is that they do their best to make themselves clear. Reassurance on this simple matter, and instruction on the essentially interior nature of religion, can do something to keep migrant Catholics in the Church. A sheet or handbook in several languages would be useful for confessors in town parishes.

Those with experience in this work tell us that that the first thing the priest has to do is to find out new Catholics in his parish; an occasional announcement from the pulpit inviting all newcomers to come to the presbytery to make themselves known would be useful, but the priest should also invite older parishioners to introduce those who do not understand what is being said. A notice to the same effect could be posted at the back of the church, in different languages. The priest needs especially to know the address of new parishioners so that he or a lay apostle can visit them. Regular reunions for newcomers might also be arranged.

Census work is difficult but essential, and lay apostles should be invited to undertake it. When visiting the house of a newcomer for the first time, the priest might bring with him as interpreter either the catechist or a compatriot of the new parishioner; if there is a lay apostle of the newcomer's tribe, he should be asked to look after him.

The Urban Apostolate

African towns are usually made up of a great number of people with very different backgrounds. In one town there will be Africans from many tribes, Indians of different religions, Catholic Goans, Europeans, Arabs; in another Lebanese, Syrians and Greeks, and probably many others. In the individual parish, as in the town as a whole, each of these groups tends to live its own life apart from the rest, and there will usually also be a large number of people who belong to none of the different groupings. Any sense of the parish as a community is difficult to achieve.

The young present a particularly acute problem in town parishes; they come to towns with high hopes of making a fortune, but many soon find themselves penniless and embittered, and they turn to crime and immorality almost out of necessity. What an argument this is for greater emphasis on agricultural and technical education which would keep many of these young people out of the towns and give them the social status they seek. The terrible housing conditions, the unjust rents, the debts they have incurred for their schooling and which are still unpaid, the bribes needed to find or to keep a job, the shock of meeting apparently devout Catholics who exploit them as unscrupulously as anyone else: all this adds up to a situation in which it is difficult not to lose faith in human nature, and only a strong character will still try to live a decent Christian life.

Associations for former pupils can help young people in towns, and priest teachers may be able to do good by visiting towns during the holidays and going to see their old students. The Young Christian Workers can do a great deal of good, and every attempt should be made to multiply decent social centres where the young can meet and enjoy some recreational facilities. Retreats and reunions might also be arranged for them.

At the same time, no amount of paternalism can really solve the problems of young people in towns; their difficulties must be resolved by themselves, and the best way to help them is to turn them into apostles, devoted to leading and uplifting those in a similar plight to themselves. Sometimes it will be possible to introduce communities of religious specially devoted to youth work, and these of course would be invaluable. Indeed the more specialized religious that can be persuaded to come to Africa the better. One might envisage congregations for special ethnic groups or social classes. They would be able to achieve what the secular priest or the overworked jack-of-all-trades, the missionary, could never hope to do.

It is in the towns that the future leaders of Africa live, and the Church must concentrate there the bigger proportion of her resources. Country parishes must still be staffed, but the shifting of emphasis from country to town which characterizes modern African must be reflected in the Church's organization of the apostolate.

The sudden, and indeed frightening increase in town population is one of the most remarkable features in an already sufficiently remarkable post-war Africa, and the Church must do all that she can to cope with the new situation. The complex, cosmopolitan and often well-educated townspeople are different from the friendly, unlettered folk of the countryside, and they need a different approach. The priest may have to re-fashion and adapt both his mentality and his methods when he is appointed to work in a town.

The Leakage Problem

In all countries, a high proportion of those who have been educated in Catholic schools lapse from the faith later on. Much has been written on the causes of the leakage, as this phenomenon is called. The kernel of the problem is certainly to be sought in environment. A careless home, a bad local spirit, bad companions at work or recreation: one or several of these factors will nearly always be found behind every lapsed Catholic. The harm done in offices and factories is notorious; men catch their manners from their neighbours, and a man needs to have an outstanding character if he is not to sink to the level of the lowest common denominator. These work places provide the lay apostle with a vital field for his zeal.

Christians seldom lose the faith. They leave the Church because they cease to observe the Christian moral code, especially that portion of it which concerns sex and marriage. When an African leaves school, he is usually not yet fully grown and he knows little of the faith. If his parents leave him to his own devices, and if he is not drawn into some youth movement where he can find an outlet for his energy and acquire the apostolic spirit, the chances of his persevering in the faith are not good. An enlightened approach to religious teaching in school can help him to relate religion and life later on, and no effort must be spared to make the teaching of religion the transmission of an urgent, personal message; but he still needs special care when he has left school.

We have already spoken of the duties of parents, and we repeat here that a persevering effort is needed to bring parents to a realization of their responsibility for their children; it is they above all who can stem the leakage. Unwearying emphasis, during the last year at school especially, on the apostolic spirit is another means of strengthening school leavers; doing instead of eternally listening may turn an indifferent Catholic into a fervent apostle. Instruction on marriage could start in Standard III; positive instruction, stressing not sex but the sacrament and the beauty of true love.

Some of those who lapse in youth make a good marriage and return to the Church after the turmoil of adolescence. Others remain faithful in youth, but fall away after a mixed marriage, or after forming an irregular union of some kind.

With all these people, the only effective means of recovery are firstly a visiting clergy, and secondly an active lay apostolate. Nearly always the fallen-away Catholic will welcome the visiting priest or lay apostle, and will talk with him freely. It must be said again that no amount of other work can ever justify the pastoral priest in cutting out visiting; it remains as it always has been the most effective instrument for the apostolate. Everywhere a visiting priest means a church-going people, and there is no other way of making contact with the lapsed. People fall away from the Church as individuals, and they must be brought back by individuals. Lay apostle and priest must of course remember that what matters most for the success of their work, and especially of their work for the lapsed, is not what they say but what they are. Men win souls, not words, and if we shed about us the good odour of Christ we will draw people to us. People still flocked to the sermons of St. John Vianney when he had lost all his teeth, and could only produce in the pulpit a scarcely audible mumbling; he was like Christ, and that made people want to be near him. The priest or lay apostle who has acquired something of the joy and patience and selfless love of Christ needs little more to win back fallen people.

Prayers for the lapsed should be said regularly in all parishes. When the community prayer, or prayer of the faithful, is restored, as foreseen by the *Constitution on the Liturgy*, the lapsed will naturally find a place in it.

Retreats

Systematic retreat work has produced excellent results in many parts of Africa. What we have to say here applies principally to the country-side, for retreats are difficult to organize in towns, where people have less leisure. Even there however an occasional triduum may be organized, perhaps through the co-operation of employers.

The following method is that described by M. Colas, S.J., in *Revue du Clergé Africain*, September 1956.

Every year each Christian receives a card inviting him to spend three days at the central parish, or at the sub-parish if accommodation can be provided. The retreat could suitably take place during the school holidays, and the retreatants could sleep in the school dormitories. On each of the three days there are four instructions, with other common exercises like the way of the cross and the rosary, and perhaps voluntary manual work. Some degree of silence might be asked of the retreatants if this is considered suitable.

The date and place of the retreat is fixed at least a month beforehand. Prayers for its success begin at once, led by the catechists in the villages and by the teachers in the schools. As far as possible separate retreats should be given for the different classes of the faithful: married men, married women, young men and young women. The invitation cards go out at least a fortnight before the retreat is due to begin, and they are best delivered personally, by a catechist or other lay apostle rather than by children. No one is to be left out, and the card has the Christian's name written on it. This is particularly appreciated in rural Africa, where people seldom receive personal invitations.

The timetable and general atmosphere of a parish retreat should be imaginatively adapted to the needs of lay people. A retreat is meant to help them to live a more Christian life in the world, and any attempt to turn them into monks or nuns for three days is out of place. Some periods of silence might be suggested for those who would know how to use them, but in many cases people would get more profit from talking with each other about their problems than from walking round waiting for the next thing to happen. Discussion groups might replace the long meditations of a retreat for religious. A certain amount of formal prayer however must be included in any timetable. Books and papers should be provided for private reading, and many would be glad of an opportunity to do some voluntary manual work. The public services should give plenty of scope for communal hymn-singing.

Many have increased in fervour as a result of these retreats, for they enable some instruction to be given in depth. They also provide the priest with an opportunity of discussing matters of common interest with the catechists and other leading Christians; and the priest who looks after a particular village might meet all the Christians from that village in a group, to talk about the religious situation and any practical matter, such as buildings that need erecting or repairing.

A particularly valuable form of retreat is that for educated people; most of these people are in towns, but it might be worth while to organize such retreats in the countryside also. Educated people feel complimented when they receive special attention in a private retreat, and they often develop a new enthusiasm for the faith as a result. Each retreatant should have a private interview with the director of the retreat, and one could arrange to keep in touch with them afterwards. Recruiting for retreats of this kind should be done by friends and lay apostles.

Apart from parish retreats, others may be given for special groups at deanery or diocesan level. In many dioceses, an annual retreat for catechists and leading lay apostles is obligatory, and an occasional, optional, deanery retreat for teachers might be envisaged.

Missions

Every parish is obliged to have a mission at least once every ten years,[1] and in some places synodal regulations require one every five years.

A mission is a valuable way of increasing the fervour of good Christians, of reclaiming the careless, and of attracting those outside the Church; in more than one place, a mission has been the starting-point for a movement of mass conversion.

Visiting priests are best for missions, but if these are not available the parish clergy might conduct a mission themselves. The central parish will always have the biggest attendance, but there may be even more need for a mission in the sub-parishes and remote villages. It should be possible for people to stay in their own homes during the mission.

Adequate preparation is essential for a good mission, and a useful system is to fix the date of the different missions in the parish at the first council of the year, and inform the people several months in advance.

[1] Can. 1349, §1.

Intensive preparation has the psychological value of making people look forward to an important event. Prayers could be asked for and invitations sent out in good time, with a prayer for the success of the mission printed on the back of the card. Catechists and lay apostles should visit the homes of careless Christians to tell them of the mission, and non-Christians might also be visited for this purpose.

A mission normally lasts at least three full days, closing if possible on a Sunday or feast day. The last day includes a renewal of baptismal vows, and perhaps a special consecration to our Lady, and all receive a card, containing some elementary prayers, as a souvenir of the mission. Large temporary structures could be erected to accommodate the crowds. The stations of the cross are best performed in the open air, and the people can put up and adorn large crosses fifty yards or so apart. Before each station the priest might improvise prayers and exhortations adapted to his audience. High Mass is the natural form of the closing ceremony; it should be as solemn as possible, and the church should be lavishly decorated. In some places, there is a closing procession which halts near a bonfire, into which all superstitious objects are thrown; all carry lighted candles and make an enthusiastic profession of faith as the fire (and the kerosene) does its work.

20 The Apostolate of the Laity

WE CONSIDERED the African lay apostolate in general in Chapter 2, and in Chapters 7 and 8 we said something of the integration of the apostolate of the laity into the parish, and of relations between the clergy and lay apostles. In this chapter we speak in more detail of the nature and organization of the lay apostolate, and especially of the principal lay apostle, the catechist.

One Apostolate Only

There is only one apostolate, the apostolate of the Church; no matter how many forms this apostolate takes, it remains the one apostolate of the Church.

This one apostolate cannot be understood unless the nature of the Church is understood. The Church has two aspects: it is a hierarchic institution and it is the community of the baptized, the People of God. These two aspects can never be separated. Some make too much of one, some too much of the other. Exclusive insistence on the first spells a priesthood without faithful; exclusive insistence on the second spells a people without priests. Either error falsifies the apostolate of the Church.

What is this one apostolate which constitutes the mission, the mandate, the work of the Church? To continue the mission, the work, the mandate of the first apostle of the Church, Christ himself, Christ who was the first sent, *missus a Patre*. His apostolate was three-fold: world evangelization, making the Church holy, establishing the kingdom of God in every dimension of life, (private, social or institutional).

It is the obligation of the whole Church to continue this apostolate of Christ. It is not just for pope, bishop and priest. For the laity, if the nature of the Church be clearly understood, are the Church, make the Church. The apostolate is given to the Church, not only as an

215

institution, but also as Christ's Mystical Body and the community of the faithful; the layman's apostolate is co-extensive (even in the temporal order) with the mission of the Church herself, saving only those functions, the power of holy orders and the power of jurisdiction, that are reserved to priesthood and episcopate.

One same calling, then, unites us all under the sole master of the apostolate, Christ. There is a sense, therefore, in which a separate lay apostolate is a misnomer. The theology of the apostolate is as simple as that. It postulates, therefore, not only a theology of the Church but a theology of the laity too.

This Theology not Always Understood

Many priests in Africa as elsewhere are not fully convinced of the need for the lay apostolate; others are, but they have, understandably, been discouraged by failure. It seems generally agreed that the chief difficulty has been that the theology of the apostolate of the laity has not been grasped. Here, we suggest, are the grounds of this misunderstanding: the true nature of the Church and therefore the nature of the Church's mission in the world has not been seized; neither has the role of the apostolate in the Church, nor the position of the laity in the Church, nor the different forms that this mission of the Church and of her members can take. So first it must be accepted that the Church is not only an institution but is also the community of the faithful. Second, that though the Church's primary role is the salvation of souls and finally God's glory, this is not its only role; its secondary and indirect role is to transform the temporal order into a suitable milieu for the salvation of souls and finally God's glory; this is principally the layman's work. Third, the position of the laity in the Church as that of God's People, a People that shares in Christ's priesthood, is not negative, to be described merely as that of neither clergy nor religious; their position is positive and demands an active apostolate.

As for the different forms which the apostolate of the Church and the laity can take, we have to understand what is the direct apostolate, the indirect apostolate (as some call it) and the apostolate of example. All three are real and active apostolates, though the third is an interior force. The indirect apostolate, *consecratio mundi*, is the purifying and redeeming of the world; it will entail forming about us a climate suitable to the growth of God's kingdom; social action (education, charitable works and the like) is one way of doing this. We define therefore the apostolate of the laity as the collaboration of all Catholics as a body with the clergy in the hierarchical activity to defend and extend the kingdom of Christ. They have an obligation to carry out this apostolate, it is not just a counsel. Their obligation is five-fold: from the precept of the Church, from the duty of charity towards God, from the duty of charity towards their neighbour, from the mandate given to them by baptism, and also from that given them by confirmation.[1]

Organization

The Church's mission is spiritual, and the apostolate has nothing to do with politics. It may sometimes be considered useful, though perhaps not often, to form Catholic associations with political, economic and social aims; but these have nothing to do with the lay apostolate.

As the aim of the lay apostle is spiritual, his methods must be spiritual also. He has only one weapon in his armoury, the charity of Christ, and any suggestion of force is quite out of place. It would be quite wrong to regard lay apostles as parish policemen, who enforce the observance of the commandments of God and of the Church in accordance with some penal code. All adult Christians should be members of the general apostolate, the local apostolic organization (called by some—though we may doubt the wisdom of the name— Catholic Action). This should be insisted on, so that people may realize that the apostolate is an essential activity of the Christian life, and a normal way of advancing in holiness. An invitation to take part in it is not to be regarded as a reward for leading a good life, and Christians who for some reason are unable to receive the sacraments should still belong to it. Even catechumens may be admitted if they are really committed to the Christian ideal.

[1] The doctrinal teaching on the lay apostolate is contained in Chapter II of the Constitution De Ecclesia. The Constitution on the Lay Apostolate, when promulgated, will be essential reading on this subject.

The majority of parishes in Africa at present are rural parishes, and each village should have its group of apostles, usually between ten and twenty-five in number. If there are not enough Christians in a single village to form a group, several villages may combine, or the out-station itself may serve as the centre for the local apostolate.

The members should meet once a week in the house of one of the Christians. The first and most important item on the agenda of any apostolate meeting must deal with the apostolate among non-Christians and in society at large; then might come various topics connected with the spiritual life of the local Christians. Stress should be laid on the spiritual progress of the apostles themselves, and there should be a spiritual talk at each meeting.

The Christians grouped in the apostolate choose their own leader; their choice is subject to the approval of the parish priest, but he should accept the people's choice as long as the person chosen is not living a scandalous life. The leaders might be elected for a period of two years. A common difficulty is that too many old people are elected; there is a great need for young and dynamic leaders, and priests should make an effort to have such people put forward for election. A married man with some standing in the district would be the best choice; catechists are ineligible, and chiefs and village headmen should be considered unsuitable too.

The leaders of the local apostolate groups might combine to form the parish lay apostolate council, which meets every month under the chairmanship of the parish priest. The meeting begins and ends with a prayer, and the leaders report on the local meetings held during the month. The priest answers any questions, and seeks to animate the leaders with apostolic zeal; if possible, he should see each of the leaders individually after the meeting. In big parishes it may be better to hold the meetings of the local leaders in the outstations, but there should be general meetings of all the leaders at least a few times a year at the parish church itself.

It is hardly necessary to say that leaders should receive no remuneration of any kind, nor should they wear any special insignia.

The apostolate leaders and the members of the parish council[1] have different fields of responsibility, but there should be friendship and close

---

[1] See above, chapter 7.

collaboration between them. The priest is always an adviser and not in charge.

Sodalities and Associations

Although all Christians should belong to the general lay apostolate, there is indeed room for specialized sodalities and associations. The general local group however should remain the backbone of the parish apostolate, and other organizations should spring from it and be ancillary to it. Evidently all members of any specialized groups must also belong to the general lay apostolate group.

Special organizations may be concerned with the direct apostolate or with the indirect apostolate; in general, it may not be wise to combine the two forms of the apostolate in the same organization. The Legion of Mary has proved itself in Africa, as all over the world, an excellent form of apostolate, and each parish should have at least one praesidium. The local praesidia, it is right to add, should be governed exactly by the Legion handbook, since it is unfair to borrow the name of the Legion of Mary for organizations which do not observe its rules. Auxiliary members of the Legion are to be welcomed, but the praesidia should be formed of truly active members, who do Legion work week by week. The Xaverian movement is a valuable African youth organization, and the Third Order of St. Francis is a useful form of the apostolate of example; each parish might have a branch of each of these also.

The Code of Canon Law,[1] reinforced by the Decree of Catechetical Instruction of 12 January 1935, requires the establishment of the Confraternity of Christian Doctrine in every parish. Members are usually required to give at least two religious instructions every week, either to Christians or to non-Christians, and it is often suggested that they recite three *Hail Marys* every day for the intentions of those whom they instruct. The parish priest is the Director of the Confraternity, and he should hold a monthly meeting of the members.

[1] Can. 711.

Catechists[1]

The lay apostle *par excellence* is the catechist. Pope John XXIII spoke in these terms of catechists in his encyclical, *Princeps Pastorum*: 'They have always been the right arm of the workers of the Lord, and they have participated in and alleviated their work to the extent that our predecessors were able to consider their recruitment and careful training among the most important matters for the diffusion of the Gospel. . . . Every effort to increase the number of these most valiant aids to the hierarchy and to make their training more adequate, every sacrifice made by catechists to carry out their task in a more apt and perfect manner, is an immediate and efficacious contribution towards the establishment and progress of new Christian communities.'

The nature of his work requires that the catechist be chosen from among the very best Christians. He should be a man wholly committed to Christ, and at the same time a real leader of men, capable of winning others to Christ. Both qualities are needed: personal piety alone cannot make a man a good catechist. Since he has to be a person who will command respect, the catechist should not be too young, and nearly always it will be preferable that he be married. On the other hand, if he is proposing to train as a full-time catechist, he should not be beyond the age of about thirty-five; an older man will be set in his ways, and it will not be easy for him to enter upon a new way of life in which he will be required to abandon all worldly ambition. Parish priests should select their catechist candidates a year before they will be expected to begin their training; this will enable the parish priest to form a good estimate of the candidate's calibre, both natural and supernatural, before he is finally accepted for training.

The catechist's training should of course fit him to explain the mysteries of the faith clearly and simply, and yet with depth, according to the principles we have expounded earlier on catechesis. In recent years, excellent catechetical centres have been opened, where the future catechist receives a thorough training in Scripture and in the liturgy, as well as in Catholic doctrine. There are now centres in Tanzania, Nigeria, Lumku, South Africa, and in a few other places. The multi-

[1] See B. VULKENS, W.F., 'Training of Catechists', in *Katigondo. Presenting the Christian Message to Africa*, op. cit.

plication of such centres must be regarded as one of the African Church's most urgent tasks. It is not surprising that all our lay congresses discuss this need of fully trained catechists. The Holy See warmly commends the idea and gives help towards capital expenditure. The main financial worry is not building but maintenance. It is to be hoped that following the principle of collegiality, the national episcopal conferences of the Old Churches will help us here. Many African dioceses still have some older catechists who began their work in circumstances different from those which now prevail. They have done fine work in the past, and are still most valuable; they need regular training, however, and where at all possible they should be given a three-day course every month at the parish church; one day's instruction each month should be regarded as the absolute minimum. In large towns, catechists could be part-time and there should be women catechists as well as men.

Members of the Confraternity of Christian Doctrine are of course voluntary catechists, and they might be used especially for the teaching of first-year catechumens and of primary school children. Catholic children who do not go to school must not be overlooked. These catechists should make a retreat every year, and this would naturally be combined with a refresher course.

The priest's most important collaborators are those catechists who have followed a full two-year course in a special institute. They have the right to expect all the help and encouragement which we can give them; nothing could be more discouraging for them, and nothing more damaging to the success of their work, than a feeling that they were being neglected by the clergy. They are educated men, and priests should repose full confidence in them, and talk openly with them of parish problems. There should be regular meetings between these catechists and all the priests of the parish, and no effort should be spared to help them to develop that power of leadership which is so necessary for their work in modern Africa. Their spiritual life will naturally be the object of the priest's special solicitude, although it may be wise for them to choose as spiritual director a priest who is not immediately involved in their work.

Catechists should be paid a salary comparable to that which they could earn in secular employment, and it might be possible to arrange for them to receive free medical attention in a Catholic hospital. The expense will be crushing, but worth it; less important works must be abandoned or curtailed to meet the costs of this first priority after the clergy themselves.

Refresher courses and extension programmes are essential for the catechist if he is to remain zealous and efficient, and these should be provided at the diocesan or inter-diocesan catechetical centre.

Lay Missionaries

More and more lay missionaries are coming to Africa from Europe and America, as teachers, secretaries and craftsmen of all kinds, and they deserve a special mention here.

Lay apostles of this kind will usually have received a fairly thorough briefing before leaving home, and they will not expect their life in Africa to be an extended tropical holiday; nevertheless, they may be in for some unpleasant surprises, and it is a good plan to appoint a priest who will be specially responsible for them. One of his first tasks will be to keep alive in them the sense of vocation which may easily be loss when their work is only indirectly apostolic. They could be reminded that their first duty is spiritual: to be present as witnesses of Christianity, a layman's Christianity, fully lived. The priest should give them a spiritual conference from time to time, and should be regularly accessible to them. Loneliness and boredom may be among their greatest trials, and an attempt should be made to enliven their social life as far as possible.

Lay missionaries usually come out for the first time on a three-year contract, and this is a wise arrangement. The contract should be drawn up in a business-like fashion, and the lay missionaries should not be asked to do work for which they have not been engaged. It is very important to tell them the full truth about their new country and work before they come. Some bishops, priests and Sisters overlook this. 'Paint me as I am', said Cromwell, 'warts and all.'

Too many today write as though the dead hand of episcopacy or clergy were the chief reason for the comparative failure of the apostolate of the laity. The truth is, as the diocesan clergy all know, that it is very hard to find lay apostles. A long-term policy is required: apostolic formation begins in Standard I: all Christian education necessarily includes formation for the apostolate.

21 The Church and Non-Catholics

WE HAVE already noted[1] that the Church is everywhere, by her nature, in a state of mission, and that Canon Law expressly instructs Ordinaries to regard all who live in the territories entrusted to them as 'commended to them in the Lord'. The priest's business in our territories is not solely, indeed not even principally, with Catholics; all those outside are his concern, for Christ died for all men, and the priest is the continued presence of Christ on earth.

Priests in Africa realize well enough their duties to non-Christians. It was to preach to them that the missionaries came to the continent in the first place, and, although in some places the shortage of priests means that the pastor's time is almost wholly taken up with looking after either catechumens or those who are already baptized, in general there is plenty of contact with those Africans who still practise the traditional animism. This is of course very important. The trend towards organized religion among all Africans is unmistakable; more and more young people are turning their backs on the traditional forms of worship and belief, and it seems likely that in one or two generations there will be very few professing pagans left. During the crucial years ahead, therefore, great efforts are needed to carry the Gospel to those Africans who are still uncommitted; if they do not become Catholics, they will almost certainly become either Protestants or Moslems.

What is not so clearly, nor so widely, recognized is that the priest's apostolic activity must also embrace those other men and women who are neither Catholics nor non-Christians: it is these whom we wish especially to consider. The existence of the Secretariat for Christian Unity on the one hand, and the Secretariat for Non-Christian Religion on the other, makes it evident that the Church is very concerned to make contact with the members of all other religions; the task of the priest in the field is to make this a contact a reality at parish level.

[1] Chapter 6.

Convert Work

There are a few who say that priests should not make individual converts from the Protestant denominations at the present time, since this damages the relations between the Churches, and jeopardizes the prospects of corporate reunion. It is not possible to subscribe to this view. There may perhaps be times and places where, by way of exception, the long-term interests of the Church demand this exceptional discretion on the part of priests in their approach to non-Catholics, and we may not always wish to disturb the good faith of convinced Protestants; nevertheless, every man who applies has the right to be accepted as a candidate for admission to the Mystical Body. A priest can never, in normal circumstances, refuse to accept for instruction in the faith anyone who seeks it, and it is not easy to envisage circumstances in which it will not be the priest's duty to take positive steps to encourage individual people to seek such instruction. Our mission is to preach Christ, and to make sure that all men are aware of the Catholic Church and its claims. If we make it a first principle not to upset anyone's beliefs, we empty the missionary life of its meaning.

There must indeed be complete respect for individual consciences. Priests are sometimes accused of seeking to swell their congregations by an unscrupulous proselytism that is interested only in counting heads and takes no account of real, interior conversion. Such accusations can rarely be well founded, but it may be well to state that anything like the party spirit is to be eschewed in priestly work; we are priests of Jesus Christ, and we seek only to win souls for him, and to win them by his methods.

When all this has been said, however, and every exception allowed for, we must add that priests *are* interested in making converts, and in seeking them. The Catholic Church is the natural home of every man; how can we not encourage people to seek admittance to their Father's house?

Ecumenism

The priest's interest in separated Christians should not be confined to those who show some desire to enter the Church; he should also be concerned to make contact with convinced and practising Protestants. This is what we mean by the ecumenical movement. It is in no sense a proselytizing movement, but an attempt to achieve greater sympathy and understanding between all Christians. The ultimate aim of the ecumenical movement is of course reunion, and no part of the Church would benefit more from reunion than the new Christian communities, for the scandal of division among them presents the weak with a special excuse for turning away from Christianity. Realism however compels us to recognize that the achievement of this ultimate aim is not in sight, and for the moment our task is simply to draw as near as we can to our separated brethren in mutual understanding and true charity. Many believe that the new good things that have come to us, the liturgical, biblical and catechetical revival, and the (in both senses) ecumenical Council have been brought about by the Holy Spirit principally to prepare the way for reunion, however distant that prospect may be. No one wants to see a continuance of the situation, unhappily not uncommon today, where religious differences are made the basis of social and political division. Most of us work at the local level, and we can do a great deal to help the ecumenical movement, for it is precisely at the local level that ignorance and suspicion are strongest.

We add a further consideration before passing on to some practical recommendations. The Church's perspective is enlarged by historical events; she does not see the conquest of souls, the making of converts, as her exclusive aim, but recognizes that, as the servant Church and the custodian of truth, she has also obligations of witness and service to the whole non-Catholic and non-Christian world. Saving souls is not the Church's only function; she must also seek to be the leaven of society, creating social conditions which sin less flagrantly against divine justice, and helping to improve material conditions simply because man's dignity demands that he live in decent circumstances.[1] The developing countries in particular have many purely human and social problems that the Church can help to solve, and she

[1] Cf. above, p. 37, remarks on religious plurality.[1]

must offer her help without any hidden strings: she wishes to help and to serve all mankind, and attaches no confessional conditions to that help. In this way, Christian principles can be integrated into national life. In many countries, different religions are firmly established; in such plural societies, national unity demands an ecumenical spirit.

It is easy to be vague about ecumenism, and many do feel confused by the term and the movement. We venture therefore to tabulate the steps to be taken at parish level, basing our remarks mainly on Pope Paul's encyclical *Ecclesiam suam*, and the second chapter of the Decree On Ecumenism (the whole of this decree[1] is of course essential reading on this subject).

First, a renewal in ourselves, as well as in our separated friends. This will mean, in the words of Pope Paul, 'a stronger determination to preserve the characteristic features which Christ has impressed on the Church', thus leading her back to her perfect form. A species of reform, therefore, in the Church and in ourselves. Next, we must pray for each other in public and in private; we could, as the *Constitution* suggests, pray for unity in each other's company. Third, we must make friends with each other. Fourth, in dialogue, we must never whittle down the truth yet must speak with charity, with precision, meekness, trust and prudence: a dialogue of this kind will seize the elements of truth in the beliefs of others.

We must now say a little more about these two last points, friendliness and the conditions of the dialogue. Our duty is to show friendliness to those who do not share our faith. Parish priests should go out of their way to show respect and deference to other religious leaders in their parish (here we include Moslems and Indians as well as Protestants). They should call on them from time to time, invite them to the priests' house, and seize every opportunity of co-operating with them in public and social work. The priest may meet with an occasional rebuff, but he must not be deterred; Christ too was rejected, and the disciple is not above his Lord.

Friendliness and affability is a beginning. When cordial relations have been established, we should try to put right those unnecessary mis-understandings which have for so long poisoned relations between Catholics and Protestants, and indeed between Moslems and Christians.

---

[1] English translation, C.T.S. London, 1965.

As regards Protestants, we should be sure that our theology is sound, and recognize that as baptized people they really are Christians. This is the basis of the ecumenical movement, and we should make the most of it; baptism truly does bind us all together in Christ, and our people are preaching false doctrine, as well as showing a lack of charity, if they say that only Catholics are Christians. There is in truth much prejudice and lack of knowledge on our side, and we must take pains to get to know what other Christians really believe. Many non-Catholic denominations have something to teach us, and we should recognize this, while not pretending that there are not profound divergences between them and ourselves, nor dissimulating the Catholic Church's claim to be the one, true Church of God.

We must of course be prepared for prejudice on the part of Orthodox and Protestants too, and we may find ourselves the object of attack. Charity must dictate our behaviour here, for meekness, patience and respect for others are the weapons that Christ has put into our hands to win souls. Skill in controversy is a dangerous gift for Christ's purposes, for we are only widening the gulf between ourselves and our separated brethren when we humiliate them by clever rejoinders; we must have larger aims in view than winning a debate. If we find our beliefs misrepresented, it will very seldom be through bad will, and we only make things worse by becoming annoyed.

Personal contacts with Protestant layfolk are best made by their Catholic friends and by lay apostles; the priest may help discreetly, perhaps by arranging study circles, but on the whole he should leave this apostolate to the laity. The priest's special contribution to the ecumenical movement should consist, in addition to cultivating friendly relations with other religious leaders, in sponsoring public demonstrations of solidarity in joint meetings with non-Catholics. Public morality is a subject on which all Christians, and indeed all good people of any belief, can work together, and we should seek to arrive at a common policy on educational, medical and social work of all kinds, so that all Christians can approach the Government through a single spokesman.

The Abbot of Downside[1] has stated that the ecumenical dialogue

---

[1] *The Tablet*, 23 May 1964, pp. 573-4, reviewing *Theology and the University*, a symposium edited by John Coulson, London, 1964.

should find its place above all in universities, since the whole problem of reunion is so largely a matter of education and understanding. Controversy is seldom useful, and polemics never, but we should seek to meet our separated brethren on a truly Christian and human level. One might envisage in Africa the setting up of Catholic institutes alongside the theological colleges or departments of other denominations, and even a special theological school in universities, staffed by qualified lecturers from the various theological colleges.

Moslems

As regards Moslems, we should realize that very many of them are sincere people, convinced of the truth of their religion. Certainly we should not pay honour to Mohammed, but we should respect good Moslems, and never discredit either them or their religion in our conversations with our own people. Charity remains always our first duty, and we can never be in a position to pass judgement on any man's condition in the eyes of God. In our conversations with Moslems, we will naturally take as a starting-point the truths we hold in common. It might be useful to illustrate what we have to say by referring to history; this fosters the critical spirit, and makes objective explanations possible. We should make full use of the treasures of the Old Testament, which Moslems honour but seldom know, and we could dwell particularly on the Messianic prophecies. Any direct comparisons between Islam and Christianity should be avoided.

In cases where truly friendly relations have been established with African Moslems and genuine discussion is possible, we should try to show the reasonableness of Catholic belief against an African background. It is obviously important to show that we are not agents of Europeanism, and that there is no opposition between Christianity and the traditional culture of Africa. Christian missionaries come to Africa simply to enlighten and to serve, bringing knowledge and skill to the people so that they can develop their own culture. We might talk about Christianity and civilization, for Moslems know that their religion has failed them here. We may try slowly to awaken in them a desire for more and higher truth, but we should proceed gradually, step by step, if we judge it suitable to embark on objective explanations of Christian doctrine. Many things in the faith will provoke a natural response in an African Moslem, and they will quickly understand the meaning of the Mystical Body and its connection with African ideas on the solidarity of family and clan. Moslems have a certain devotion to our Lady, and we should make full use of it. The name Fatima has special associations for them, and if every diocese had a parish church dedicated to our Lady of Fatima, it could become a place of pilgrimage for both Moslems and Christians. The presence of Moslems at outdoor processions and other devotions to our Lady should be welcomed. We might aim too, in conversations with individual Moslems, at seeking to make them act more out of charity, even to make acts of love and sorrow, in order to make them more responsive to God's promptings, for in this way we can draw them under the influence of grace. A combined Christian influence on Islamic culture is surely required to help Islam to become more open and to adapt itself to plural society. Dioceses that are experiencing difficulties from Moslem governments should not give up hope but should continue the approach of brotherly love, together with concern for the country's good.[1]

True respect for Islam will naturally show itself in the way we treat Moslem children in our schools. They should be allowed to observe their own religious holidays, and if they feel strongly about it they should be provided with meat that has been ritually slaughtered. There is no reason why Catholic children should not eat this too. Islamic teachers must be allowed to teach religion to Moslem children in Catholic schools, and if the Church is invited to open a school in a predominantly Moslem district, the invitation should be accepted.[2]

We have spoken of our brothers the Moslems because they are so numerous amongst us in this continent. But we have other brothers too; the Jews, sons of the Covenant before us, and the many other non-Christian religions. Pope Paul has spoken with warmth of his wish to make contact with them, especially those of the great non-Christian monotheistic religions. We too must be in touch with them, by praying for them to God, our common Father.

[1] Cf. BISHOP JOSEPH BLOMJOUS, W. F., 'Ecumenism and Conversions', in *The Ecumenist*, January–February 1964.
[2] Record of East African Interterritorial Episcopal Meeting, 1961.

22 The Presence of the Church in the World

ANY Christian philosophy must always be based on the importance and dignity of the individual human being, and in the last analysis the whole of the Church's apostolate is directed towards the salvation of individuals. The individual however cannot be saved in isolation; he lives in society, and the kind of society he lives in will largely determine whether he is more or less responsive to the call of Christ in the Church. The Church must seek therefore to influence the individual by being present to the world.

Social Presence

'The aim of social action,' said Pope John XXIII in *Mater et Magistra,* 'is to bring about social conditions which permit and favour the development of the personality of each member of the human race.'

The Church has a well-developed social doctrine, and the first step in Christian social reform is to make this doctrine known. Priests and lay apostles must first be sure that they themselves understand the Church's teaching. Students in major seminaries should have courses in Christian sociology, but this is not enough: they should also be given the opportunity of taking an active part in social work as part of their training; this might be in the local parish, or work in prisons or hospitals might be taken on as the special responsibility of the seminary. Practical experts in social action, such as members of Y.C.W. teams, could be invited to address the students from time to time, and give them instruction on such matters as the organization of a group of social workers and the training of office-bearers. In this way priests leaving the seminary will be equipped to play their part in passing on to others the Church's social teaching.

Primary school teachers probably constitute the largest body of educated people in Africa, and they have wide influence; it is therefore important that they be instructed in Christian social ethics during their years of professional training; only then can they communicate to their pupils, and to all with whom they come into contact, the principles on which alone a Christian society can be built. Study groups can do much good among adults, especially those composed of members with the same professional interests.

The aim of the priest must be to ensure that all Christians have a clear idea of the Church's teaching on those matters which are becoming more and more objects of discussion in Africa: the just wage, industrial relations, trade unions, security of labour, small ownership, the right of private property, co-operatives, credit unions, housing, agricultural methods, the need for small industries in rural areas, social amenities such as recreation centres: on all these matters the Church has stated her position. We may refer here to Chapter 14 for some remarks on the bride-price,[1] so important in any discussion of social life in Africa.

The Church must of course lend her full support to all government efforts to improve housing conditions and to encourage more enlightened agricultural methods. It is sometimes argued that the real reason for the African's reluctance to co-operate with agricultural schemes is that he has no security of tenure; the land is owned communally, and the individual has no guarantee that he will be able to profit from any improvements he makes. This may be true in some places, and occasionally the Church might be able to help by suggesting some system of private ownership. It is clear however that the Church must loyally support the laws of the country if they prescribe some other system. One wishes that governments would fix as low as possible the minimum acreage required to qualify for government facilities and grants.

People should be instructed in the absolute need of co-operatives if they are to hold their own in the economic conditions of contemporary Africa, and here is another opportunity for the Church to collaborate with national governments. Experience has shown that it is seldom wise for the Church to undertake the management of a co-operative society; the priest's role should be purely advisory, showing the people the advantages of co-operation, and if necessary explaining how to

1 Pp. 152–4.

organize a co-operative, either in collaboration with the government or on a purely private basis. On the whole, it seems preferable that co-operatives remain under private management, rather than pass under government control.

Consecrating the World

The Church is the guardian of the natural law as well as the custodian of revealed truth; it is in the former capacity especially that she seeks to influence the public life of countries with plural societies. By insisting on the natural virtues of justice and fraternal equality, she can make herself accepted as a social teacher even by those who reject her as the oracle of God; for what she says then must find an echo in the heart of every man.

The Catholic's social apostolate will best be exercised, for the most part, simply by a layman's being an excellent worker and citizen, while remaining of course an excellent Christian. The lay apostle is involved in every department of the social order—commercial, industrial, agricultural, medical and political—and his task is to christianize society through and through. He must be taught that it is a mistake for a Catholic to think that he can contract out of society and concentrate on saving his own soul. The good Christian is really concerned about the common good and anxious to play a leading part in building up a world where men can live in peace and dignity, free from poverty and disease and civil disturbance. Only the layman can build up such a world, and here again the priest's role is simply advisory; his work is the formation of apostles of the temporal order whose faith is reasonable and free, who are filled with a perceptive charity, and whom non-Catholics are glad to know and glad to work with.

What is this social apostolate but the fulfilling of the third of the three tasks that constituted the sacred mission of Christ, and constitute the mission of the Church today?—world evangelization, sanctification of the Church, establishment of the kingdom of God in every dimension of life. This is the Christian restoration of the temporal order, the forming of conditions which make it possible and easy for others to live lives that are truly human and Christian. This is the consecration of the world, the indirect apostolate, unobtrusively carried out by dedicated men who are not necessarily labelled lay apostles and perhaps do not even belong to any particular group.

Political Presence

The Church has no politics, and she is prepared to work with any political party which is not in opposition to Christian principles. Most political parties in Africa are compatible with Christianity, and Christians should be told that they are free to vote for the party which, in their judgement, is most fitted to advance the welfare of the country. At the same time, the Church has of course the right and duty to teach the Christian principles which govern the civil life of nations.

It is very important to instruct people in their political responsibilities, and in particular they should realize that they have a duty to vote. Many African governments really want to know what the people think, but the people themselves are reluctant to express opinions or to form pressure groups. It might be explained to them that pressure groups are a normal feature of a democratic society, and that they cannot expect the Government to meet their wishes unless those wishes have been clearly put forward. They must speak up for their rights, insisting, for example, on the responsibility of parents for their children's education, on the establishment of co-operative societies, and any other matter of local interest. The widespread belief among Catholics in Africa that the priest should do all the protesting is one more manifestation of that clericalism which it is so desirable to destroy. Groups such as School Committees and Parents' Associations help to educate the people in their civic duties, and also bring forward the Catholic point of view.

Some care is needed when Christians ask if they should join societies with social or political aims. In general it is very desirable that a Christian influence be brought to bear on all the activities of society, but there are associations which are so bound up with immoral or anti-Christian aims or methods that Catholics can hardly join them without practically denying their faith. In this matter, as indeed in all others, it is important that all priests follow the same policy; this policy will be plainly laid down by the bishop.

Since the Church cannot identify herself with any single political party, it is seldom advisable for priests to join a party, and they may not put themselves forward for election as members of a legislative assembly. Political activity is good and necessary for the layman, but it is essentially of this world, and the priest's interests extend beyond this world.

The Catholic Politician

Catholics should enter political life and work whole-heartedly for the worldly welfare of their country. The Catholic politician is to be free from all sectarian bias; his duty is to support the party, or the person, who will do most to promote the moral and material good of the country; he should not give his vote automatically to anyone who is a Catholic, or a Catholic sympathizer, whether he agrees with such a person's policy or not.

The Catholic politician needs training, and the parish priest should do what he can to help him acquire knowledge of political practice and organization, as well as of the Church's social teaching. There are several social institutes which provide good courses, and needless to say, the aspiring politician must be encouraged to do a great deal of reading. Any practical experience he can gain of leadership at the local level will be valuable. Priests and laity should seek to win his confidence and make him feel that they are his loyal friends; he will then be more inclined to turn to them for help and advice later on.

The Priest in the School

However poor he may be with children, the priest has a central part to play in a school; diocesan synods often require him to give several instructions a week to children in Catholic schools. His seminary training may not have equipped him to teach religion in school, and he might well wish to do some reading on the subject.[1] Where there are well-trained teachers of religion in a school, the priest's task will be mainly to supervise and encourage. But his presence should always be felt. As a sympathetic counsellor, he can do much to encourage the

---

[1] A small but useful book is Fr. KEVIN CRONIN, *Teaching the Religious Lesson*, Paternoster Publications, London.

teaching staff, and he can also give positive help in guiding the children in the choice of a career, whether in the world, or in the religious or priestly life. There is no substitute for the priest in the school.

It is of importance to provide good material conditions in Catholic schools, and to maintain high academic standards. Technical and commercial schools are important in modern Africa, and where they do not exist the Church should seek to introduce them.

In the case of schools under Church management, teachers should be both guided and protected by a written code of regulations. There should be a standard procedure for investigating complaints against a teacher, with statutes determining the disciplinary action to be taken against a teacher found guilty of a serious fault. Dismissal must evidently be regarded as a last resort.

Inferior housing is sometimes a grievance with teachers. Every effort should be made to provide them with suitable accommodation, where they can live decently with their families and work in comfort. Domestic harmony will benefit from reducing the educational disparity often found between teachers and their wives, and an attempt might be made to provide suitable courses to raise the cultural level of teachers' wives.

Headmasters and headmistresses should be appointed on the strength of their qualifications and general suitability; racial considerations should be irrelevant, as far as the local situation allows, and the posts should not be restricted to religious. The headmaster's position must be respected, and all directives to the staff, whether religious or lay, should come from him.

If a priest is in charge of a school, he should hold a meeting with all the teachers at least once a month.

The importance of religious instruction in state schools is obvious, and the priest has to be very attentive to Catholic children in such schools. Most African governments give Catholic priests the right of entry into state schools, and full advantage must be taken of this permission. It is useful to have Catholic teachers in government schools; priests should point out to them the special apostolic opportunities of their position, not only with regard to Catholic children, but also to the non-Catholic children and to their colleagues on the staff. These teachers should be well-trained in catechetics; if the day should come when Catholic schools have to be abandoned, well-qualified and apostolically-minded Catholic teachers of this kind would be invaluable in coping with the large influx of Catholic children into state schools.

Adult Education

In most African countries, there is still a great deal of illiteracy among adults, and at the same time a widespread clamour for education. Mass education is therefore a necessity, and the Church should work to provide literacy classes and other courses for adults. Religious Sisters can do good work for women, both at home and in social welfare centres. Youth clubs and associations like the Young Farmers can also be used for educational purposes. In the towns, classes can usually be given only in the evenings, but in the countryside people are often free during the day, and classes could be arranged either in the outstations or in private houses. Technical and agricultural training programmes often draw financial support from the government. Teachers could be invited to give their services for an hour or two each week, and lay apostles might also help; all this must be on a voluntary basis.

Medical Work

The Church has been specially commanded by our Lord to 'heal the sick',[1] and this essential work of charity has always engaged the attention of Christians. The Church heals the sick simply because this is a work of charity; she has no hidden motives.[2] It is part of her task of perfecting creation on every level of human existence. We may call it a by-product of the Church's essential activity of bringing men to God, and, as a by-product, it is to be left in the hands of Brothers, Sisters and laity; the priest has been ordained for another purpose, and he must be on his guard against the natural temptation of getting too deeply involved in secondary occupations, to the detriment of his primary task, which is to plant the Church.

Our witness here is to the great commandment of the law; a Catholic hospital which is inspired by any motive other than genuine love is a

[1] See above, Chapter 19, p. 199.   [2] See above, Chapter 2, p. 21.

contradiction. It will therefore be obvious that Catholic hospitals will welcome sick people of every race, religion and tribe. There must be no rivalry between state hospitals and Catholic hospitals; in her medical work, as in all her social activity, the Church seeks, not her own external glory, but the happiness and general well-being of men, and she is glad to collaborate with the state in every way possible. Governments have an obligation to make sure that their citizens are being well looked after; Catholic hospitals should therefore welcome supervision, and should even seek integration into the national medical service. It is evident too that the government has the right to inquire into how public money is being spent in Catholic hospitals, and it may also lay down minimum qualifications for the staff. The laity should be members of the hospital committee and a lay administrator for a hospital is often wise. Joint Christian councils for health services, and indeed for education and every other form of social aid are very desirable.

Mass Publicity Media

'Everyone knows,' wrote Pope Pius XII in his encyclical *Evangelii Praecones*, 'how effectively newspapers, magazines and reviews can be employed either to present truth and virtue in their proper light, and thus to impress them on men's minds, or to expose fallacies masquerading under the guise of truth. . . . We warmly commend those bishops who interest themselves in the widest possible distribution of printed works of this sort, which have been carefully edited. Though much has been done in this regard, much still remains to be done.'

The importance of mass media in forming men's minds and shaping attitudes has been underlined by the *Constitution* on the subject issued by the Second Vatican Council. The *Constitution* urges that a Christian influence be brought to bear in the field of communications, and that they be used to preach the Gospel.[1] The Church cannot ignore the fact that most people are affected far more by what they see in the cinema or on the television screen than by what they hear in the pulpit, and that the popular press is a most powerful instrument for influencing a

---

[1] Clearly seminarists training in Europe for the missions should be instructed in methods of communication; provision for this is expected at the fourth session of the Council.

literate population. Certainly it is necessary to point out any un-Christian elements in these mass media, but condemnation is obviously not enough: every effort must be made positively to influence the mass media in a Christian direction.

Newspapers and radio and television centres are usually glad to receive Catholic news, and priests should help the Catholic Press Secretariats which are being set up in Africa by sending in items of news as quickly as possible; a delay of twenty-four hours often means that another opportunity has been lost of bringing the Church into public notice.

The Catholic Press

In addition to seeking to influence the national organs of publicity, the Church also seeks to have her own vigorous publications, where the Catholic position on current affairs can be explained at length, and in which the faithful can find real instruction. Catholic journalists need all the help they can get to encourage them to persevere in their difficult work.

A principal aim of the Catholic press in Africa today must be to spread knowledge of the Church's social doctrine; the local press should be studied, so that any mistakes concerning the Church may be put right. This is best done by an article in the paper in which the mistake occurred, but if this is not possible then a Catholic paper should make the position clear. Catholic newspapers often languish for lack of support, and in many cases a concerted effort from the pulpits of the country could turn a failing publication into a flourishing and lively instrument of the apostolate; lay apostles come in here.

The publication of Catholic books and pamphlets in the vernacular becomes a matter of ever greater urgency as more and more people in Africa become literate. The main difficulty is not so much the writing and preparing of such publications as the problem of financing them; this can only be solved by ensuring the greatest possible sale for Catholic books. The Church should not be afraid to imitate the methods of the business world, in so far as these are honest, to persuade people to buy Catholic publications.

Cinema and Television

The cinema and television are two of the four important means of communication mentioned by Pope Paul VI when he set up the Pontifical Commission for the Means of Social Communication; the other two are the press and the radio.

The influence of the cinema, and now of the television screen, is enormous in developed countries, and it is probably even greater in countries where the habit of reading is not widespread. No effort should be spared to realize the potential for good which the cinema contains. So far, the Church in Africa seems to have done little with regard to the cinema except to condemn bad films, and this is surely not enough; there is needed a positive effort to found Catholic agencies to distribute good films, and to place them at the disposal of parishes for educational purposes. Of course Christians have to be protected from bad films, and associations like the Legion of Decency in America, which publishes a judgement on the moral value of individual films, should be established in every country. At the same time, cinema clubs in schools can do much good by teaching children intelligent discrimination in the use of films; the showing and discussion of films in youth clubs is another way of educating people in this important matter.

Governments and commercial undertakings use their best men for publicity work, and the Church should do the same. This is of course principally a work for lay apostles; the priest's role, as in all departments of the lay apostolate, is advisory.

Radio

The wireless is another powerful means of forming public opinion, and the way in which Moscow, Peking and Cairo spend so much of their resources in broadcasts to Africa is a lesson to the Church. There have been daily broadcasts to Africa on the Vatican Radio since November 1961; the times of these programmes, and the stations on which they can be heard, should be mentioned in the pulpit from time to time. In schools or recreation centres, the programmes could be recorde,d and played back at a suitable time.

It seems to be true that the Church as a whole makes insufficient use of information services; the Church in Africa needs alerting to the importance of the press, the wireless, cinema and television, and it should seek to be present in these mass media while they are still in a more or less formative stage.

Epilogue

WHAT does the future hold for the African Church and the Churches of the other lands of mission? When the Council fathers have packed their bags at the end of Vatican II and gone back to their dioceses, will these young churches be in any better case than before?

Excepting missionary adaptation, they will be in little better case unless they receive two things, both of which depend on collegiality: an overall plan of world evangelization and the direct co-operation in mission aid of the national episcopal conferences of the old churches with the national episcopal conferences of the young churches. Episcopal collegiality brings obligation as well as privilege; the universal college shares the burden of the universal Pastor: his chief burden is to plant the Church where it does not exist, and then to sustain it until it becomes capable of standing alone. Every bishop is consecrated for the salvation of the whole world rather than for one diocese.[1]

Neither world evangelization nor the direct co-operation of the episcopal conferences of the older countries with those of the new can succeed without the backing of the entire episcopal college. This means in effect that the necessary steps can be planned and decreed only by the Council; only a Council has the necessary authority and prestige to ensure that the plans made would become effective.

What world evangelization most needs is the sending of priests to those parts of the world where they are most needed. At present, some eighty per cent of the world is mission territory; yet only twelve per cent of the priests of the world are working there. Eighty-eight per cent of all Catholic priests are concentrated in that one-fifth of the world where the Church has long been planted. In round figures, of the 392,000 Catholic priests in the world, 359,000 are working in the older

---

[1] A point that was clearly made at the third session of the Council, and is expected to receive further emphasis when the Schema on the Missions comes up again at the fourth session.

Christian countries, while only 33,000 are working in the remaining four-fifths of the world.

The shortage of priests in Africa is having disastrous results for the Church. There are many missions, with between twenty and forty thousand Christians, staffed by three priests, if so many. Some fifteen years ago, a town in West Africa asked the local Catholic bishop to give them a priest. The bishop had no priest to give them. That town has now over a million inhabitants, all Moslem. When there is talk therefore of a shortage of priests in the older Christian countries, it is clear that the term is being used in a very relative sense.

A just apportioning of the priests of the world to those places which need them most is the first contribution which it is hoped that the General Council will make to the work of evangelizing mankind. The second contribution must be material aid. Hitherto, the material needs of the Church in countries of mission were met exclusively by the missionary congregations and by the Congregation for the Propagation of the Faith, with its associated Pontifical Mission Aid Societies. It must be our hope now that the national episcopal conferences of Europe and America, recognizing their responsibilities for the Universal Church, will come to the aid of their poverty-stricken brethren. Already the German and American Episcopal Conferences have done great things, each collecting more money for the missions each year than the Pontifical Mission Aid Societies have been able to collect from the whole world. It is this kind of direct co-operation between the bishops of the older churches and those of the younger that will make episcopal collegiality something more than an academic thesis. Obviously the sending out of priests, Brothers, Sisters and lay missionaries, as part of the scheme of world evangelization would be done, under the guidance of the Holy See, through the national episcopal conferences.

Organization on a world scale is needed if the Church in lands of mission is not to perish for want of men and want of money. The opportunity for decisive action provided by the Council may not come again for centuries. The Church cannot afford to wait. The Christianization of millions is at stake.

Appendix

THE APOSTOLIC FACULTIES

IT WAS at first proposed to give a chapter to the Apostolic Faculties, containing some general remarks together with a commentary on any particular faculty of the sixty-eight that seemed to require comment. We have instead, however, decided merely to make this brief general note.

Writing for the whole of Africa, it is not possible to decide which faculties need comment in South Africa, which in Central Africa, which in the East, North, or West. It would be different if one were writing a monograph. Then, again, Pope Paul on 3 December 1964 extended these faculties, with slight variations, to all the residential bishops of the world (*Motu Proprio, Pastorale Munus*). Already, a spate of commentaries on these faculties is beginning to appear in the old countries. To be sure, they will be written against a European background, but much of their insight will apply to Africa as well. Again, these universal faculties will presumably be inserted in their immediate cadre in the proposed revision of the Code, and this will imply changes in phrasing. All of this makes it obvious that any detailed comment we might have made in this book on particular faculties would soon have become out of date. For the same reason, we have thought it advisable not to include an English text of the Faculties as was suggested to us by several priests.

The reader will always have at hand, meanwhile, the ubiquitous and down to earth commentary on the Faculties by Bishop John de Reeper, *A Missionary Companion*. We throw in here for good measure the *Facultates Decennales* of Father J. Buijs, S.J., of the Gregorian University, Rome (Gregorian Press, 1961). Note that the current Faculties were granted on 1 January 1961, and lapse on 31 December 1970.

Many bishops have the excellent practice of issuing to the clergy lists telling them which of these faculties they grant to them: *O si sic omnes,* sigh the other priests. There is, too, in some areas, concern that few dispensations, for example marriage dispensations, are being granted.

BIBLIOGRAPHY

Acta et Decreta Primi Concilii Plenarii Indiae, Ranchi, 1951.

Actes de la VIe Assemblée Plénière de l'Episcopat du Congo, Léopoldville, 1961.

Actus Congressus Catechistici Internationalis, Vatican Press, 1950.

AERTYNS, J., *Theologia Pastoralis Tradens Practicam Institutionem; Confessarii,* Gulpen, 1936.

AJOULAT, L. P., *Aujourd'hui l'Afrique,* Tournai, Paris, 1958.

ALBERIONE, G., *Appunti di Teologia Pastorale,* Alba, 1960.

The Art of Teaching the Catechism, Catholic Centre, Hong Kong.

BEA, CARDINAL A., *The Unity of Christians,* London, 1963.

BENEDICT, RUTH, *Patterns of Culture,* New York, 1960.

BOISSARD, E., *Questions théologiques sur le mariage,* Paris, 1948.

BOULARD, F., *An Introduction to Religious Sociology,* London, 1960.

BÜHLTMANN, W., *Afrika: die Kirche unter den Völkern,* Mainz, 1963.

The Catholic Church in an Independent Nigeria (Nigerian Hierarchy Letter), 1960.

CHARLES, P., *Les dossiers de l'action missionnaire,* Louvain, 1938.

Christian Responsibility and World Poverty (a symposium edited by A. McCORMACK, M.H.), London, 1963.

CONGAR, YVES, *Lay People in the Church,* London, 1962.

CONSIDINE, J. M., *The Missionary Role in Socio-Economic Betterment,* Westminster, Maryland.

COUTURIER, C., *The Mission of the Church,* London, 1960.

DANIÉLOU, J., *Advent,* London, 1950.

DAVIS, H., *Moral and Pastoral Theology,* 4 vols., London, 1949.

Directoire en matière sociale, Paris, 1954.

Directoire pour la pastorale des sacrements, Paris, 1951.

Directoire pour les actes administratifs des sacrements, Paris, 1954.

Directoire pour la pastorale de la messe, Paris, 1957. (All French Hierarchy.)

DRINKWATER, F. H., *Telling the Good News,* London, 1960.

DUMÉRY, H., *Les trois tentations de l'apostolat moderne,* Paris, 1948.

East African Lay Apostolate Congress, Nyegezi, 1961.

Eglise et apostolat, Tournai, 1957 (A. CHAVASSE AND OTHERS).

FRASSINETTI, J., *Parish Priest's Manual,* London, 1885. (Background value.)

GÉNICOT-GORTEBEKE, *Institutiones Theologiae Moralis,* 2 vols., Brussels and Bruges, 1951.

GILLEMAN, G., *The Primacy of Charity in Moral Theology,* London, 1959.

GONSÁLEZ, M., *Theologia Pastoralis*, Valladolid, 1936.

HÄRING, B., *The Law of Christ*, 2 vols., Cork, Ireland, 1963; *Macht und Ohnmacht der Religion*, Salzburg, 1956.

HOFINGER, J., *Worship, The Life of the Missions*, Washington, 1958; *Teaching all Nations*, London, 1961; (contains record of the Eichstätt Study week, pp. 394–400).

JOYCE, G. H., *Christian Marriage*, London, 1933.

JUNGMANN, J. A., *Handing on the Faith*, New York, 1959.

LEDOGAR, R. (ed.), *Katigondo, Presenting the Christian Message to Africa* (report of Pan-African Catechetical Study Week, Katigondo, 1964), London, 1965.

LITHARD, V., *Précis de théologie pastorale*, Paris, 1936.

LUBAC, H. DE, *Catholicism*, London, 1950; *Le fondement théologique des missions*, Paris, 1946.

MATHYSSEK-RICARD, *Mémento de pastorale*, Paris, 1942.

Mezzi di comunicazione di massa (encyclicals, letters, addresses of Popes Pius XI, Pius XII, and John XXIII on mass media). Edited by D.A.

MICHONNEAU, G., *Revolution in a City Parish*, Blackfriars, Oxford, 1949.

National Catholic Educational Association, Washington, D.C., Aug., 1948.

NIEDERGANG, G., *Le clergé paroissial*, Paris, 1927.

NOLDIN-SCHMITT, *Summa Theologiae Moralis*, 3 vols., Barcelona, 1957.

Novella Ecclesiae Germina (missionary studies in German, French and English), Nijmegen–Utrecht, 1963.

OLIVER, R., *The Missionary Factor in East Africa*, London, 1952.

Papal Encyclicals. Missionary Activity: *Maximum illud*, Benedict XV, 1919; *Rerum Ecclesiae*, Pius XI, 1926; *Evangelii praecones*, 1951, also *Fidei donum*, 1957, Pius XII; *Princeps pastorum*, John XXIII 1959. Education: *Divini illius Magistri*, Pius XI, 1929. Cinema: *Vigilanti cura*, Pius XI, 1936. Cinema, radio, television: *Miranda prorsus*, Pius XII, 1957. Social: *Mater et magistra*, John XXIII, 1963. Mystical Body: *Mystici Corporis*, Pius XII, 1945. Church, ecumenism: *Ecclesiam suam*, Paul VI, 1964. Marriage: *Casti Connubii*, Pius XI, 1930. Sacred Music: *Musicae sacrae disciplina*, Pius XII, 1955.

Pastorale, oeuvre commune (National Congress of Versailles), Paris, 1956.

Problèmes de l'adaptation en apostolat (collection of articles from *Nouvelle Révue Théologique*—general, not missionary), Tournai, 1949.

REEPER, BISHOP J. DE, *The Sacraments on the Missions*, Dublin, 1957; *A Missionary Companion* (commentary on the Apostolic Faculties), Westminster, Maryland, 1952.

ROBINSON, JOHN M., *The Family Apostolate and Africa*, Dublin, 1964.

SCHULTZE, F., *Manual of Pastoral Theology*, St. Louis, U.S.A., and London, 1923. (Background value.)

Second World Congress for the Lay Apostolate, 2 vols., Rome, 1957.

Semaine de missiologie de Louvain, 1926, 1927, 1929, 1946.

Social Study Week, Dar-es-Salaam, 1962.

Sociologie de la Soc. Religieuse (International Conference of Religious Sociology), Paris, 1959.

SOUTH AFRICAN BISHOPS' CONFERENCE, *Letter* of 1960 (nationalism politics, unity of all men), Catholic Secretariat, Pretoria.

STANG, W., *Pastoral Theology*, New York, 1897. (Background value.)

STOCCHIERO, G., *Pratica Pastorale*, Vicenza, Italy, 1936.

SUENENS, CARDINAL L. J., *Theology of the Apostolate of the Legion of Mary*, Westminster, Maryland, 1954; *The Nun in the World*, London, 1962.

Unity and Freedom (Tanzania Hierarchy Letter), 1962.

VERMEERSCH, A., *Theologia Moralis*, 4 vols., Rome, 1937.

VILLENEUVE, CARDINAL, *Le sacrement de la confirmation; Le mariage* (I, II, III), Québec, 1946.

ZALBA, M., *Theologiae Moralis Compendium*, 2 vols., Madrid, 1958.

LEADING REVIEWS CONSULTED

Action Catholique et Mission, Lille.

Africa, London International Institute, London.

African Abstracts, London International Institute, London.

African Affairs, London International Institute, London.

African Ecclesiastical Review, Masaka, Uganda.

African Studies, Johannesburg.

African World, London.

American Catholic Sociological Review, Marquette University, Milwaukee.

American Ecclesiastical Review, Washington University.

L'Ami du Clergé, Langres.

Anthropological Quarterly, Washington.

Blackfriars, London.

Bulletin des Missions, St. André, Bruges.

Cahiers d'Action Religeuse et Sociale, Paris.

Cahiers du Clergé Rural, Sèvres, Paris.

Canon Law Abstracts, Melrose, Scotland.

Catholic Action Reprints, Dayton, Ohio.

Catholic Herald, London.

Catholic Times, London.

Centre d'Etudes des Problèmes Sociaux Indigènes, Elizabethville, Congo-Léo.

Centre d'Informations pour l'Afrique (C.I.P.A.), White Fathers, Rome.

Christ to the World, Rome.

Christus, Paris.

Clergy Monthly, Ranchi, India.

Clergy Review, London.

Concilium, London (English Version).

Conference Bulletin, Archdiocese of New York, New York.

Digest Religioso, Naples.
Documentation Catholique, Paris.
East Africa and Rhodesia, London.
The Ecumenist, New York.
Ephemerides Iuris Canonici, Officium Libri Catholici, Rome.
Etudes, Paris.
Fiches de Pédagogie Religieuse, Strasbourg.
The Furrow, Maynooth, Ireland.
Homiletic and Pastoral Review, New York.
Informazione Fides, Rome.
The Jurist, Washington University.
Kongo Oversee, Antwerp.
Lumen Vitae, Brussels.
La Maison-Dieu, Centre de Pastorale Liturgique, Paris.
Masses Ouvrières, Paris.
Monde Non-Chrétien, Paris.
The Month, London.
Notes et Documents, White Fathers, Rome.
Notes de Pastorale Liturgique, Paris.
Nouvelle Révue Théologique, Louvain.
Paroisse et Liturgie, St. André, Bruges.
Parole et Mission, Paris.
Pastoral Life, Canfield, Ohio.
Periodica, Gregorian University, Rome.
Présence Africaine, Paris.
The Priest, Huntington, Indiana.
Problèmes d'Afrique Centrale, Brussels.
Questions Liturgiques et Paroissiales, Mont César, Louvain.
Reader's Digest, London.
Révue du Clergé Africain, Mayidi-Inkisi, Congo-Léo.
Rythmes du Monde, St. André, Bruges.
The Tablet, London.
Tanganyika Notes and Records, Dar-es-Salaam.
Tanganyika Weekly News, Dar-es-Salaam.
Theological Studies, Baltimore, U.S.A.
L'Union, Paris.
La Vie Spirituelle, Paris.
La Vie Spirituelle, Supplément, Paris.
Vivante Afrique, Namur.
World Mission, New York.
Worship, Minnesota.

Index

249

Church dues: collection of, 57–8; non-payment of, 135–7
Ciborium, consecration of, 117
Cicognani, Cardinal, 47
Cinema, influence of, 239
Citizen, the, and the State, 6
Clergy Monthly, 132, 135n
Clergy Review, 157n, 167n
Clericalism, 85–6, 233
Colas, M., on parish retreat, 212
'Commitment' ceremony, 108
Communion, Holy: link with Mass, 118; four effects of, 118–19; first communion; 119; frequency of, 120–1; danger of routine, 120; necessity for right intention, 120–1; need to avoid sacrilegious communions, 123–5; taken to the sick, 125; admittance of public sinners, 125–6; reservation of the Blessed Sacrament, 126–8; Benediction of, 128–129
Communism, principles of, 8; in Africa, 10
Confession: before Mass, 123, 124–5, 145; the priest as father, 131–2; his need to keep abreast of thought, 132; his questioning of the penitent, 132–3; importance of contrition, 133–4; absolution, 134–7; penance, imposition of, 137–8; importance of the admonition, 138–9; secrecy of, 139–40; children and, 140–2; habitual sinners, 142; men and boys, 142–4; the seriously ill, 144; outside Church, 145; general confessions, 145; exchange of priests, 145; sea voyages, 145–6; language difficulties, 146
Confessor, the, responsibilities of, 78–9
Confirmation: as initiation sacrament, 107; most suitable age for, 107; preceding first communion, 107; instruction for, 108–9; need for reappraisal of, 109; preparation for, 109; duties of sponsors, 110–11; of adults, 111; invocation of name of saint taken, 112
Confraternity of Christian Doctrine, 219, 221
Congo, the: part played by Christians in, 16; Plenary Assembly of Bishops of (1961), 23 and n, 26; tragedy in, 27; establishment of hierarchy in, 49; instructions to missionaries in, on baptism, 99; the bishops: on imposition of penance, 137; on sick calls for priests, 203

Congregation for the Propagation of the Faith, 242
Congregation of the Sacraments, the, 107
Coninck, L. de, 42n
Constitution on the Lay Apostolate, 217n
Constitution on the Liturgy, 94, 95, 104, 112, 114, 116, 151, 159, 163, 164, 168, 169, 171, 172, 174, 176, 211
Contraception, 156–8
Conversion, 224: as aim of the catechist, 184–5
Converts, first confession of, 101
Co-operation, need for, between episcopal conferences of older and new countries, 241
Co-operatives, 231–2
Coptic rite, suggestion for use of in Africa, 172–3
Crawley, Fr. Matteo, 130
Cremation, church's attitude to, 166–7
Crichton, J. D., 169n
Cronin, Fr. Kevin, 234n
Cures, effected by Christ, 160

D

Dalrymple, J., 83n
Davis, C., 60n, 160n, 163n
Dawson, Christopher, 11
Deaf, the: and confession, 145; problem of, 206–7
Deaf mutes, baptism of, 99
Dean, the: appointment of by bishops, 53; presence at deanery meetings, 53; and at parochial inductions, 53
Deanery, the: Canon Law provision for, 52; meetings of, 52–3
Death: respect for dead body, 164; need for joyful attitude, 164–5; burial of baptized infants, 165
De Ecclesia, 217n
De Ecumenismo, 226
Doepfner, Cardinal, quoted, 19
Downside, Abbot of, on ecumenism in universities, 227–28
Dramatization, and education, 190–1
Drawing, and education, 191
Drinkwater, F. H., 186n
Drunkenness, 194–5
Dupanloup, quoted, 56